Basic Skills for Effective Reading

*Dedicated with much love to Sara Ophira Sternstein,
Moses Elchanan Sternstein, Lily Idra Wilf,
and Isaac Zev Wilf.*

Basic Skills for Effective Reading

fourth edition

SELMA WILF

Phoenix College

PRENTICE HALL
Upper Saddle River, New Jersey 07458

Library of Congress Cataloging-in-Publication Data

Wilf, Selma
  Basic skills for effective reading/Selma Wilf.—4th ed.
    p. cm.
  Includes bibliographical references and index.
  ISBN 0-13-533852-2
  1. Reading (Adult education)—United States. 2. Reading—Phoenetic
method. I. title.
  LC5225.R4W54 1998
  428.4'07115--dc21

                                                        98-5891
                                                          CIP

Editor in chief: *Charlyce Jones Owen*
Acquisitions editor: *Maggie Barbieri*
Editorial assistant: *Joan Polk*
Managing editor: *Bonnie Biller*
Production liaison: *Fran Russello*
Editorial/production supervision: *Kerry Reardon*
Prepress and manufacturing buyer: *Mary Ann Gloriande*
Cover director: Jayne Conte
Cover designer: Kiwi Design

This book was set in 11/13 Bookman Light by KR Publishing Services and
was printed and bound by R.R. Donnelley and Sons Company. The cover was
printed by Phoenix Color Corp.

 ©1999, 1994, 1988, 1983 Prentice-Hall, Inc.
Simon & Schuster/A Viacom Company
Upper Saddle River, New Jersey 07458

10   9   8   7   6   5   4   3   2

ISBN 0-13-533852-2

Prentice-Hall International (UK) Limited, *London*
Prentice-Hall of Australia Pty. Limited, *Sydney*
Prentice-Hall Canada Inc., *Toronto*
Prentice-Hall Hispanoamericana, *S.A., Mexico*
Prentice-Hall of India Private Limited, *New Delhi*
Prentice-Hall of Japan, *Tokyo*
Simon & Schuster Asia Pte. Ltd., *Singapore*
Editora Prentice-Hall do Brasil, Ltda., *Rio de Janeiro*

Contents

Preface

The fourth edition of *Basic Skills for Effective Reading* continues to address the needs of students with limited reading skills. Like the first three editions, it offers a step-by-step approach to reading skill development and application. The purpose of this textbook is to bring students closer to college level reading.

Basic Skills for Effective Reading has been designed to provide students with a hands-on approach to skill development. Each skill is explained and then learned through the use of Guided Practice exercises. Immediate feedback is provided upon completion of the Guided Practice exercises. Where appropriate, skills are subdivided into sections and learned in small units. Skill development is reinforced in Skill Practice exercises that follow each section within the chapter. Each of the eleven skills in *Basic Skills for Effective Reading* prepares students for those which follow.

The fourth edition of *Basic Skills for Effective Reading* is divided into four parts. Part One, Working with Words, develops word attack skills such as phonics and syllabication and teaches students to apply what they have learned to both real and nonsense words. Part Two, Building Vocabulary, develops skills related to the use of context clues, word parts, a dictionary, and a personal vocabulary system that can be adapted to the individual student's specific needs. Part Three, Improving Comprehension, stresses the formation of packages of related information through the identification of main ideas and details in paragraphs and longer selections. Paragraphs and selections are mapped to show these packages of related information. The fourth part, Extending Your Reading Skills, provides ten reading selections. The selections follow the eleven skill development chapters to allow instructors the flexibility of using them at any time rather than at the end of each chapter. These selections have been chosen because they have been found interesting to students and have an appropriate readability level. The Reading Selections are presented in a sequence of increasing level of readability. The ten questions, which follow each Reading Practice, are intended to enhance student comprehension of its content. Students are also asked to write their reactions to each selection.

There are changes in the fourth edition of *Basic Skills for Effective Reading:*

- Additional graphic organizers in the form of informal maps have been included in chapters where concepts to be mastered are numerous. They will aid students to understand and retain these concepts.

- Practice materials have been modified or replaced as suggested by users of this textbook.

- Dictionary entries and the dictionary page in Chapter Six have been enlarged to enhance their clarity.

- An eleventh skill has been added in a separate chapter. Once students have mastered main ideas and details in paragraphs and selections, a natural extension is to develop mapping skills to be applied to reading materials as needed. Students in reading classes at all levels have responded most positively to mapping. It has proven to be very helpful for students as they are required to understand and remember more difficult reading materials.

- To involve students to a greater extent in the development of their reading skills, beginning with Chapter Three, Skill Practices include skill application from sources other than this textbook. Students are asked to apply what they have learned in the skill development chapters to reading materials of their choice.

Feedback from students and instructors who have used earlier editions of *Basic Skills for Effective Reading* has continued to be more positive. At Phoenix College, where the concept for this book was born and where it continues to be used for students with limited reading skills, *Basic Skills for Effective Reading* has been successful in preparing such student for more advanced reading courses and in coping with daily reading tasks. It is hoped that the changes presented in this fourth edition will help make it an even more valuable tool for the teaching and learning of basic reading skills.

ACKNOWLEDGMENTS

Special thanks are extended to Maggie Barbieri and Joan Polk at Prentice Hall, two wonderful women who were always there to help. Their encouragement and ongoing support has been crucial to the completion of this new edition of *Basic Skills for Effective Reading.*

The generosity of Joyce M. Ewell, who provided the first two phonics summary sheets and the inspiration to create additional graphics to clarify concepts that might be difficult for some students, continues to be greatly appreciated.

The author is grateful to Kerry Reardon, a fine production editor. With skill and amazing patience, she has worked very hard to produce a quality textbook.

Thanks to the reviewers who provided valuable feedback: Doreen Keller, *Rio Hondo College*; Vicki Raine, *Penn Valley Community College*; Shelley Beard, *Owens Community College*; Anna-Marie Schlender, *California State University—Howard*; and Ted Walkup, *Clayton State College*.

Finally, thanks to the following sources for allowing use of the materials:

Pages 182–198: Copyright © 1992 by Houghton Mifflin Company. Reproduced by permission from *The American Heritage Dictionary of the English Language,* third edition.

Pages 217–218, Skill Practice: Reprinted by permission of United Press International.

Page 229, paragraph 5: Adapted from "Man," *Illustrated World Encyclopedia,* 1977, p. 1025. Printed with permission of Bobley Publishing Corporation.

Page 231, paragraph 3: Adapted from "Dietary Guidelines for Americans," Susan Welsh, *Research for Tomorrow,* U.S. Department of Agriculture Yearbook, 1986, pp. 193, 194.

Page 231, paragraph 4: Adapted from "How to Use Music to: Calm Yourself Down, Stir Someone Up, Put Him in the Mood for Love," Ruth Winter, *Glamour*, March 1980, p. 42. Copyright © 1980 by Condé Nast Publications, Inc. Printed with permission of the author.

Pages 232, paragraph 6: Adapted from *What's to Eat*, U.S. Department of Agriculture Yearbook, 1979, p. 98.

Page 232, paragraph 7: Adapted from John Biesanz and Mavis Biesanz, *Introduction to Sociology*, Prentice Hall, 1979, p. 500.

Page 232, paragraph 8: Adapted from "Move Over, Milky Way—Our Cows Are Stars, Too," R. P. Niedermeier, G. Bokstedt, and C. A. Baumann, *That We May Eat*, U.S. Department of Agriculture Yearbook, 1975, p. 139.

Page 232, paragraph 9: Adapted from *Consumers Tell It to the Judge: Small Claims Courts and Consumer Complaints*, U.S. Department of Justice, Office of the Attorney General, December 1980.

Page 232, paragraph 10: Adapted from "Endangered: Handle with Care—The Manatee," Alan Rosenthal, *Discovery*, Spring 1979, p. 35. Printed with permission of the publisher.

Page 234, sample B: Adapted from *How to Buy Potatoes*, U.S. Department of Agriculture, Consumer and Marketing Service, Home and Garden Bulletin 198, February 1971.

Page 235, paragraph 1: Adapted from *Protecting Your Housing Investment*, U.S. Department of Housing and Urban Development, p. 6.

Page 236, paragraph 2: Adapted from "They Call It 'Rough-Water Swimming'—Watch or Join," *Sunset*, July 1981, p. 36D. Printed with permission of the publisher.

Page 243, paragraph 1: Adapted from *Women's Day*, November 4, 1980. Printed with permission of the publisher.

Page 243, paragraph 3: Adapted from "Fire! Surviving in a High-Rise Building," *Phoenix Gazette*, March 23, 1981, p. 4. Printed with permission of the *Phoenix Gazette*.

Page 244, paragraph 4: Adapted from "Checking Belts and Hoses," Walt Voron, *Gemco Courier*, April 1980, p. 38. Printed with permission of Gemco Membership Department Stores.

Page 244, paragraph 5: Adapted from "The Ringed Planet," *Voyages to Saturn*, David Morrison, Scientific and Technical Information Branch, NASA, 1982.

Page 244, paragraph 6: Adapted from *Protecting Your Housing Investment*, U.S. Department of Housing and Urban Development, p. 6.

Page 245, paragraph 7: Adapted from "Shades of Summer," James R. Gregg, *Travel and Leisure*, June 1981, p. 54. Reprinted with permission of *Travel and Leisure*.

Page 245, paragraph 8: Adapted from "Don't Rush Out for a Ski Outfit: Make Sure It's Your Snowflake," Bill Keil, *1973 Yearbook of Agriculture*, U.S. Department of Agriculture, p. 344.

Page 247, paragraph 1: Adapted from *What's to Eat*, U.S. Department of Agriculture Yearbook, 1979, p. 119.

Page 247, paragraph 2: Adapted from *Successful Jogging*. Printed with permission of the American Running and Fitness Association.

Page 247, paragraph 3: Adapted from "An Hour or Less from Phoenix or Tucson, *Sunset*, June 1980, p. 95. Printed with permission of the publisher.

Page 248, paragraph 4: Adapted from *Your Right to Federal Records*, U.S. General Services Administration and U.S. Department of Justice, p. 1.

Page 248, paragraph 5: Adapted from "November Gardening in the Desert," *Sunset*, November 1980, p. 228. Printed with permission of the publisher.

Page 248, paragraph 6: Adapted from "Bubbling Up for the Holidays," Emanuel and Madeline Greenberg, *Travel and Leisure*, December 1980, p. 86. Reprinted with permission of *Travel and Leisure*.

Page 249, paragraph 7: Adapted from "Dietary Guidelines for Americans," Susan Welsh, *Research for Tomorrow*. U.S. Department of Agriculture Yearbook, 1986, pp. 193, 194.

Page 249, paragraph 8: Adapted from "How to Use Music to Calm Yourself Down, Stir Someone Up, Put Him in the Mood for Love," Ruth Winter, *Glamour*, March 1980, p. 42. Copyright © 1980 by Condé Nast Publications, Inc. Printed with permission of the author.

Page 250, paragraph 9: Adapted from "Gimme Shelter—Outdoors," Joseph Steed, *Travel and Leisure*, June 1981, p. 145. Reprinted with permission of *Travel and Leisure*.

Page 250, paragraph 10: Adapted from "Think Snow," Storm Field, *Travel and Leisure*, February 1980, p. 12. Reprinted with permission of *Travel and Leisure*.

Page 258, paragraph 1: Adapted from "From the Horse's Mouth—How Not to Ride for a Fall," Larry L. Finks, *1974 Yearbook of Agriculture—Shopper's Guide*, U.S. Department of Agriculture, p. 321.

Page 258, paragraph 2: Adapted from "All About Brick and the 10,000 Ways It Comes," G. William Detty, *1974 Yearbook of Agriculture—Shopper's Guide*, U.S. Department of Agriculture, p. 93.

Page 259, paragraph 3: Adapted from *More Than a Dream: Being Your Own Boss*, U.S. Department of Labor, Employment, and Training Administration, 1980.

Page 259, paragraph 4: Adapted from "Imaginative Ways with Bathrooms," Alexandra Kira, *1974 Yearbook of Agriculture—Shopper's Guide*, U.S. Department of Agriculture, p. 174.

Page 259, paragraph 5: Adapted from "Microwave Savvy," Marlene Scribner, *Gemco Courier*, April 1980, p. 40. Reprinted with permission of Gemco Membership Department Stores.

Page 261, paragraph B: Adapted from "Wide Awake Walls ... with Sheets," Jean Rountree, *Gemco Courier*, April 1980, p. 18. Printed with permission of Gemco Membership Department Stores.

Page 263, paragraph 4: Adapted from "Robert E. Lee," *Illustrated World Encyclopedia*, 1977, p. 963. Reprinted with permission of Bobley Publishing Co.

Page 263, paragraph 5: Adapted from *Consumer Handbook to Credit Protection Laws*, Board of Governors of the Federal Reserve System, p. 3

Page 263, paragraph 1: Adapted from "Swapping Homes ... U.S.A., Canada, Europe," *Sunset,* April 1979, p. 54. Printed with permission of the publisher.

Page 265, paragraph 4: Adapted from *More Than a Dream: Being Your Own Boss,* U.S. Department of Labor, Employment, and Training Administration, 1980.

Page 267, number 3: Adapted from *Woman's Day,* November 4, 1980. Printed with permission of the publisher.

Page 268, number 4: Adapted from "Hong Kong Post Report," U.S. Department of State, 1981, p. 9.

Page 269, paragraph 1: Adapted from "Carrying It Off in Style! The Role of Clothing," Marilyn J. Horn, *1973 Yearbook of Agriculture,* U.S. Department of Agriculture, p. 316.

Page 269, paragraph 2: Adapted from "Don't Rush Out for a Ski Outfit: Make Sure It's Your Snowflake," Bill Keil, *1973 Yearbook of Agriculture,* U.S. Department of Agriculture, p. 344.

Page 269, paragraph 3: Adapted from "Your Own Pool to Get in the Swim," William P. Markert, *1973 Yearbook of Agriculture,* U.S. Department of Agriculture, p. 123.

Page 272, paragraph B: Adapted from "Bats," *Illustrated World Encyclopedia,* 1977, p. 190. Printed with permission of Bobley Publishing Corporation.

Page 273, paragraph 4: Adapted from *When You Move—Do's and Don'ts.* Interstate Commerce Commission, p. 272.

Page 273, paragraph 5: Adapted from *Woman's Day,* November 4, 1980, p. 30. Printed with permission of the publisher.

Page 274, paragraph 1: Adapted from *Gasoline—More Miles per Gallon,* U.S. Department of Transportation, Office of Public and Consumer Affairs, p. 5.

Page 274, paragraph 2: Adapted from "Australia Is Another World," *Sunset,* November 1980, p. 85. Printed with permission of the publisher.

Page 274, paragraph 3: Adapted from "Seaborne Hunt for a Kodiak," Jim Carmichel, *Outdoor Life,* January 1981, p. 53. Printed with permission of the publisher.

Page 274, paragraph 4: Adapted from "How to Get Control of Your Feelings," Gene Church Schulz, *Listen,* October 1979, p. 13. Printed with permission of the publisher.

Page 274, paragraph 5: Adapted from "Bow and Arrow Hunting Gear," Tink Nathan, *1974 Yearbook of Agriculture—Shopper's Guide,* U.S. Department of Agriculture, p. 348.

Page 275, number 2: Adapted from *Sewing Menswear Patterns,* U.S. Department of Agriculture, 1975, p. 3.

Page 275, number 3: Adapted from *Discovering Prince William Forest Park,* National Park Service, U.S. Department of the Interior, p. 1.

Page 276, number 4: Adapted from *Backpacking,* U.S. Department of Agriculture, Forest Service, 1979, p. 12.

Page 276, number 5: Adapted from *From Sundials to Atomic Clocks— Understanding Time and Frequency,* U.S. Department of Commerce, 1977, p. 96.

Page 277, paragraph 1: Adapted from *Everglades Wildlife,* National Park Service, U.S. Department of the Interior, p. 45.

Page 277, paragraph 2: Adapted from *Mountaineering—Mt. McKinley National Park, Alaska,* National Park Service, U.S. Department of the Interior, 1975, p. 12.

Page 278, paragraph 3: Adapted from *Pollination and the Honey Bee,* U.S. Department of Agriculture, 1975, pp. 8, 9.

Page 279, paragraph A: Adapted from *Beekeeping for Beginners,* U.S. Department of Agriculture, Home and Garden Bulletin 158, revised, 1979.

Page 280, paragraph B: Adapted from *Consumers Tell It to the Judge—Small Claims Court and Consumer Complaints,* U.S. Department of Justice, Office of Attorney General, December, 1980.

Page 281, paragraph 2: Adapted from *Consumer Handbook to Credit Protection Laws,* Board of Governors of the Federal Reserve System, June 1980, p. 22.

Page 281, paragraph 3: Adapted from "Keeping Your Pet Healthy," *FDA Consumer,* March 1979, U.S. Department of Health and Human Services.

Page 281, paragraph 4: Adapted from *Guide to Health Insurance for People with Medicare,* U.S. Department of Health and Human Services, Health Care Financing Administration, January 1981, p. 4.

Page 282, pargaraph 5:: Adapted form "Hungry People," *What's to Eat,* U.S. Department of Agriculture Yearbook, 1979, p. 117.

Page 286, paragraph 5: Adapted from "Keeping Your Pet Healthy," *FDA Consumer,* U.S. Department of Health and Human Services, 1979.

Page 286, paragraph 1: Adapted from *Handbook to Credit Protection Laws,* Board of Governors of U.S. Federal Reserve System, June 1980, pp. 22, 23.

Page 287, paragraph 2: Adapted from *The Auto Safety Belt Fact Book,* U.S. Department of Transportation, 1977, p. 13.

Page 293, Selection A: Adapted from *What You Should Know About Smoke Detectors,* U.S. Consumer Product Safety Commission.

Page 294, Selection B: Adapted from *Protecting Your Housing Investment,* U.S. Department of Housing and Urban Development, February 1980, p. 14.

Page 295, Selection 1: Adapted from *Trees of Our National Forests,* U.S. Department of Agriculture, Forest Service, 1980, p. 1.

Page 297, Selection 2: Adapted from *Can Your Kitchen Pass the Food Storage Test?,* Jane Heenan, FDA Consumer, U.S. Department of Health and Human Services, March 1974.

Page 298, Selection 3: Adapted from *Consumers Tell It to the Judge—Small Claims Courts and Consumer Complaints,* U.S. Department of Justice, December 1980, p. 19.

Page 299, Selection 4: Adapted from "What's in a Name?" *In Touch with People,* U.S. Department of the Interior, 1973.

Page 300, Selection 5: Adapted from "What Does AIDS Mean to You?" U.S. Department of Health and Human Services, Public Health Service Center for Disease Control, April 1991.

Page 303, Selection 1: Adapted from "A Prickly Problem," Elizabeth Welborn, *McCall's*, June 1981. Reprinted with permission of the McCall Publishing Company.

Page 303, Selection 2: Adapted from "Our Planets at a Glance," *NASA Facts*, Educational Publication of NASA, 1982.

Page 304, Selection 3: Adapted from "What's Happening to the Old Time Madstone?" Mary Whatley Clarke, *Frontier Times, March 1981. Reprinted with permission of the author.*

Page 305, Selection 4: Adapted from *Can I Really Get Free or Cheap Public Land?* U.S. Department of the Interior, 1980.

Page 305, Selection 5: Adapted from *From Sundials to Atomic Clocks—Understanding Time and Frequency*, U.S. Department of Commerce, 1977.

Page 313, Selection 1: Adapted from "Health Claims: Separating Fact from Fiction," *Facts for Consumers from the Federal Trade Commission*, April 1986.

Page 314, Selection 2: Adapted from *Can Your Kitchen Pass the Food Storage Test?*, Jane Heenan, FDA Consumer, U.S. Department of Health and Human Services, 1974.

Page 315, Selection 3: Adapted from *Common Sense in Buying a New Car*, U.S. Department of Transportation, 1978.

Page 315, Selection 4: Adapted from "Full Moon Madness," Andy Schweich, *McCall's*, July 1981, p. 41. Reprinted with permission of McCall Publishing Company.

Page 316, Selection 5: Adapted from "Toward a Drug-Free Generation: A Nation's Responsibility," National Commission on Drug-Free Schools Final Report, September 1990, pp. 17, 18.

Page 319, Selection 1: Adapted from "Daydream Your Problems Away," Janet Chan, *McCall's*, March 1978, p. 44. Reprinted with permission of McCall Publishing Company.

Page 320, Selection 2: Adapted from "Forests: On the Wildside," U.S. Department of Agriculture, Forest Service Wildlife and Fisheries Staff, September 1991.

Page 321, Selection 3: Adapted from "How to Be a Water Miser," Merri Rosenberg, *McCall's*, June 1981, p. 45. Reprinted with permission of McCall Publishing Company.

Page 322, Selection 4: Adapted from *Our Flag*, Joint Committee on Printing, U.S. Congress. U.S. Government Printing Office, 1989, pp. 7, 8.

Page 324, Selection 5: Adapted from "How Can You Mend a Broken Heart?" by Ludmilla Alexander, *Listen*, November 1979. Printed with permission of the publisher.

Page 329, Sample A: Adapted from "Imaginative Ways with Bathrooms," Alexandra Kira, *1974 Yearbook of Agriculture—Shopper's Guide*, U.S. Department of Agriculture, p. 174.

Page 331, Paragraph 1: Adapted from *More than a Dream: Being Your Own Boss*, U.S. Department of Labor, Employment, and Training Administration, 1980.

Page 332, Paragraph 2: Adapted from "Don't Rush Out for a Ski Outfit: Make Sure

It's Your Snowflake," Bill Keil, *1973 Yearbook of Agriculture*, U.S. Department of Agriculture, p. 344.

Page 333, Sample C: Adapted from "Health Claims: Separating Fact from Fiction," *Facts for Consumers from the Federal Trade Commission*, April 1986.

Page 335, Selection 1: Adapted from "How to Be a Water Miser," Merri Rosenberg, *McCall's*, June 1981, p. 45. Reprinted with permission of McCall Publishing Company.

Page 337, Selection 2: Adapted from *Protecting Your Housing Investment*, U.S. Department of Housing and Urban Development, February, 1980, p. 14.

Page 339, Paragraph: Adapted from Jon R. Waltz, *Introduction to Criminal Evidence, 2nd Edition*, Nelson-Hall, 1985, p. 12.

Page 340, Selection: Adapted from Paul J. Rosch and Kenneth R. Pelletier, "Designing Worksite Stress Management Programs," *Stress Management in Work Settings*, U.S. Department of Health and Human Services, Center for Disease Control, National Institute for Occupational Safety and Health, May 1987, p. 78.

Page 343, Reading Selection 1: Adapted from *National Geographic World*, © July 1981. Courtesy National Geographic Society.

Page 347, Reading Selection 2: Adapted from "Water over the Dam," by Frank E. Heard, Listen, October 1979. Printed with permission of the publisher.

Page 351, Reading Selection 3: Adapted from Selma Wilf, *Techniques for Success–College Reading and Study Skills*, NJ: Prentice Hall, © 1986, pp. 20–30.

Page 357, Reading Selection 4: Adapted from *Outdoor Life*, July 1979, pp. 74–75. Printed with permission of the publisher.

Page 361, Reading Selection 5: Adapted from "It's the Books That Changed Me" by Peter Swet, *Parade Magazine*, May 10, 1992, pp. 4, 5.

Page 365, Reading Selection 6: "Practice Makes Perfect" by Patricia Barnes-Svarney. Reprinted with permission of the author.

Page 369, Reading Selection 7: Adapted from *Walnut Canyon*, National Park Service, U.S. Department of the Interior.

Page 373, Reading Selection 8: Adapted with permission from the November 1980 *Reader's Digest*. Copyright © 1980 by The Reader's Digest Assn., Inc.

Page 371, Reading Selection 9: From Cobblestone's October 1986 issue: *Witchcraft*, © 1986, Cobblestone Publishing, 30 Grove Street, Suite C, Peterborough, NH 03458. Reprinted with permission of the publisher.

Page 381, Reading Selection 10: "Block Island Lights" by Elinor DeWire, *Mariners Weather Log*, Spring 1992, pp. 30–32.

Basic Skills for Effective Reading

Getting Started

Getting started can be very exciting. It can open doors to new worlds. You may learn many new things. You may form different ideas. And you may develop important skills. Once you have started, you are never quite the same person as you were before.

Basic Skills for Effective Reading has been written to get you started on becoming a better reader. This book will help you learn the reading skills you need to do better in school or on the job. Then, as you master each skill, you will be on your way toward becoming an effective reader.

What will you be like as an effective reader? First, you will have mastered a number of different reading skills. Thus, you will be a *flexible* reader—one who can choose from among these skills according to what you need as you read. For example, if you need to figure out words you do not know at sight, you will have a number of skills to put to work to help you. Second, you will be able to understand and remember what you read. Finally, you will begin to find it easier to read different kinds of materials.

Any skill is easier to master if you understand what you need to do and how to do it. For example, if you want to become a good golfer, you must learn what the game is all about. Then, you must master a number of basic golf skills. You have to learn how to choose the right club for each different shot, how to grip a golf club, how to stand, and how to hit the ball.

The same kind of learning is needed to read well, to read effectively. But in this case, you need to find out what reading is all about and which reading skills need to be mastered. You will find out about reading and about these skills in this "Getting Started" part of *Basic Skills for Effective Reading.*

A LOOK AT READING

A good way to learn what reading is all about is for you to "learn to read." We will use a cartoon to take you back to the time when you couldn't read. Do you remember how strange printed words looked to you? All those funny marks meant nothing. Then, as you began to learn what they stood for, the groups of marks took on meaning. You had begun to read.

Since you already know English letters, other marks will be used here. When you look at these marks for the first time, you will not be able to read them. They will look just as strange to you as English letters did before you learned what they were.

Now look at the cartoon on page 4. Examine each of the four boxes. Try to read pictures just as you did before you learned to read words. Then write down what you think is happening.

Did you come up with a very broad idea of what is happening? Check what you wrote against the following facts. The cartoon is about two monkeys, one female and one male. Both are on the branch of a tree. The male monkey seems to be reading a book in different ways. Why is he reading in a different way in each box? And what is the female monkey saying to him? To answer these questions and make sense out of the cartoon, you need to know more about what the two monkeys are saying to each other. Look at the cartoon as it appears on pages 5 and 6. What you need to know is written in strange marks below each box.

The first step to understanding what is written under each box is to figure out, or decode, each of the strange marks. They must be changed into English letters. Each mark stands for an English letter and its sound. Groups of marks stand for words. Large marks stand for capital letters. Punctuation marks are the same as those you already know.

Use the following steps to decode what is printed under each box of the cartoon:

1. *Decode words from left to right.*
2. *Look at the shape of each mark.*
3. *Find that shape in the code on the right-hand side of the page.*
4. *Write the English letter the mark stands for in the space directly below it.*
5. *Read the English words.*

The first two words have been done for you. As you decode the marks, something will happen to you. Think about what you are doing and how you are "learning to read."

What do you think is happening?

_____

_____

_____

_____

◇⊡◐◑:◆⊡◐○◇ ○▲◐ ★△◇ ⊕△▯▲◧?
S h e : W h a t

⊡○◈:⊙◐◑▯△□ ○△ ◑●●◑▯◈◇▯◈◐ ▲○○⊕◐▲.

◇⊡◐◑:◆⊡◐○◇ ○▲◐ ★△◇ ⊕△▯▲◧?

⊡○◈:⊙◐◑▯△□ ○△ ◑●●◑▯◈◇▯◈◐ ▲○○⊕◐▲.

Code

○	=a
◉	=b
◑	=c
⊕	=d
◐	=e
●	=f
□	=g
⊡	=h
▯	=i
⊞	=j
◧	=k
■	=l
△	=m
◮	=n
△	=o
⟁	=p
▲	=q
▲	=r
◇	=s
◈	=t
◇	=u
⊕	=v
◖	=w
◆	=x
★	=y
✡	=z

◇▣◐:△△◆ ◐▣○◇ ○▲◐ ★▲◇ ⊕▲▤▲□?

▣◐:◉▣▤△□ ○△ ●●●●◐◍◍◆▤⊕◐ ▲◐○⊕◐▲.

◇▣◐:▤ ⊕▲△'◇ ◇△⊕◐▲△◇◇◇○△⊕!

▣◐:○▲ ◉●●◐◍◍◆▤⊕◐ ▲◐○⊕◐▲ ▤◇ ●■◐ ▥◉■◐.

▤'△ ◈▲★▣△□ ◇△ ◐◐ ●■◐◆▤◉■◐!

Code

Symbol	Letter
○	=a
◉	=b
◍	=c
⊕	=d
◐	=e
●	=f
□	=g
▣	=h
▥	=i
⊞	=j
◧	=k
■	=l
△	=m
◬	=n
◭	=o
⟁	=p
◺	=q
▲	=r
◇	=s
◈	=t
◍	=u
⬦	=v
◖	=w
◆	=x
★	=y
✡	=z

Check your decoding.

Box 1

She: What are you doing?
 He: Being an effective reader.

Box 2

She: What are you doing?
 He: Being an effective reader.

Box 3

She: Now what are you doing?
 He: Being an effective reader.

Box 4

She: I don't understand!
 He: An effective reader is flexible. I'm trying to be flexible!

What happened to you as you decoded the marks? Did you find that you did not need to decode words that were used over and over again? Did you begin to know them after seeing them one or two times? This usually happens with words such as "what," "doing," "effective," and "reader." Each of these words is used in all or most of the four boxes. You began to know each of these words. This is called developing a **sight vocabulary,** or words you know when you look at them. When you did not know words on sight, you used the code to change the marks into English letters. Then you were able to blend the sounds the English letters stand for into words. This is called using **phonics.** Thus, using both your new sight vocabulary and phonics, you learned to read words in a strange, new language. If you were to keep on using this language, you would probably become very comfortable with it. You would become a reader of this language just as you have become a reader of English.

Some people learn to read by first developing a sight vocabulary. Others learn to read by decoding, as you did with the strange marks. However, having a good sight vocabulary and being able to use phonics are both very important to an effective reader. Think how difficult it would be to work out every word as you read. The more words you know on sight, the easier and smoother your reading will be. But, as you read more difficult things, you will find many words you do not know on sight. Then phonics will become an important tool to have. While English letters do not always stand for the sounds you expect them to have, they do stand for the same sounds often enough to make phonics a useful tool for the effective reader. It has been found that phonics can be used to work out about 85 percent (85 out of 100) of the words in the English language. (For words that cannot be worked out with phonics, you can use a dictionary. What you know about letters and their sounds will also be of great help when you use the dictionary to pronounce words.)

Developing a good sight vocabulary and being able to use phonics are only the first steps toward effective reading. Once you know what the words are, you are ready for the second important step—understanding those words. There are a number of ways to figure out word meanings. When you work out words but do not understand what the writer is trying to tell you, you are still not really reading. Every writer uses written words to give the reader a message. It is up to you, the reader, to receive this message. Thus, reading must include thinking, putting ideas together, and finally, understanding the writer's message. That is the final, and most important, step in reading anything.

HOW TO USE THIS BOOK

Basic Skills for Effective Reading will help you master the kinds of skills you became aware of while working with the cartoon. The book is divided into four main parts. In Part One, Working with Words, you will learn to work out new words by using phonics and syllables. In Part Two, Building Vocabulary, you will find out how to build a bigger and better reading vocabulary by using context clues, word structure, the dictionary, and a personal way to learn new words. Part Three, Improving Comprehension, will show you how to understand writers' messages. Here you will learn how to find main ideas, how to select details that are related to those main ideas, and how to map paragraphs and selections that may be hard to understand and remember. You will apply your skills to the ten selections in Part Four.

Eleven basic skills are taught in the first three parts of this book. These skills have been chosen because they can help you form a strong base from which to learn more advanced skills later on. Each skill in *Basic Skills for Effective Reading* is presented in the same way:

1. The skill is described.
2. Samples are given to show you how to use the skill.
3. The skill is used in Guided Practice exercises. In these parts of the chapter, you may be told to check your answers after you complete the exercises. It is very important that you do *not* look at the answers until you have done the Guided Practice. Guided Practice exercises let you know if you are learning the skill.
4. The skill is practiced and mastered with Skill Practice exercises. Here you apply what you have learned in Guided Practice.

As you work through the Reading Selections in Part Four, Extending Your Reading Skills, use your basic reading skills as needed. Use phonics and syllables to pronounce words you do not know at sight. Once you have said these words aloud, you may find that you already know them. Perhaps it was only their written form you did not know. Then, if you do not know the meanings of any words, use context clues and word parts. If you need to, use a dictionary to help with pronunciations and meanings. You may decide to make these words part of your vocabulary. If so, use the Personal Vocabulary System. As you read, be aware of the main ideas and details. They will help you understand and remember what you read. If you have not covered all eleven basic skills, apply those you can. If what you are reading is hard to understand, you may decide to map it.

Read the introduction to the selection. It will give you a very good idea of what the selection is about. Then read the selection and answer the questions that follow it. Finally, write your reaction to what you have read.

As you go through Part Four, the selections become more difficult. If you can still answer the questions well, you are making good gains toward becoming an effective reader.

Learning to be an effective reader is like learning any other skill. You need to practice. Some practice is provided in the Guided Practice and Skill Practice parts of each chapter. Additional practice is given with the reading selections in Part Four. Here you have a chance to apply your reading skills as you learn them. However, all the reading you will do in this textbook is still not enough practice. You must also begin to read as much as you can on your own.

Read newspapers, magazines, books—anything that interests you. Remember, a champion swimmer does not become a winner by swimming four laps across a pool every Monday, Wednesday, and Friday. A tennis star does not practice only one hour a week. Anyone who wants to do well with any skill must take the time to practice daily. If you master the skills in *Basic Skills for Effective Reading* and practice every day, you will find that reading will become easier for you. And, as you read with ease, you will begin to enjoy it.

Now, let's get started!

CHAPTER 1

Phonics: Consonants

Phonics is a tool for decoding words you do not know at sight. When you use phonics, you apply what you know about the letters of the English alphabet and the sounds they stand for to decode, to work out, unknown words. As you found in "Getting Started," decoding can be a very important first step if you are to understand a writer's message.

In Chapters One and Two, you will usually apply what you learn about single letters and groups of letters to short words. In Chapter Three, you will use what you know about phonics in working out longer words. In all three chapters, it is very important that you say the sounds of letters aloud and listen carefully to hear if you have correctly blended the sounds into words.

There are two kinds of letters in the English alphabet, **consonants** and **vowels.** In Chapter One you will learn about consonant letters, and Chapter Two will cover vowel letters.

The following drawing shows what is included in Chapter One. You can use it as a map to guide you through the chapter. A Summary Sheet of consonants and examples of the sounds they stand for is found on pages 47 and 48. It will help you to remember what you have learned in Chapter One.

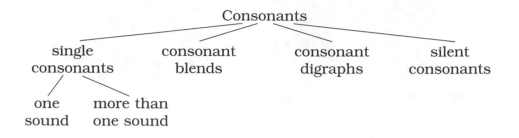

Twenty-one of the letters in the English alphabet are consonants:

b c d f g h j k l m n p q r s t v
w x y z

Each consonant letter stands for one or more sounds that are made when a speaker's breath is blocked by the tongue, teeth, or lips.

As you work with consonant letters, you will find that a consonant can stand for more than one sound. You will also find that more than one consonant can stand for the same speech sound. Three consonant letters, **c, q,** and **x,** do not have speech sounds of their own. Instead, they use the sounds of other consonants.

In this chapter, you will learn the sounds that consonant letters usually stand for. You will learn about

1. Single consonants that stand for only one speech sound.
2. Single consonants that stand for more than one speech sound.
3. Two or three letters that form consonant blends.
4. Two letters that form consonant digraphs.
5. Special cases where consonants are silent.

It is important that you say the words with the speech sounds out loud so that you can relate consonant letters with their sounds as you learn them.

SINGLE CONSONANTS THAT STAND FOR ONLY ONE SOUND

The following letters stand for only one consonant speech sound:

<pre>
b   f   h   j   k   l   m   p   r   t   v
w*   y (as a vowel, see Chapter Two)
</pre>

This sound is the same no matter where the letter is found in a word.

The following sample words will give you practice in seeing these consonant letters and relating their speech sounds to them. As you say each word aloud, notice what happens in your mouth when you say the underlined consonant letter. Notice that your breath is blocked by your tongue, teeth, or lips.

b	base	obey	tub
f	fast	drift	loaf
h	home	beehive	perhaps
j	jump	inject	major
k	kept	taken	book
l	lamp	failed	level
m	money	crime	mom
p	pint	ripen	pop
r	ride	rerun	scare
t	take	boating	toot
v	vine	never	move
w	wise	rewind	aware
y	yet	beyond	yank

SINGLE CONSONANTS THAT STAND FOR MORE THAN ONE SOUND

The following consonants each stand for more than one speech sound:

<pre>
c   d   g   n   q   s   x   y (as a vowel, see Chapter Two)
z
</pre>

*Although the consonant letter **w** seems to stand for a number of different sounds, it is probably safe to say that **w** stands for only one sound of its own. As you will find later in Chapter One, when next to **h**, the **w** is sometimes silent. At other times the **wh** is a digraph in which **w** keeps its own sound. In Chapter Two, **w plus a vowel has no sound of its own.** Sometimes **w** is silent, and at other times it becomes a part of a brand new sound. This new sound is not shown in the dictionary pronunciation as having the sound of **w** at all.

1. Sounds of c

The letter **c** does not stand for a speech sound of its own. Instead, the letter **c** may use the speech sound of **s** or **k**.

When the letter **c** is followed by **e, i,** or **y,** it usually stands for the speech sound of **s** (s̲un). This is called the **soft** sound of the letter **c.** The following words all have the soft sound of **c.** Say the words and listen for that soft sound of **c.**

c̲ell	c̲igar	c̲ity
c̲ent	ric̲e	c̲yst
ac̲e	c̲ircle	bic̲ycle

When the letter **c** is followed by any letters other than **e, i,** or **y,** it usually stands for the speech sound of **k** (k̲ite). This is called the **hard** sound of the letter **c.** The following words all have the hard sound of **c.** Say the words and listen for the hard sound of **c.**

c̲ast	c̲urb	c̲ome
c̲oin	Drac̲ula	rec̲ount
c̲oal	C̲oc̲a C̲ola	c̲opper

Guided Practice 1–1: Sounds of c

Directions: Say the following words. Listen for the sound of **c** in each word. If the **c** has a soft sound (c̲ent), write **s** next to the word. If the **c** has a hard sound (c̲an), write **k** next to the word.

1. onc̲e _____
2. fenc̲e _____
3. c̲ollege _____
4. spruc̲e _____
5. rec̲ount _____

6. c̲ool _____
7. dec̲ide _____
8. c̲ourse _____
9. c̲ommon _____
10. peac̲e _____

2. Sounds of d

The letter **d** usually stands for the speech sound you hear in dog. Say the following words and listen for the usual sound of **d**.

down	rider	cord
dust	fade	freed
dirt	dad	binder

Sometimes the letter **d** may stand for the speech sound of **j** (jump). The following words have the **j** sound of **d**. Say the words and listen for this sound of the letter **d**.

soldier	graduate	schedule

Guided Practice 1–2: Sounds of d

Directions: Say the following words. Listen to the speech sound of **d** in each word. Mark **d** if the sound of **d** is the same sound you hear in dime. Mark **j** if the sound of **d** is the same sound you hear in jar.

1. dark _____	5. does _____
2. hide _____	6. education _____
3. diet _____	7. stored _____
4. gradual _____	8. lady _____

3. Sounds of g

When the letter **g** is followed by **e, i,** or **y,** it often stands for the speech sound of **j** (jump). This is called the **soft** sound of the letter **g**. Say the following words and listen for the soft sound of **g**.

germ	gin	gym
bidge	ginger	gypsy
cage	giant	page

When the letter **g** is followed by any letter other than **e, i,** or **y,** it usually stands for the speech sound you hear in gate. This is called the **hard** sound of **g.** Say the following words and listen for the hard sound of **g.**

good	piglet	drug
goat	begun	stag
got	tugboat	gag

Guided Practice 1–3: Sounds of g

Directions: Listen to the sound of **g** in each of the following words. If the sound of **g** is a **j** sound (jam), write a **j** next to the word. If the sound of **g** is the same sound you hear in give, write a **g** next to the word.

1. hinge _____

2. gold _____

3. urge _____

4. gift _____

5. ranger _____

6. stage _____

7. gum _____

8. lodge _____

9. govern _____

10. rage _____

4. Sounds of n

The letter **n** usually stands for the speech sound you hear in not. Say the following words and listen for the usual speech sound of **n.**

north	nine	run
name	none	brown
note	inside	twin

When the letter **n** comes before a letter that stands for the **k** sound, the **n** sounds like **ng** (bang). Some people find it hard to hear the **g** sound in words such as bank. However, it is there. If you look at words that have **nk** in a dictionary you will find that **n** followed by **k** is shown to have a different sound that **n** followed by other letters. Some dictionaries show this **ng** in bank as bangk, while other dictionaries use the special mark η, as in baηk. Say the following words and listen for this **ng** sound.

ba<u>n</u>ker	dri<u>n</u>king	u<u>n</u>cle
tru<u>n</u>k	mo<u>n</u>ks	dra<u>n</u>k
bri<u>n</u>k	sli<u>n</u>ky	hu<u>n</u>k

Guided Practice 1–4: Sounds of n

Directions: Listen to the sound of **n** in each of the following words. If the sound of **n** is its usual sound, write **n** next to the word. If the sound of **n** is the same sound you hear in bank, write **ng** next to the word.

1. ma<u>n</u>y _____ 6. a<u>n</u>swer _____

2. i<u>n</u>k _____ 7. wi<u>n</u>k _____

3. <u>n</u>otice _____ 8. ope<u>n</u> _____

4. la<u>n</u>ky _____ 9. a<u>n</u>kle _____

5. mo<u>n</u>ey _____ 10. <u>n</u>u<u>n</u> _____

5. Sounds of q

In English words, the letter **q** is always followed by a **u**. The **qu** does not have a speech sound of its own. It usually stands for a **kw** sound. Say the following words and listen for the **kw** sound.

question	quack	quickly
quiet	quilt	quarter
queen	require	quit

However, the **qu** may sometimes have a **k** sound. Say the following words and listen for the **k** sound of **qu**.

liquor	plaque
bouquet	antique

6. Sounds of s

The letter **s** can stand for four different sounds. The **s** usually stands for the sound you hear in <u>s</u>on. Say the following words and listen for the usual sound of **s**.

<u>s</u>illy	sen<u>s</u>e	mutt<u>s</u>
<u>s</u>orry	rip<u>s</u>aw	<u>s</u>i<u>s</u>
<u>s</u>oap	hand<u>s</u>ome	ye<u>s</u>

The letter **s** sometimes stands for the **z** sound you hear in <u>z</u>ip. Say the following words and listen for this sound of **s**. Notice that the **z** sound of **s** is usually found in the middle or at the end of the word.

ha<u>s</u>	clo<u>s</u>et	u<u>s</u>ed
i<u>s</u>	ri<u>s</u>er	ro<u>s</u>y
crab<u>s</u>	rea<u>s</u>on	friend<u>s</u>

The other two sounds of **s** are not found very often. The **s** may stand for an **sh** (<u>sh</u>ip) sound. Say the following words and listen for the **sh** sound of **s**.

<u>s</u>ugar	<u>s</u>ure

The **s** may also stand for the **zh** sound. Say the following words and listen for the **zh** sound of **s**.

trea<u>s</u>ure	vi<u>s</u>ion
colli<u>s</u>ion	deci<u>s</u>ion

Guided Practice 1–5: Sounds of s

Directions: Listen to the sound of **s** in each of the following words. If the **s** in the word has its usual sound (<u>s</u>on), write an **s** next to the word. If the **s** in the word stands for the **z** sound (<u>z</u>ip), write a **z** next to the word. If the **s** in the word stands for the **zh** sound (trea<u>s</u>ure), write a **zh** next to the word.

1. shore<u>s</u> _____
2. <u>s</u>andy _____
3. pipe<u>s</u> _____
4. avoid<u>s</u> _____
5. lei<u>s</u>ure _____

6. perhap<u>s</u> _____
7. trade<u>s</u> _____
8. plea<u>s</u>ure _____
9. cho<u>s</u>e _____
10. Thur<u>s</u>day _____

7. Sounds of x

The letter **x** does not have a speech sound of its own. It usually stands for a **ks** sound. Say these words and listen for the **ks** sound of **x**.

hex   bo<u>x</u>es   fo<u>x</u>y
mi<u>x</u>   fi<u>x</u>ing   o<u>x</u>en

The letter **x** may also stand for a **gz** sound. Say these words and listen for the **gz** sound of **x**.

e<u>x</u>am   e<u>x</u>ile
e<u>x</u>it   e<u>x</u>ert

In a few cases, the **x** may stand for the sound of **z** (<u>z</u>oom), as in <u>x</u>ylophone.

Guided Practice 1–6: Sounds of x

Directions: Listen to the sound of **x** in each of the following words. If the **x** in the words sounds like **ks**, write **ks** next to the word. If the **x** in the word sounds like **gz**, write **gz** next to the word.

1. e<u>x</u>haust _____
2. e<u>x</u>cite _____
3. si<u>x</u>ty _____
4. e<u>x</u>ample _____
5. ne<u>x</u>t _____

6. coa<u>x</u> _____
7. e<u>x</u>ist _____
8. e<u>x</u>cept _____
9. e<u>x</u>cuse _____
10. e<u>x</u>amine _____

8. Sounds of z

The letter **z** usually stands for the sound you hear in zip. Say the following words and listen for the **z** sound.

zoom	blazing	froze
zipper	hazy	amaze
zone	razor	quiz

The letter **z** may also have the sound of **zh**. Say the following words and listen for the **zh** sound of **z**.

seizure   azure (meaning: color of the blue sky)

Finally, the letter **z** may have the sound of **s** (sun), as in waltz.

SKILL PRACTICE: SINGLE CONSONANTS

A. Directions: Circle all the consonant letters that usually stand for more than one speech sound.

b c d f g h j k l m n p q
r s t v w x y z

B. Directions. Write the letter or letters that stand for the sound of the underlined part of each word.

n ng s z kw ks gz d j

1. Te<u>x</u>as _____ 11. <u>d</u>ump _____

2. bun<u>k</u> _____ 12. <u>qu</u>est _____

3. e<u>xp</u>lode _____ 13. su<u>n</u>ken _____

4. ba<u>s</u>eball _____ 14. dungeon _____

5. e<u>qu</u>al _____ 15. e<u>x</u>act _____

6. agai<u>n</u> _____ 16. <u>s</u>ome _____

7. wi<u>s</u>e _____ 17. la<u>z</u>y _____

8. <u>qu</u>iet _____ 18. e<u>d</u>ucate _____

9. drin<u>k</u> _____ 19. pro<u>d</u>uct _____

10. chee<u>s</u>e _____ 20. ri<u>n</u>k _____

C. Directions: Read the following paragraph. Each underlined word has a sound of **c** in it. If the **c** has a soft sound, write **s** on the numbered line below the paragraph. If the **c** has a hard sound, write **k** on the numbered line below the paragraph.

1   2   3   4   5

Janice and Lance loved to camp out in their cabin. Twice they

6   7

took a couple of friends with them to help with the cooking and

8   9

headed for the scenic woods. They took their cameras just in case

10

they might meet some animals face to face.

1. _____	6. _____
2. _____	7. _____
3. _____	8. _____
4. _____	9. _____
5. _____	10. _____

D. Directions: Read the following paragraph. Each underlined word has a sound of **g** in it. If the **g** has a soft sound, write **j** on the numbered line below the paragraph. If the **g** has a hard sound, write **g** on the numbered line below the paragraph.

1   2   3   4   5

Gary, the gentle giant, got a present for his birthday in August.

6   7   8

His friend, George, gave him a stuffed toy giraffe. The giraffe wore

9   10

a gold ribbon around its long neck and a garter around its leg.

1. _____	6. _____
2. _____	7. _____
3. _____	8. _____
4. _____	9. _____
5. _____	10. _____

E. Directions: The same consonant is found twice in each of the following words. If the two letters stand for the same sound, write **s** after the word. If the two letters stand for different sounds, write **d** after the word.

1. <u>c</u>o<u>c</u>onut _____

2. en<u>g</u>a<u>g</u>e _____

3. <u>n</u>i<u>n</u>e _____

4. <u>c</u>ir<u>c</u>us _____

5. u<u>ns</u>i<u>n</u>kable _____

6. <u>X</u>ero<u>x</u> _____

7. po<u>t</u>a<u>t</u>oes _____

8. <u>g</u>ad<u>g</u>et _____

9. <u>s</u>ea<u>s</u>ons _____

10. <u>g</u>a<u>g</u> _____

CONSONANT BLENDS

When two or three consonant letters next to each other in a word keep their own speech sounds, these groups of letters are called **consonant blends.** Consonant blends can be found in the beginning, in the middle, or at the end of a word. Since each consonant in the blend keeps its own special sound, these sounds can be heard when you say the blend. For example, when you say the following words, you will be able to hear the sound of each of the consonants in the underlined blend.

b<u>l</u>ue	un<u>scr</u>ew	se<u>nd</u>
grass	wa<u>st</u>e	la<u>st</u>
<u>dr</u>ag	af<u>l</u>oat	te<u>nt</u>

The consonant blends are easier to learn when they are put into groups. The following are some often-used groups of consonant blends.

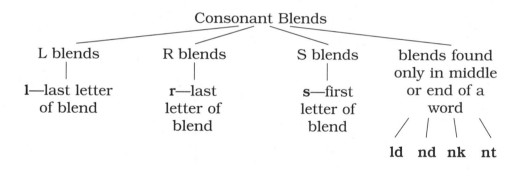

1. L blends all have l as the last letter of the blend.

bl   cl   fl   gl   pl   sl   spl

bl	<u>bl</u>ack	<u>bl</u>ow	re<u>bl</u>ot
cl	<u>cl</u>ap	<u>cl</u>og	un<u>cl</u>ean
fl	<u>fl</u>y	<u>fl</u>ower	<u>fl</u>ag
gl	glass	glow	glee
pl	plate	plop	plum
sl	<u>sl</u>ice	<u>sl</u>ate	<u>sl</u>ow
spl	splash	splice	splint

Guided Practice 1–7: L Blends

Directions: Say each of the following words. Circle each l blend you hear.

1. place
2. clock
3. sleet
4. fleet
5. glue
6. flop
7. claw
8. split
9. plot
10. bleed

2. **R** blends all have **r** as the last letter of the blend.

br   cr   dr   fr   gr   pr   tr

br	brown	brand	umbrella
cr	crab	cross	crank
dr	drag	dry	drop
fr	fry	fret	refresh
gr	green	grape	grunt
pr	prize	prank	surprise
tr	train	try	subtract

Guided Practice 1–8: R Blends

Directions: Say each of the following words. Circle each r blend you hear.

1. trip
2. unfriendly
3. pretty
4. brat
5. drug
6. frank
7. cry
8. preach
9. track
10. unbreakable

3. **S** blends all have **s** as the beginning letter of the blend.

sc   sk   sm   sn   sp   st   sw
scr   spr   squ   str

(**sl** and **spl** can be **l** blends or **s** blends. They have been put in the l blend group.)

sc	<u>sc</u>ale	<u>sc</u>old	<u>sc</u>um
sk	<u>sk</u>ip	<u>sk</u>ate	a<u>sk</u>
sm	<u>sm</u>ile	<u>sm</u>ack	<u>sm</u>oke
sn	<u>sn</u>ake	<u>sn</u>ip	un<u>sn</u>ap
sp	<u>sp</u>ider	<u>sp</u>eak	cla<u>sp</u>
st	<u>st</u>ill	<u>st</u>and	lo<u>st</u>
sw	<u>sw</u>eet	<u>sw</u>im	<u>sw</u>ab
scr	<u>scr</u>ub	<u>scr</u>ap	un<u>scr</u>ew
spr	<u>spr</u>ing	spray	sprout
squ	squaw	square	squint
str	<u>str</u>ing	<u>str</u>ap	<u>str</u>uck

Guided Practice 1–9: S Blends

Directions: Say each of the following words. Circle each **s** blend you hear.

1. scat
2. sprinkle
3. Scotch
4. screen
5. smear
6. swear
7. snoop
8. stretch
9. first
10. desk

4. Other often-used consonant blends are usually found in the middle or at the end of a word.

ld   nd   nk   nt

ld	co<u>ld</u>	ba<u>ld</u>	he<u>ld</u>
nd	fou<u>nd</u>	sa<u>nd</u>lot	wi<u>nd</u>ing
nk	tha<u>nk</u>less	su<u>nk</u>en	wi<u>nk</u>
nt	hu<u>nt</u>	pla<u>nt</u>ed	spli<u>nt</u>er

Guided Practice 1–10: Other Blends

Directions: Say each of the following words. Circle each consonant blend you hear.

1. bunk
2. field
3. painter
4. landing
5. fender

6. holder
7. wanted
8. send
9. rank
10. welder

SKILL PRACTICE: CONSONANT BLENDS

A. Directions: Circle the consonant blends you hear in the words in each of the following groups. Some words have more than one consonant blend. Other words do not have any blends at all.

1. grind	greet	gold
2. trapper	tailor	trailer
3. clearest	fastest	cradle
4. subject	swallow	splint
5. pretend	placement	passage
6. skunk	grasp	blunt
7. favor	flavor	frame
8. blend	sorrow	strike
9. brain	blame	bold
10. improve	instant	insist

B. Directions: Complete the following sentences using only words that have consonant blends.

1. The lion's sharp _____ hurt the hunter.

(tail   teeth   claws)

2. The factory workers would like to _____ work

(skip   miss   not)

today and go fishing.

3. All week Susan _____ about the man

(chatted   talked   dreamed)

she had met at the dance.

4. A warm _____ will always help you make

(heart   hello   smile)

new friends.

5. The heavy rain made the river _____ over its

(flow   reach   go)

banks.

6. _____ was her best color.
   (Brown   Red   Yellow)

7. Janet loved to _____ from the big
   (hop down   swing   jump down)

   oak tree.

8. The money was safe in the _____.
   (box   bank   case)

9. It was time to _____ the new class.
   (greet   meet   open)

10. I love to see new plants begin to grow in the _____
    (fall   summer

    _____.
    spring)

C. **Directions:** Use the following consonant blends to form
words.

1. **bl   cl   fl   gl   pl   sl**

_____ ump   _____ ump   _____ ump

_____ ay   _____ ay   _____ ay

_____ ot   _____ ot   _____ ot   _____ ot

_____ ing   _____ ing   _____ ing

_____ am   _____ am

2. **br   cr   dr   fr   gr   pr   tr**

_____ own _____ own _____ own _____ own _____own

_____ ess _____ ess

_____ am _____ am _____ am

_____ ack _____ ack

_____ op _____ op _____ op

3. sc sk sm sn sp sw st

_____ an   _____ an   _____ an

_____ ip   _____ ip

_____ im   _____ im

_____ in   _____ in

_____ oke   _____ oke   _____ oke

4. ld nd nk nt

ba _____   ba _____   ba _____

bu _____   bu _____

te _____   te _____

to _____

wa _____   wa _____

CONSONANT DIGRAPHS

When two consonants that are next to each other stand for *only one* speech sound, they are called **consonant digraphs.** Some consonant digraphs stand for a new sound—one that is different from the sounds either of the consonants would stand for if it stood alone. Other consonant digraphs stand for the sound of a single consonant. Again, the sound of the consonant digraph is not the same sound either consonant usually stands for. One consonant digraph, **ch** may stand for a new sound, the sound of another consonant, or the sound of another digraph. See the following drawing of this part of Chapter One.

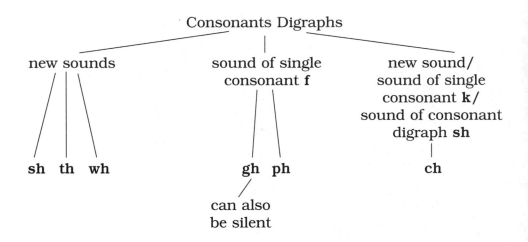

1. Consonant Digraphs **Sh, Th,** and **Wh** That Stand for New Sounds

Be aware as you work with consonant digraphs **sh, th,** and **wh** that they stand for new sounds that are different from the usual sounds of these single consonants.

sh

The following words all have the **sh** consonant digraph. Say the words and listen for the new speech sound.

shell	washer	cash
shine	fishing	fresh
shape	splashed	hush

th

The consonant digraph **th** stands for two new speech sounds. One **th** sound is called **voiced** and is heard in that, the, there, mother, and weather. The other **th** sound is called **unvoiced** and can be heard in thin, thank, thick, both, and birthday. Most dictionaries show that **th** stands for two different sounds. Look at page 186. It includes a dictionary key to pronouncing words. Notice the **th** is shown with two different sounds.

The difference in the two sounds of **th** may be hard for you to hear. Sometimes the difference between the voiced **th** and unvoiced **th** sounds is easier to hear if you say words that have each sound one after the other. In addition to hearing the difference between the two sounds of **th**, you can also feel the difference in your throat. Place your hand on your throat and say a word with the voiced **th**. You can feel your throat vibrate as you say this **th** sound. Your throat does not vibrate when you say the unvoiced **th** sound.

Practice saying the following pairs of words to help you hear and feel the two sounds of **th**.

Voiced **th**	*Unvoiced* **th**
them	third
thou	thump
these	thing
leather	faithful
bathe	bath

wh

The **wh** digraph sometimes stands for the sound of **hw**. Listen for the **hw** sound in the following words. This **hw** is another sound that is hard to hear. However, if you check your dictionary for the way to say any of the words below, you will find the wh digraph presented as hw.

wheel	when	while
what	where	white

Guided Practice 1–11: Consonant Digraphs—New Speech Sound

Directions: Say each of the following words. Circle each consonant digraph that stands for a new speech sound.

1. shoe	6. wish
2. wheeze	7. mother
3. ship	8. whisk
4. whip	9. flasher
5. fourth	10. sharp

2. Consonant Digraphs Gh and Ph Stand for the Sound of F

The consonant digraph **gh** stands for the sound of **f** (f̲un) in the following words. Listen for that **f** sound.

laugh	cough	rough

The consonant digraph **ph** also stands for the **f** (f̲un) sound in the following words.

phone	alphabet	graph
photo	nephew	phrase
phonics	orphan	geography

3. Consonant Digraph Ch Stands for a New Speech Sound, the Sound of a Single Consonant, or the Sound of Another Consonant Digraph

The consonant digraph **ch** may stand for three different sounds. The most often-used sound of **ch** is the new sound you can hear in the following words.

chur<u>ch</u>	<u>ch</u>apter	mar<u>ch</u>
<u>ch</u>eese	pea<u>ch</u>	brun<u>ch</u>
<u>ch</u>in	cat<u>ch</u>er	pin<u>ch</u>

Sometimes the consonant digraph **ch** can stand for the sound of **k** (<u>k</u>ite), as in the following words.

<u>Ch</u>rist	s<u>ch</u>ool	a<u>ch</u>e

Finally, consonant digraph **ch** can stand for the sound of another consonant digraph, **sh** (<u>sh</u>oot). Listen for the **sh** sound in the following words.

<u>ch</u>ef	<u>ch</u>ute	ma<u>ch</u>ine

Guided Practice 1–12: Consonant Digraph Ch

Directions: Read the following words and listen for the sounds of **ch**. If the **ch** sounds like the **ch** in <u>ch</u>ip, put a **ch** next to the word. If the **ch** sounds like a **k** (<u>k</u>ind), put a **k** next to the word. If the **ch** sounds like **sh** (<u>sh</u>e), put a **sh** next to the word.

1. reach _____	6. Christmas _____
2. backache _____	7. branch _____
3. Chicago _____	8. ditch _____
4. change _____	9. chorus _____
5. moustache _____	10. choke _____

SKILL PRACTICE: CONSONANT DIGRAPHS

A. Directions: Circle the consonant digraphs in the following words. There may be more than one digraph in a word.

1. whether
2. exchange
3. bashful
4. truthful
5. photograph
6. search
7. chemistry
8. tough
9. thrush
10. Charles

B. Directions: Use the following consonant digraphs to make new words.

ch   sh   wh

_____ ine	_____ ine	
_____ y	_____ y	
_____ ip	_____ ip	_____ ip
_____ ack		
_____ op	_____ op	
_____ in	_____ in	
_____ eat	_____ eat	
_____ erry		
_____ ale		
_____ eer	_____ eer	

C. Directions: Use only words that have consonant digraphs to finish the following sentences.

1. The storekeeper did not give Bob the right _____
   (food   drugs

   _____.
   change)

2. The church _____ was so good that it was
   (group   choir   team)
   asked to sing all over the state.

3. Ranchers have to _____ their sheep every
   (shear   sell   rope)
   spring.

4. Mrs. Smith feeds the baby every _____ hours.
   (four   two   three)

5. Prices are so high that it is hard to _____ a
   (feed   clothe   house)
   large family.

6. It is not unusual to get a _____ in your
   (pain   sound   wheeze)
   chest when you have a bad cold.

7. The bully was so _____ that the
   (tough   unfriendly   unhappy)
   other workers stayed away from him.

8. Families are usually asked to _____ food for
   (cook   make   share)
   potluck dinners.

9. The cook's best dish is made with _____.
   (squash   carrots   peas)

10. The people who live in the new house have asked us to come

    over for _____.
    (breakfast   lunch   dinner)

D. Directions: Read the following paragraph. Write the letters that stand for the consonant digraph sound or sounds you hear in each underlined word.

On the fourth[1] of July, the Finch[2] family took a train ride to Philadelphia. Because they were not rich[4] and could not take a berth[5], they all rode in the coach. The children took off their shoes[6] and outer clothes[7] and tried to sleep, but the screech[8] of the wheels[9] on the tracks made their heads ache[10]. It was such a rough[11] ride that they were glad when it was finished[12].

1. _____   7. _____

2. _____   8. _____

3. _____ _____   9. _____

4. _____   10. _____

5. _____   11. _____

6. _____   12. _____

SILENT CONSONANTS

When two consonants are next to each other in a word, sometimes one of them is silent. You do not hear it at all when you say the word.

The following are some examples of silent consonants. Say the words in the examples. You should *not* hear the underlined letters.

1. Two of the Same Consonant Letters

When two of the same consonant letters are next to each other, only one sound is heard.

egg	oddest	purring
bill	putt	missed

2. Examples of Silent Consonants

Silent b

b silent after **m**

lamb   climb   bomber

b silent before t

debt   doubt

Silent c

c silent before **k**

black   duck   nickel

c sometimes silent after **s** (Remember, in other words **sc** is a consonant blend and you hear both sounds.)

scene   muscle

scissors   science

Silent g

g silent before **n**

gnat   gnash

sign   design

Silent gh digraph

gh silent after **i**

sight	weigh
high	neighbor

Silent h

ghost	honest	hour

Silent k

k silent before **n**

knife	knit	knee

Silent l

calf	half	talk

Silent n

n silent after **m**

autumn	damn	hymn

Silent p

psalm	raspberry	cupboard

Silent s

isle	island	aisle

Silent t

castle	often	fasten

(Remember, in other words **st** is a consonant blend and you hear both sounds.)

Silent w

w silent before **r**

wrong	write	wrap

w silent before **h**

who	whom	whole
wholly	whose	whoever

(Remember, in other words **wh** is a consonant digraph with the new sound **hw.**)

Guided Practice 1–13: Silent Consonants

Directions: Say each of the following words. Cross out any consonant or consonants you do not hear.

1. listen
2. thumb
3. sigh
4. scent
5. stalk

6. psychology
7. pillow
8. wreck
9. assign
10. knight

SKILL PRACTICE: SILENT CONSONANTS

A. Directions: Say each of the following words. Cross out any consonant letters you do not hear.

1. ah
2. swordfish
3. walk
4. design
5. numb

6. racket
7. kinfolk
8. picket
9. knob
10. doubtful

11. fight
12. scenic
13. column
14. whistle
15. honor

B. Directions: Finish the following sentences by using only words with silent consonant letters.

1. For Hallowe'en, Jody wore a _____ hat.
   (clown   funny   green)

2. In many cities, if you _____ across the street
   (run   walk   skip)
   when the light is red, you can get a ticket from the police.

3. Hikers should make sure their _____
   (sleeping bags   tents
   _____ are packed very tightly.
   knapsacks)

4. The judge did not make the man's sentence _____
   (lighter   longer
   _____ even though there seemed to be a reason for the crime.
   shorter)

5. The bell in the church steeple rang _____.
   (loudly   softly   hourly)

6. Did you get many _____
   (birthday   Christmas   Valentine's Day)
   gifts this year?

7. Many tennis players wear bands to help their _____
   (legs   ankles)
   _____.
   wrists)

8. A _____ flying around the room can be a bother
   (bug   gnat   fly)
   when you are trying to study.

9. _____ of the Round Table were supposed
   (Knights   Men   Leaders)
   to do good deeds.
10. It was so _____ that night, he could not see
    (dark   rainy   black)
    the road.

C. Directions: Read the clue for the word needed on each line. Each word will have a silent letter in it. Then fill in the blanks to the right of the clues.

1. Land with water all around it is an __ s __ __ __ __.

2. The opposite of day is __ i __ __ __.

3. A baby sheep is called a l __ __ __.

4. A play may have three __ __ e __ __ __.

5. If you match the lottery numbers, you will be a __ __ n __ __ __ __.

6. If your car won't start, you may need a new __ __ t __ __ __ __ __.

7. Kings may live in c __ __ __ __ __ __ __.

8. If something is not right, it is __ __ o __ __.

9. If you are only a little hungry, take a __ n __ __ __.

10. When one is not happy in a job, it may be best to __ __ s __ __ __.

11. Sixty minutes equal one __ o __ __.

12. A good-looking man is __ __ n __ __ __ __ __.

13. Instead of jogging, some people would rather __ a __ __ __.

14. In church you sing __ __ __ n __.

15. A dead body may be found in a t __ __ __.

16. Turtles can draw into their s __ __ __ __ __.

SKILL PRACTICE: CONSONANTS

A. Directions: Choose the consonant letter that finishes the sentence.

b   c   d   f   g   h   j   k   l   m   n   p   q   r   s   t   v
   w   x   y   z

1. A _____ followed by **e, i,** or **y** is called "soft" and has the sound of **s** (s̲un).

2. Three consonant letters, _____, _____, and _____, do not have speech sounds of their own.

3. In English words, _____ is always followed by the letter **u.**

4. If **c** is not followed by **e, i,** or **y,** it has the sound of _____.

5. In the word cheese, the **s** has a _____ sound.

6. In the word soldier, the **d** has a _____ sound.

7. An _____ followed by **k** has the sound of **ng.**

8. The letter _____ can be a consonant or a vowel.

9. An _____ may have the sound of **gz** in some words.

10. A _____ followed by **e, i,** or **y** is called "soft" and has the sound of **j** (jam).

B. Directions: Each of the following words has a consonant blend, a consonant digraph, or both. Underline the blends and circle the digraphs.

1. swish
2. brisk
3. orphan
4. plush
5. squash
6. thick
7. blanket
8. drench
9. sprint
10. shoulder
11. inspect
12. whisker
13. paragraph
14. chest
15. zebra
16. flush
17. friend
18. lasting
19. splinter
20. glands

C. Directions: Write the letter or letters that stand for the sound of the underlined part of each word. If the letter is silent, write a zero (0) next to the word.

1. urge _____
2. bla<u>n</u>k _____
3. germ _____
4. night _____
5. <u>c</u>arpet _____
6. equal _____
7. gra<u>d</u>ual _____
8. mu<u>s</u>ic _____
9. <u>k</u>nit _____
10. <u>Ch</u>rysler _____

11. <u>c</u>inder _____
12. nephew _____
13. twig _____
14. <u>s</u>upper _____
15. com<u>b</u> _____
16. e<u>x</u>hale _____
17. tough _____
18. liq<u>u</u>or _____
19. para<u>ch</u>ute _____
20. <u>wh</u>irl _____

SUMMARY SHEET: CONSONANTS

SINGLE CONSONANTS

ONE SOUND	MORE THAN ONE SOUND
b base	c soft (s) cell
f fast	(c followed by e, i, y)
h home	hard (k) coin
j jump	d (d) down
k kept	(j) soldier
l lamp	g soft (j) germ
m money	(g followed by e, i, y)
p pint	hard (g) got
r ride	n (n) note
t take	(ng) bank
v vine	q (kw) quit
w wise	(k) liquor
y yet	s (s) soap
	(z) has
	(sh) sure
	(zh) treasure
	x (ks) fox
	(gz) exact
	(z) xylophone
	z (z) zoom
	(s) waltz
	(zh) azure

CONSONANT BLENDS

L		R		S	
bl	black	br	brown	sc	scale
cl	clap	cr	crab	sk	skip
fl	fly	dr	drag	sm	smile
gl	glass	fr	fry	sn	snake
pl	plate	gr	green	sp	spider
sl	slice	pr	prize	st	still
spl	splash	tr	train	sw	sweet
				scr	scrub
				spr	spring
				squ	squaw
				str	string

FOUND IN MIDDLE OR END OF WORD ONLY

ld	coldest
nd	found
nk	thankless
nt	hunt

CONSONANT DIGRAPHS

NEW SOUNDS	SOUND OF SINGLE CONSONANT	NEW SOUND / SOUND OF SINGLE CONSONANT / SOUND OF ANOTHER DIGRAPH
sh	**gh** (f) laugh	**ch** (ch) church
th (voiced) that	**ph** (f) phone	(k) school
(unvoiced) thank		(sh) chef
wh (hw) when		

SILENT CONSONANTS

two of the same consonant letters
only hear one sound egg

b	after **m** lamb
	before **t** debt
c	before **k** black
	after **s** scene
g	before **n** gnat
gh	after **i** sight
h	ghost
k	before **n** knife
l	calf
n	after **m** damn
p	psalm
s	island
t	castle
w	before **r** wrong
	before **h** who

CHAPTER 2

Phonics: Vowels

Five of the 26 letters of the English alphabet are vowels:

a   e   i   o   u

Sometimes the consonant letters **w** and **y** also act as vowels. Vowel letters stand for sounds that are made when the speaker's breath is *not* blocked by the tongue, teeth, or lips. Each of the vowel letters stands for more than one speech sound. Also, more than one vowel letter may stand for the same sound. Be sure to pronounce the words with the speech sounds out loud so that you can relate vowel letters and their sounds as you learn them.

In this chapter, you will learn about

1. Single long vowels.
2. Single short vowels.
3. Single vowels + **r.**
4. **Y** as a vowel.
5. Double vowels—with one vowel silent.
6. Double vowels—new single sounds.
7. Using what you have learned about consonants and vowels to decode and pronounce new words.

The following drawing shows what is included in Chapter Two. You can use it as a map to guide you through the chapter and when you need to remember which information about vowels goes together.

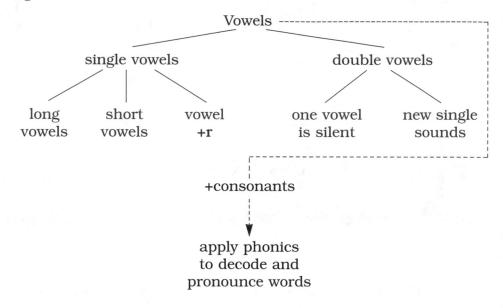

A Summary Sheet of vowels and examples of the sounds they stand for is found on page 72. It will help you to remember what you have learned in this part of Chapter Two.

SINGLE LONG VOWELS

Use the following drawing to help you understand and remember the five possible sounds of single vowels.

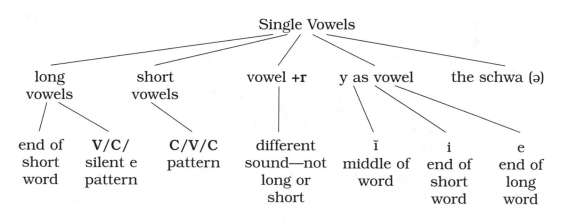

When the sound of a vowel is the same as its name, the vowel sound is said to be **long**.

Say each of the following words and listen for the sounds of the vowel's name. A bar (–) is used above a vowel letter to show that the letter stands for a long vowel sound.

ace eve ice oh use

Guided Practice 2–1: Long Vowels

Directions: Say each of the following words and listen for the name of the vowel letter. Then mark the long vowel that you hear.

1. base	6. choke	11. wipe
2. Utah	7. Pete	12. she
3. tote	8. hope	13. late
4. flute	9. kite	14. we
5. high	10. flake	15. chute

1. Single Vowel at the End of a Short Word

A single vowel at the end of a short word usually stands for a long vowel sound. Say the following short words and listen for the long vowel sound in each.

be go she hi

2. Silent e at the End of a Word

When a word has a | vowel | | consonant | | silent e | pattern, the vowel sometimes stands for a long sound. The following words are examples of this pattern. Notice that the final **e** is silent in each word and that the first vowel has a long sound.

tape these bite nose rude

Guided Practice 2–2: Silent e

Directions: Say the following words. You will not hear any long vowel sounds. Then add an **e** to each word. Now mark the long vowel sound you hear in each word.

fat   hop   mad   us   ton

fat ____   hop ____   mad ____   us ____   ton ____

SINGLE SHORT VOWELS

A curved line (˘) is used above a vowel letter to show that the letter stands for a short vowel sound. Vowel letters may stand for more than one short sound. An often-used short sound that each vowel letter stands for is given in the following words. Say each word and listen for the short vowel sound.

hăt ĕnd ĭn hŏp bŭt

When a word has a ⎡consonant⎤ ⎡vowel⎤ ⎡consonant⎤ pattern, the vowel letter usually stands for a short sound. The following words all have that pattern. Say each word and listen for short vowel sounds.

stop	map	win
man	red	must
get	cod	rid
cut	ran	men

Guided Practice 2–3: Long and Short Vowels

Directions: Say each of the following words and mark the vowels as long (–) or short (˘). If there are two vowels in a word, mark only the first one.

1. like
2. truck
3. tube
4. home
5. will

6. pass
7. slot
8. game
9. yet
10. these

SINGLE VOWEL + R

The letter **r** following a vowel letter changes the sound of that vowel. The resulting vowel sound is neither long nor short. As you say the following words, listen for the **different sound** each vowel stands for when it is followed by an **r**. Notice also that **er, ir,** and **ur** stand for the same sound.

m<u>ar</u>	h<u>er</u>	b<u>ir</u>d
t<u>ur</u>n	c<u>ar</u>	f<u>er</u>n
d<u>ir</u>t	l<u>ur</u>k	sp<u>ar</u>k
f<u>or</u>	h<u>ur</u>t	st<u>or</u>m
s<u>ir</u>	b<u>er</u>th	w<u>or</u>th

Y AS A VOWEL

The letter **y** can act as either a consonant or vowel letter. The letter **y** found at the beginning of a word stands for the consonant sound in yet. When the letter y **is found in the middle or at the end of a word, it stands for a vowel sound.**

1. Short i Sound of y

When the letter **y** is in the middle of a word, it usually stands for a **short i** sound. Listen for the short i sound of **y** in the following words.

gym   hymn   oxygen

2. Long i Sound of y

As the last sound of a short word, the letter **y** usually stands for the **long i** sound heard in the following words.

dry   fry   my

Long e Sound of y

When the letter **y** is the last letter in a word that has more than one part, it usually stands for a **long e** sound. Listen for the long e sound at the end of each of the following words.

baby   candy   happy

Guided Practice 2–4: Vowel Sounds of y

Directions: Say the following words and write the vowel sound of **y** you hear in each word.

ĭ   i   e

1. sky   _____
2. jelly   _____
3. symbol   _____
4. nasty   _____
5. system   _____

6. busy   _____
7. fly   _____
8. hungry   _____
9. myth   _____
10. mystery   _____   _____

THE SCHWA

Long words are usually broken down into parts. Each part is called a syllable. As you pronounce these syllables you do not stress each in the same way. For example, the word errand is broken down into two syllables: **er** + **rand**. Stress is put on pronouncing **er**, the first syllable. Now, a strange thing happens. The vowel in the unstressed syllable **rand** does not have the short single vowel sound you would expect it to have. Instead, it is pronounced like a weak **short u** such as you would hear in the word **up**. This **weak short u** is called a **schwa** and is shown in the dictionary by an upside-down **e** (ə). The word errand is pronounced **er-ənd**. (Remember that one consonant is silent in a pair of matching consonants. Thus, only one **r** is shown in the pronunciation of errand.)

The schwa is not a letter of the alphabet. However, it can stand for all five vowels and even for a vowel that is followed by r in unstressed syllables. If you skim through your dictionary looking for words that are pronounced with a schwa, you will probably be surprised to find how often the schwa sound is used.

Read the following words and listen for the sound of the schwa in each. The vowel in the unstressed syllable has been underlined for you.

potato   waiter
ago   golden
super   parachute
lantern   lava
China   mistake

Name _____

SKILL PRACTICE: SINGLE VOWELS

A. Directions: Say the following words and listen for the sound of each vowel. Write the letter that stands for the sound you hear and mark it as long or short. If the sound of the vowel is changed by an **r**, write that vowel + **r** on the line.

1. fly _____

2. cute _____

3. me _____

4. floppy _____ _____

5. gyp _____

6. torn _____

7. warm _____

8. pitch _____

9. place _____

10. lumpy _____ _____

11. branch _____

12. verse _____

13. like _____

14. shaky _____ _____

15. home _____

16. hike _____

17. burn _____

18. kit _____

19. fret _____

20. lurch _____

B. Directions: Finish the following sentences by drawing circles around words with long vowel sounds.

1. In Rome, I saw the _____ come to the window
   (king   Pope   nun)
   to bless the people.

2. One way to get dust out of a mop is to _____
   (wash   rinse
   _____ it.
   shake)

3. The new golf clubs were a gift for _____.
   (Jack   Sally   Bob)

4. Some people like to _____ after dinner.
   (smoke   drink   chat)

5. Jack only likes to be seen with _____ women.
   (tall   smart   cute)

6. Our family stayed in a cabin by a _____ every
   (lake   pond   river)
   summer.

7. Americans have to pay any taxes that they _____
   (can   should
   _____ by April 15.
   owe)

8. Because the _____ was wrong, the new
   (size   color   panel)
   drapes had to be sent back.

9. A small _____ of special skin cream can cost
   (jar   bottle   tube)
   a lot of money.

10. You can expect to live longer, and be in better health, if you
    don't _____.
    (overeat   drink j   jog)

C. Directions: Read the following paragraph. Write the vowel sound you hear in each underlined word. If the word has more than one vowel, write the sounds of both vowels. Show long vowels, short vowels, vowels + **r, y** acting as a vowel, and the ə sound. The first one has been done for you.

               1   2   3   4   5
Not <u>so</u> many years in the past, <u>children</u> could hardly wait <u>for</u>
        6   7   8   9   10   11
the <u>first</u> snow of <u>winter</u> to <u>start</u>. It was <u>fun</u> to <u>dash</u> into the <u>cold</u>
12   13   14   15   16   17 18
<u>white</u> <u>stuff</u>. <u>These</u> days, it is not <u>quite</u> the <u>same</u>. The snow gets very
  19   20   21   22 23
dirty. It is gray from <u>cars</u> that pass by and may even <u>be</u> <u>full</u> of lead
24 25   26   27   28   29
if <u>traffic</u> <u>has</u> been heavy. Who would <u>like</u> to play in that <u>mess</u>? <u>Not</u>
              30
anyone <u>smart</u>!

1. __o__   16. _____

2. _____   17. _____

3. _____ _____   18. _____ _____

4. _____ _____   19. _____ _____

5. _____   20. _____

6. _____   21. _____

7. _____ _____   22. _____

8. _____   23. _____

9. _____   24. _____

10. _____   25. _____ _____

11. _____   26. _____

12. _____   27. _____

13. _____   28. _____

14. _____   29. _____

15. _____   30. _____

DOUBLE VOWELS

Use the following drawing to help you understand and remember the three kinds of sounds that double vowels can stand for.

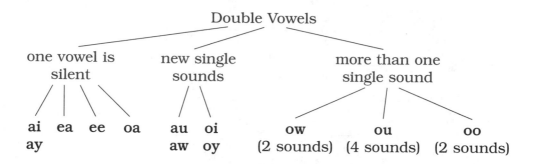

DOUBLE VOWELS—ONE VOWEL IS SILENT

When two vowels are next to each other in a word, they sometimes act as if they were only one vowel. Some double vowels stand for the sound of only one vowel, with the other vowel silent. The following double vowels usually act as though they were single vowels. The first vowel stands for the sound you hear. The second vowel is silent.

1. Sound of **ai** and **ay**

The double vowels **ai** and **ay** usually stand for only one sound, **long a.** The **i** and **y** are silent. Say the following words and listen for the sound of long **a.**

aid	tray	stain
main	waist	pray
laid	clay	wait

2. Sounds of **ea**

The double vowel **ea** sometimes stands for a **long e** sound. The **a** is silent. Say the following words and listen for the long **e** sound.

clean	please	weak
sea	treat	grease

The double vowel **ea** may also stand for a **short e** sound. The **a** is still silent. Say the following words and listen for the short **e** sound.

bread   wealth   breast
death   deaf   dead

3. Sound of **ee**

The double vowel **ee** usually stands for the single **long e** sound. Say the following words and listen for the long **e** sound.

week   eel   queen
peep   Greek   teen

4. Sound of **oa**

The double vowel **oa** usually stands for the **long o** sound. The **a** is silent. Listen for the long **o** sound as you say the following words.

soap   cloak   boat
coal   foam   oak

DOUBLE VOWELS—NEW SINGLE SOUNDS

Some double vowels stand for a single sound that is different from that of either vowel when it stands alone. These single sounds are neither long nor short. They arc **new** sounds.

1. Sound of **au** and **aw**

Both **au** and **aw** stand for the new single vowel sound you hear in the following words.

cause   awe   fault
squaw   haul   saw

Notice that the **w** loses its own sound when it follows **a** in these words.

Look up any of the **au** or **aw** words above in a dictionary. You will find **au** and **aw** shown with a single sound that is new.

2. Sound of **oi** and **oy**

Double vowels **oi** and **oy** stand for the new single vowel sound you hear in the following words.

boy	c<u>oi</u>n	toy
v<u>oi</u>ce	joy	sp<u>oi</u>l

Notice that **y** acts as a vowel when it is part of the double vowel **oy.**

Guided Practice 2–5: Sound of au and aw, Sound of oi and oy

Directions: Say each of the following words. If you hear the sound of **aw** (sh<u>aw</u>l), write **aw** next to the word. If you hear the sound of **oy** (joy), write **oy** next to the word.

1. enjoy _____		6. auto _____
2. rejoice _____		7. crawl _____
3. caught _____		8. noise _____
4. lawn _____		9. Paul _____
5. coil _____		10. destroy _____

DOUBLE VOWELS THAT STAND FOR MORE THAN ONE SINGLE SOUND

The double vowel **ow** may stand for a **long o** sound. In this case, the **w** is silent. Say the following words and listen for a long **o** sound in each.

bl<u>ow</u>	<u>ow</u>n	t<u>ow</u>
gr<u>ow</u>	sn<u>ow</u>	gl<u>ow</u>

Sometimes the **ow** may stand for the sound heard in the following words.

h<u>ow</u>	br<u>ow</u>n	c<u>ow</u>
<u>ow</u>l	cr<u>ow</u>d	h<u>ow</u>l

This sound of **ow** is the same sound as that of **ou** in some words. Check the words above in a dictionary and you will find the **ow** shown as **ou**. For example, **howl** is shown to be pronounced as h<u>ou</u>l.

Guided Practice 2–6: Sounds of ow

Directions: Say cach of the following words and listen for the two sounds of **ow**. If the word has the **ow** sound you hear in sn<u>ow</u>, write an **a** next to the word. If the word has the **ow** sound you hear in h<u>ow</u>, write a **b** next to the word.

1. power _____
2. brown _____
3. flow _____
4. growing _____
5. flower _____

6. now _____
7. town _____
8. show _____
9. prowl _____
10. slow _____

2. Sounds of **ou**

The double vowel **ou** usually stands for the same **ow** sound that you hear in <u>ow</u>l.

bl<u>ou</u>se	fl<u>ou</u>r	<u>ou</u>r
<u>ou</u>t	gr<u>ou</u>nd	sc<u>ou</u>t

The double vowel **ou** may also stand for three other sounds. In the following words, the double vowel **ou** stands for a long **o** sound. The **u** is silent. Listen for the long **o** sound in the following words.

d<u>ou</u>gh	s<u>ou</u>l	th<u>ou</u>gh

The double vowel **ou** may also stand for a **short u** sound. Then the **o** is silent. Listen for the short **u** sound in the following words.

cousin   double   tough

Finally, **ou** may stand for the **u** sound you can hear in the following words. The **o** is again silent. Say the words and listen for the sound of **u**.

group   route   soup

(Note that this sound of **ou** matches the long **oo** sound you will learn later in this chapter.)

Guided Practice 2–7: Sounds of ou

Directions: Say the following words and listen for the sounds of **ou**. Write **a**, **b**, or **c** to show which sound of **ou** you hear: **a** = sound in out, **b** = sound in double, **c** = sound in group.

1. country _____   6. cougar _____

2. youth _____   7. ounce _____

3. count _____   8. rough _____

4. house _____   9. trouble _____

5. enough _____   10. coupon _____

Sounds of oo

The double vowel **oo** may stand for two different sounds. One **oo** sound is heard in the following words. It is called the **long oo** sound (oo). Listen for the **long oo** sound as you say the following words.

room   mood   noon
snoop   too   food

The other **oo** sound is heard in the following words. It is called the **short oo** sound (o͝o). Say the following words and listen for the short **oo** sound.

foot   hood   crook
book   stood   soot

Guided Practice 2–8: Sounds of oo

Directions: Listen to the **oo** sound in each of the following words. Mark the oo as long (boot) or short (ho͝od) in each word. (Be sure that your mark covers both o's.)

1. zoo
2. brook
3. shook
4. bloom
5. noose

6. hood
7. groom
8. wool
9. proof
10. rooster

SKILL PRACTICE: DOUBLE VOWELS

A. Directions: Underline the word or words in each row that have the same vowel sound you *hear* in the key word.

Key Words

1. m<u>ai</u>n	gray	stage	cast	plain
2. t<u>ea</u>	seam	tense	teeth	press
3. br<u>ea</u>d	scene	spread	wreck	leak
4. w<u>e</u>ck	beef	fresh	beach	lean
5. b<u>oa</u>t	note	float	post	prove
6. bl<u>ow</u>	soap	stove	cow	froze
7. c<u>ow</u>	bounce	drown	flow	wow
8. s<u>aw</u>	sauce	rant	taught	dawn
9. <u>oi</u>l	coy	noise	some	moist
10. c<u>oo</u>l	droop	shook	choose	hook

B. Directions: Finish the following sentences by drawing circles around words with double vowels.

1. Mel's leg was so sore that he could not _____
    (walk   chase
   _____ his horse.
   mount)

2. Alice is glad that her birthday is in _____,
    (June   July   August)
   when she is home from college.

3. The shaggy dog put his _____ on his master's
    (nose   paw   leg)
   new chair.

4. A new _____ can be very useful when
    (broom   mop   duster)
   cleaning the house.

5. A polite person always says, _____

   ("Thanks"   "Pardon me"

   _____.

   "Please")

6. Many drivers try to limit their use of _____

   (gas   filters   oil)

   because of its cost.

7. There is a story in the Bible about Joseph and his _____

   (coat

   _____ of many colors.

   cape   hat)

8. Did you _____ your lecture notes before you

   (tape   read   study)

   took the test?

9. I was in such a hurry that I could _____ no

   (sit   wait   watch)

   longer.

10. Being a _____ is not a safe

    (firefighter   police officer   beekeeper)

    and easy job.

C. Directions: Use the following double vowels to finish words.
Then check to be sure you have formed a real word.

   ai   ea (h<u>ea</u>t)   **oa**

   1. r_____n   6. sp_____k

   2. pr_____ch   7. g_____l

   3. t_____l   8. m_____l m_____l

   4. r_____st   9. cl_____k

   5. w_____st   10. f_____nt

ay   ee   ow (sn<u>ow</u>)

1. cl_____   6. f_____d

2. m_____ed   7. sl_____   sl_____

3. b_____l   8. g_____ly

4. gr_____n gr_____n   9. _____n

5. str_____   10. cr_____k

au   aw   ou (<u>ou</u>t)   **oy**

1. gr_____nd   6. _____ch

2. c_____   c_____   7. h_____nt

3. t_____ght   8. pr_____d

4. p_____t   9. enj_____

5. b_____s   10. sh_____l

aw   oi   ow (<u>ow</u>l)

1. br_____n br_____ny   6. cl_____n

2. fr_____n   7. p_____nt

3. cr_____l   8. j_____n

4. cr_____n   9. pl_____

5. str_____   10. ch_____ce

Name _____

SKILL PRACTICE: VOWELS

A. Directions: Fill in the blanks using these four terms: **long, short,** or **vowel + r,** or **schwa ə.**

1. Single vowels can have _____, _____, _____, or _____ sounds.
2. The letter **y** in the middle of a short word usually has a _____ i sound.
3. In a word with the vowel/consonant/silent **e** pattern, the vowel sometimes has a _____ sound.
4. A vowel marked with a curved line above it usually has a _____ sound.
5. When a word has a consonant/vowel/consonant pattern, the vowel usually has a _____ sound.
6. As the last sound in a short word, the letter **y** usually has a _____ i sound.
7. When the sound of a vowel is the same as its name, the vowel is said to be _____.
8. A _____ has a different vowel sound that is neither long nor short.
9. When **y** is the last letter in a word with more than one part, it usually has a _____ e sound.
10. A vowel in an unstressed syllable is often pronounced with the _____ sound.

B. Directions: Write the single or double vowel sound(s) you hear in each of the numbered words. Use the marks that show vowels as long or short where needed. Mark each single vowel + r by writing the vowel letter that stands for the sound + r. Mark the sound of **y** and each schwa with ə.

    1   2   3   4   5   6
Steve, Joan, and Paul are part of a team that shows up at the

7   8   9   10   11   12   13   14   15
gym each day at dawn. They don't just fool themselves and fly

   16   17   18   19   20   21
through a tough workout. Instead, they work hard daily and are

happy to keep fit. Steve, Joan, and Paul feel good when they
leave the gym. They are now ready to face the rest of the day.

22   23   24 25
26   27 28 29   30

1. _____   16. _____

2. _____   17. _____

3. _____   18. _____   _____

4. _____   19. _____   _____

5. _____   20. _____

6. _____   21. _____   _____

7. _____   22. _____   _____

8. _____   23. _____

9. _____   24. _____

10. _____   25. _____

11. _____   26. _____

12. _____   27. _____

13. _____   28. _____   _____

14. _____   _____   29. _____

15. _____   30. _____

C. Directions: Finish these statements.

1. The double vowel **oa** usually stands for the single _____ sound.

2. Double vowel **ee** stands for a single _____ sound.

3. In the double vowel **oy**, the letter **y** acts as a _____.

4. The sound of **au** that you hear in **cause** is the same sound as that of double vowel _____.

5. Double vowel **ow** may stand for the sound you hear in **how,** or it may stand for the _____ sound.

6. Double vowel _____ may stand for the **ow** sound the **o** sound, the **ŭ** sound, or the **oo** sound.

7. In the word **wood,** the **oo** has a _____ sound.

8. Double vowels **ai** and **ay** usually stand for the single _____ sound.

9. The **oo** in **gloom** has a _____ sound.

10. Double vowel **ea** may stand for two single vowel sounds, _____ and _____ .

SUMMARY SHEET: VOWELS

SINGLE VOWEL SOUND

LONG VOWELS

a ace
e eve
i ice
o oh
u use

at end of short word:
be
go
she
hi

silent e at end of word (vowel/consonant/silent e):
tape
these
bite
nose
rude

SHORT VOWELS

a hăt
e ĕnd
i ĭn
o hŏp
u bŭt

middle of short word, between two consonants (consonant/vowel/consonant):
răn
mĕn
rĭd
cŏd
mŭst

DOUBLE VOWELS

VOWEL +R

mar
her
bird
for
hurt

Y AS A VOWEL

middle of short word
ĭ gym

last lstter of short word:
i dry

last letter of word with more than one part:
e baby

ONE VOWEL SILENT

ai $\searrow$ a

ay — aid, clay

ea — e clean, ĕ bread

ee — e week

oa — o soap

NEW SINGLE SOUNDS

au/aw — cause, saw

oi/oy — coin, joy

MORE THAN ONE SINGLE SOUND

ow — o blow, ow how

ou — ow blouse, o dough, ŭ cousin, soup

oo — room, ŏŏ foot

USING PHONICS TO DECODE AND PRONOUNCE WORDS

You have learned sounds that letters of the English alphabet usually stand for. You are now ready to use these sounds to decode and pronounce unknown words. The words you will decode in this part of the chapter are nonsense words. They have been made up for you to practice on; **they do not exist.** This practice will help you learn to use phonics whenever you need to decode and pronounce real words that you do not know at sight.

The key steps in using phonics to decode and pronounce words are as follows:

1. *Look at the letters that make up the word very carefully. Use what you know about consonant blends, consonant digraphs, and double vowels to help you spot letters that go together.*
2. *Say the sounds that letters and pairs of letters stand for. Be careful not to say silent letters.*
3. *After you have said all the sounds of the letters, say them again while blending the sounds together so that the result is the sound of the new word.*

Three nonsense words will be decoded for you. Follow the steps carefully so that you understand what has been done. Then you will practice on words that you will be able to check afterward. See if you are able to decode and pronounce them correctly. Finally, you will work with words on your own in Skill Practice.

1. **Word:** skoaph

   sk = blend—go together

   oa = o

   ph = **f** sound

   sk + **o** + **f**

   Pronounced: skof

2. **Word:** maghe

   m- = usual consonant sound

   ☐ vowel ☐ ☐ consonant ☐ ☐ silent e ☐ pattern—a = **a**

   gh = **f** sound

   m + **a** + **f**

   Pronounced: maf

3. **Word:** wrisp

wr usually = silent **w**

| consonant | | vowel | | consonant | pattern—i = ĭ

sp = consonant blend—go together

r + ĭ + sp

Pronounced: rĭsp

Guided Practice 2–9: Decoding Nonsense Words

Directions: Use the three key steps to decode these nonsense words. Use the space under each word to show how you decoded it. If you need help, go back and look at the sample decoding above.

1. **Word:** caild   Pronounced: _____

2. **Word:** sproad   Pronounced: _____

3. **Word:** wremb   Pronounced: _____

SKILL PRACTICE: USING PHONICS TO DECODE AND PRONOUNCE WORDS

A. Directions: Use what you know about letters and their sounds to say each of the following words. Then write its correct English spelling. These are real words. For example,

terckee = turkey
cele = seal

1. psope = _____

2. wramb = _____

3 cou = _____

4. kwik = _____

5. phite = _____

6. shigh = _____

7. cyk = _____

8. ghlag = _____

9. wrabit = _____

10. doun = _____

B. Directions: Use what you know about letters and their sounds to pronounce the following nonsense words. Show how each word may be pronounced. Some of these nonsense words may be pronounced in more than one way. An example has been done for you.

Word: spluew (silent **e**)   Pronounced: __spluw__

1. cild   Pronounced: _____

2. gayck   Pronounced: _____

3. quaish   Pronounced: _____

   (use the sound   or: _____
   of **sh** as in <u>sh</u>e)

4. cormn   Pronounced: _____

5. scawbt   Pronounced: _____

6. gese (silent **e**)   Pronounced: _____

7. treang   Pronounced: _____

                or: _____

8. snerc   Pronounced: _____

9. flysp   Pronounced: _____

10. wraske (silent **e**) Pronounced: _____

11. choogh (long **oo**) Pronounced: _____

                or: _____

                or: _____

12. sny   Pronounced: _____

13. clooph (short **oo**) Pronounced: _____

14. scaffy   Pronounced: _____

15. gumbe (silent **e**) Pronounced: _____

CHAPTER 3

Syllables

In Chapters One and Two, you learned the speech sounds the letters of the English alphabet stand for. Then you used these sounds to decode and pronounce words. All the work with words that you have done thus far has been with fairly short words. An effective reader, however, must also know how to decode and pronounce long words. The best way to decode long unknown words is to break them down into smaller parts called **syllables** and then to work with each part. In this chapter, you will learn how to

1. Hear syllables in words.
2. Use visible clues for dividing words into syllables.
3. Put together what you know about phonics and syllables to decode and pronounce long words.

HEARING SYLLABLES

As you read in Chapter Two, syllables are parts of words. A word may have one or more syllables. Each syllable, or word part, is made up of groups of letters that are said together. Each syllable may have one or more consonant sounds, but it never has more than one vowel sound. A group of letters is *not* a syllable if it has more than one vowel sound. On the other hand, a group of letters is *not* a syllable if it does not have a vowel sound in it.

Sometimes a vowel may stand alone as a syllable. As long as that vowel stands for a sound, the syllable need not have consonants. The following words are examples of vowels standing alone as syllables.

a̲/bout	ra/di/o̲	e̲/quip
o̲/pen	I̲	cap/i̲/tal

A syllable may make up a whole word if the word has only one vowel sound. The following words are all one-syllable words. Say each word and listen for a single vowel sound. The vowel sound you hear may be a long sound, short sound, or vowel + **r** sound.

snag	dark	climb
no	prim	hurt
spill	hand	led
blunt	spy	monk

When words have double vowels that are next to each other, they are still one-syllable words if only one vowel sound is heard. The following words each have two vowels next to each other, but only one vowel sound is heard. Listen for the single vowel sound in each word.

boast	sound	green
head	foil	haul
mail	leap	clue

Short words that have a ⎡vowel⎤ ⎡consonant⎤ ⎡silent **e**⎤ pattern are one-syllable words because only one vowel sound is heard—that of the first vowel. The following words all have that pattern. As you say these words, notice that the one vowel sound you hear may be long or short or made by a vowel + **r**.

verse	fare	edge
safe	give	those
were	done	name

A word has the same number of syllables, or parts, as it has vowel sounds. Thus, if you want to know how many syllables there are in a word, you need to listen for vowel sounds rather than count the number of vowel letters in the word. Find out how many syllables there are in each of the following words by saying the word and listening for vowel sounds. Then check to see if the number of vowel sounds you heard is the same as the number next to the word.

invent	(2)	ability	(4)
shawl	(1)	hockey	(2)
lullaby	(3)	branch	(1)
mermaid	(2)	graze	(1)
ordinary	(4)	uncomfortable	(5)

Guided Practice 3–1: Hearing Syllables

Directions: Say the following words and listen for vowel sounds. Write the number of syllables you hear in each word.

1. window _____

2. please _____

3. addresses _____

4. altogether _____

5. property _____

6. accept _____

7. during _____

8. count _____

9. danger _____

10. quarter _____

SKILL PRACTICE: HEARING SYLLABLES

A. Directions: Each of the following one-syllable words has more than one vowel letter but only one vowel sound. Read the words and write the vowel sound you hear. The vowel sound may be long, short, vowel + **r,** or a double vowel with one sound.

1. house _____	11. jade _____
2. point _____	12. stoke _____
3. perch _____	13. give _____
4. huge _____	14. coin _____
5. preach _____	15. spine _____
6. ounce _____	16. coat _____
7. faint _____	17. sauce _____
8. spurt _____	18. east _____
9. caught _____	19. hinge _____
10. grease _____	20. broil _____

B. Directions: Tell how many syllables you hear in each of the following words.

1. peace _____	6. uninvited _____
2. explain _____	7. tender _____
3. forgetful _____	8. brave _____
4. October _____	9. funeral _____
5. marvelous _____	10. justice _____

11. merry _____   16. produce _____

12. hamburger _____   17. recently _____

13. governor _____   18. secretary _____

14. slender _____   19. easy _____

15. device _____   20. machinery _____

C. Directions: Circle only two-syllable words to finish each of the following sentences.

1. Every four years, the American people _____
   (elect   pick   choose)

   a president.

2. If you have a dog who likes to roam, it is wise to _____
   (fence

   _____ your yard.
   enclose   shrub)

3. Today, more people than ever are going to _____
   (college   work

   _____ for the first time.
   school)

4. The family lost many things of great _____
   (importance   worth

   _____ during the fire.
   value)

5. Many restaurants now have special _____
   (parts   sections   seats)

   for nonsmokers.

6. Each year, there seem to be new _____
   (styles   fashions   fads)

   in women's clothing.

7. On a short airplane trip, only _____
   (liquids   drinks   beverages)

   such as coffee, tea, and milk are served.

8. It is usually a _____ to be with good

        (joy   holiday   pleasure)

   friends.

9. Many of the _____ highways across

        (county   state   interstate)

   the United States are heavily used.

10. A book is usually divided into _____.

                            (parts   chapters   paragraphs)

VISIBLE CLUES FOR DIVIDING WORDS INTO SYLLABLES

So far in learning about syllables, you have been able to hear the number of syllables in words you already know how to pronounce. When you meet a long new word, however, you cannot depend on hearing alone to help you divide the word into syllables. With an unknown word, you can only depend on what you see. All you see are letters of the alphabet placed to form a word. If you know what to look for, the placement of letters can give you **visible clues,** clues you can see, to dividing the word.

Four visible clues are presented in this chapter. A fifth visible clue will be given later when you work with word structure in Chapter Five. If you learn these visible clues and practice using them, you will be able to look at new words and divide them into syllables quickly and easily.

1. Visible Clue 1

$$\boxed{\text{Vowel}} \; \boxed{\text{Consonant}} \; / \; \boxed{\text{Consonant}} \; \boxed{\text{Vowel}} \; \textbf{(VC/CV)}$$

If two vowels in a word are separated by two consonants, divide between the consonants. The following words are all divided **VC/CV.** Look at each word very carefully to be sure you understand the visible clue for dividing that word into two syllables.

tun/nel	ob/ject	den/tist
com/mon	pow/der	sur/round
ar/range	lum/ber	dif/fer

Consonant blends may or may not be separated when you divide words. In some words, they are treated like two single consonants. For example, look at **dentist,** which is separated between the **nt** blend. In other words the consonants remain as blends and the division is made before or after the blend. There isn't any sure way to know how a blend will be treated in a word.

Digraphs are never separated. They are treated as single consonants, and the division is made before or after the digraph. If you do split a consonant digraph, you will have very strange results. For example, father will become fat/her.

Look at the following words for examples of consonant blends and digraphs kept together. Note that the words have been divided before or after blends or digraphs in these examples.

ath/lete   fath/er   sur/prise
ex/change   in/stant   gam/bler
far/ther   ap/prove   im/press

Notice that the first syllable in all the words divided **VC/CV** ends with a consonant. Syllables that end with a consonant are called **closed syllables.** The vowel in a closed syllable usually stands for a short sound, the sound made by a vowel + **r,** or the schwa sound (ə).

Guided Practice 3–2: Visible Clue 1—VC/CV

Directions: Divide each of the following words into syllables using Visible Clue **VC/CV.** The first syllable will be closed. Check to see if the vowel sound is a short one, is the sound made by vowel + **r,** or is the schwa sound. Mark the first vowel (˘) if it stands for a short vowel sound. Be careful not to separate consonant blends or consonant digraphs.

1. pitcher
2. enjoy
3. handsome
4. explain
5. worship

6. further
7. motto
8. convince
9. swallow
10. pretzel

2. Visible Clue 2

Vowel Consonant Vowel (VCV)

The **VCV** pattern is not always divided in the same way. Sometimes this pattern of letters is divided **V/CV.** At other times, it is divided **VC/V.** There is no way for the reader to know in advance where to divide the pattern. When you see a **VCV** pattern of letters in a word, try **V/CV** first, since it seems to be used more often than the other pattern. Depend on you ears. If the word does not sound right when you try to pronounce it, try the **VC/V** pattern. Both ways of dividing **VCV** into syllables are given here. Be sure to notice what happens to the sound of the first vowel in **VCV** when you divide the pattern each way.

Vowel / Consonant Vowel (V/CV)

When a vowel is followed by a single consonant letter, the word is often divided after that vowel. Look at the following words carefully and see how they are divided **V/CV**.

pa/per	to/tal	la/bor
de/mon	na/tive	si/lent
ba/by	mo/tor	de/cent

Notice that the first syllable of each of these words ends with a vowel letter. Syllables that end with vowels are called **open syllables** and usually have **long** vowel sounds.

Guided Practice 3–3: Visible Clue 2—V/CV

Directions: Divide each of the following words using **V/CV**. Mark the vowel in each open syllable (–) to show that it stands for a long vowel sound.

1. equal
2. Utah
3. notion
4. reflect
5. spoken
6. preview
7. title
8. nature
9. open
10. treason

Vowel Consonant / Vowel (VC/V)

Sometimes words with a **VCV** pattern are divided after the consonant (**VC/V**). The following words are divided **VC/V**. Look at each word carefully and note how it has been divided. Note that the first syllables are **closed syllables** and the vowels are not long ones.

lim/it	cab/in	sol/id
rob/in	sev/en	nov/el
wag/on	pow/er	riv/er

Guided Practice 3–4: Visible Clue 2—VC/V

Directions: Notice that the first syllable of each of these words ends with a consonant letter. Remember, syllables that end with consonants are closed syllables. Vowels in closed syllables usually have a short sound, the sound made by vowel + **r**, or the schwa sound. Divide the following words using **VC/V**.

1. second
2. habit
3. taxi
4. pity
5. Latin

6. devil
7. weapon
8. level
9. prison
10. olive

Visible Clue 3

$$\boxed{\text{Consonant}} + \textbf{le}$$

A consonant followed by **le** at the end of a word usually forms the last syllable of that word and the **le** sounds like ə**l**. Look at each of the following examples of words that have a consonant + **le** forming the last syllable.

tur/tle	cir/cle	ti/tle
gen/tle	han/dle	ap/ple
sta/ple	top/ple	ta/ble

There is one case in which a consonant does *not* join with the **le** at then end of a word to form a syllable. When **ck** comes before **le**, the **le** forms a separate syllable and still sounds like ə**l**.

$$\boxed{\underline{\qquad}\text{ck}} / \boxed{\text{le}}$$

Look at the following words to see how the **ck** and **le** are divided so that **le** forms a separate syllable.

chuck/le	crack/le	tack/le

Here is a hint to help you to use Visible Clue 3. Look at the end of a word you want to divide into syllables. If the word ends in

le, look at the letters before the **l.** If they are **ck,** you know the **ck** forms a separate syllable. Otherwise, the last syllable will include the consonant before the **le.** You now have the final syllable of the word.

Guided Practice 3–5: Visible Clue 3—Consonant + le

Directions: Show how you would divide the following into syllables by using Visible Clue 3.

1. buckle
2. tumble
3. pickle
4. stable
5. rifle
6. cripple
7. double
8. spackle
9. dangle
10. wrinkle

4. Visible Clue 4

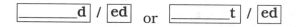

When a **d** or **t** at the end of a word is followed by **ed,** the **ed** forms a separate syllable. Each of the following words is an example of a word in which **d** or **t** appears at the end of that word, followed by **ed.** Notice that in each example, the **ed** forms a separate syllable. When the **ed** does not form a separate syllable, the **e** may be silent. For example, the word **lived** is pronounced **lĭvd.**

want/ed	need/ed	hunt/ed
frost/ed	mind/ed	chart/ed
wait/ed	stat/ed	pound/ed

As you did when using Visible Clue 3, look at the end of the word you want to divide into syllables. If the word ends in **ed,** look at the letter before the **ed.** If that letter is a **d** or **t,** you know the **ed** forms a separate syllable. Again, you now have the final syllable of the word.

Guided Practice 3–6: Visible Clue 4—d or t + ed

Directions: Look at each of the following words. Use Visible

Clue 4 to show how each word is divided into syllables.

1. gained
2. elected
3. herded
4. toured
5. hoped

6. sighted
7. scaled
8. branded
9. greeted
10. lasted

Use the Summary Sheet on page 90 to help you remember the four visible clues for dividing words into syllables.

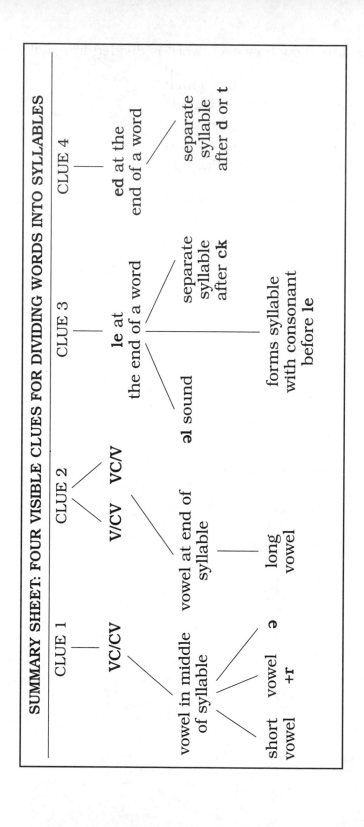

SUMMARY SHEET: FOUR VISIBLE CLUES FOR DIVIDING WORDS INTO SYLLABLES

CLUE 1

VC/CV

vowel in middle of syllable

short vowel

vowel + r

ə

CLUE 2

V/CV   VC/V

vowel at end of syllable

long vowel

ə sound

CLUE 3

le at the end of a word

separate syllable after ck

forms syllable with consonant before le

CLUE 4

ed at the end of a word

separate syllable after d or t

SKILL PRACTICE: VISIBLE CLUES FOR DIVIDING WORDS INTO SYLLABLES

A. Directions: Look at the letter patterns in the following words. Divide each word into syllables using **V/CV** or **VC/CV**. Then say the word aloud. It should sound like a real word to you. If it doesn't, go back and see if you have correctly divided it into syllables.

1. student	11. marry
2. nylon	12. ocean
3. effort	13. hotel
4. barber	14. locate
5. major	15. insist
6. drowsy	16. surround
7. moment	17. frozen
8. nonsense	18. forget
9. pilot	19. label
10. convince	20. grocer

B. Directions: Look at the letter patterns in the following words. Divide each word into syllables using **VC/V** or **VC/CV**. Then say the word aloud. Again, it should sound like a real word to you. If it doesn't, go back and see if you have correctly divided it into syllables.

1. concrete	7. orlon
2. damage	8. talent
3. batter	9. beckon
4. washer	10. income
5. passage	11. written
6. feather	12. atom

13. honey   17. convert

14. travel   18. Saturn

15. vanish   19. vowel

16. savage   20. perfect

C. Directions: Divide the following words into syllables.

1. puzzle	8. twinkle	15. marble
2. sniffle	9. trickle	16. tickle
3. freckle	10. ripple	17. wiggle
4. grumble	11. maple	18. dangle
5. shackle	12. fickle	19. fable
6. purple	13. idle	20. ankle
7. muddle	14. needle	

D. Directions: Put an **x** next to any of the words that should be divided into syllables. Then divide each of those words.

1. flushed _____		11. armed _____
2. wasted _____		12. halted _____
3. harmed _____		13. coasted _____
4. loved _____		14. waded _____
5. voted _____		15. fenced _____
6. clouded _____		16. raked _____
7. proved _____		17. mounted _____
8. seemed _____		18. hushed _____
9. doubted _____		19. trusted _____
10. founded _____		20. marched _____

DECODING WORDS WITH MORE THAN ONE SYLLABLE

Now you are ready to use what you have learned about phonics and syllables. When you meet an unknown word in your reading, use the following three steps to help you decode it:

1. *Use visible clues to divide the word into syllables. Write the V or C over each letter so that you can easily see patterns.*
2. *Use phonics to decode and pronounce each syllable.*
3. *Blend the syllables together to form the word again. Now pronounce the whole word.*

As you learn to use these three steps, write down what you do in each. Later, you should be able to decode unknown words quickly in your mind. You will not need to write down the three steps.

The words you will use to practice decoding skills are nonsense words that have been made up for this purpose. Nonsense words are used instead of real words to provide you with totally unknown words. Several words will be done for you to show how the three steps are used. Follow each step carefully so that you will see how to use it on your own. Next, you will decode words in Guided Practice. Finally, you will decode other words in Skill Practice.

Word: snalpop

1. *Use visible clues to divide the word into syllables.*

   c   vccvc
   (sn) alpop
   VC/CV pattern
   two-syllable word—snal/pop

2. *Use phonics to decode and pronounce each syllable.*

   snal

   sn = consonant blend—say together
   CVC pattern = closed syllable—a = ă
   l = usual sound
   pronounce syllable: snăl

pop

p = usual sound
CVC pattern = closed syllable—o = ŏ
p = usual sound
pronounce syllable: pŏp

3. *Blend the syllables together to form the word again. Now pronounce the word:*

snălpŏp

Word: glotern

1. *Use visible clues to divide the word into syllables.*

   c vcvcc

(gl)otern

VCV pattern—use **V/CV**
two-syllable word—glo/tern

2. *Use phonics to decode and pronounce each syllable.*

glo

gl = consonant blend—say together
o at end of syllable = open syllable—a = o
pronounce syllable: glo

tern

t = usual sound
er = vowel + **r** sound
n = usual sound
pronounce syllable: tern

3. *Blend the syllables together to form the word again. Now pronounce the word:*

glotern

Word: agonbran

1. *Use visible clues to divide the word into syllables.*

vcvc c vc

agon (br) an

VCV pattern—(use VC/V)—ag/o
VCCV pattern—n/br—split before consonant blend br
three-syllable word—ag/on/bran

2. *Use phonics to decode and pronounce each syllable.*

ag
ag = closed syllable—a = ă
g not followed by e, i, y = hard g sound
pronounce syllable: ăg

on
closed syllable—o = ŏ
n = usual sound
pronounce syllable: ŏn

bran
br = consonant blend—say together
closed syllable—a = ă
n = usual sound
pronounce syllable: brăn

3. *Blend the syllables together to form the word again. Now pronounce the word:*

| ăgŏnbrăn |

Guided Practice 3–7: Decoding Nonsense Words

Directions: Try the next three words on your own. If you find
the **VCV** pattern in a word, use the **V/CV** pattern.

Word: daiblod

1. Use visible clues to divide the word into syllables.

2. Use phonics to decode and pronounce each syllable.

3. Blend the syllables together to form the word again. Now pronounce the word.

Word: makoded

1. Use visible clues to divide the word into syllables.

2. Use phonics to decode and pronounce each syllable.

3. Blend the syllables together to form the word again. Now pronounce the word.

This time, see if you can go through the steps without having them written out for you.

Word: tobklackle

1.

2.

3.

Name _____

SKILL PRACTICE: DECODING WORDS

Directions: Use the following three steps to decode words. Try to complete the steps without writing them out.

1. Use visible clues to divide the words into syllables. Write a **V** or **C** above each letter so that you can easily see visible clues.
2. Use phonics to decode and pronounce each syllable.
3. Blend the syllables together to form the word again. Now pronounce the word.

Then show how you would divide and pronounce each word. For example:

Divide	Pronounce
c vcv c	
(fl) aso (th)	
fla/soth	fla/sōth

A. For the first ten nonsense words, use **V/CV** when you have a **VCV** pattern. If a letter or letters has more than one sound, show only one of those sounds in pronouncing the word.

Divide	Pronounce
1. slubbate (silent e)	_____
2. hollarded	_____
3. peleck	_____
4. deplunckle	_____
5. rubranted	_____
6. murphen	_____
7. swishflike (silent e)	_____

8. robungle   _____

9. tinayded   _____

10. quaprait   _____

B. For the next ten nonsense words, use **VC/V** when you have a **VCV** pattern.

Divide	*Pronounce*
1. seckranckle	_____
2. warflonged	_____
3. splatcher	_____
4. turbail	_____
5. hipaulted	_____
6. clatimble	_____
7. pithshample	_____
8. coybiled	_____
9. zampenner	_____
10. vilaphlord	_____

C. The following are real words. Use everything you know about phonics and syllables to show how you would divide and pronounce each word. Depend on your ears. Once pronounced, it should sound like a word you know. If the word does not sound like a real word to you, go over the way you divided it into syllables.

Divide	*Pronounce*
1. anchor	_____
2. decency	_____
3. leeway	_____
4. contribute	_____
5. scraggly	_____

6. relay _____

7. marketable _____

8. gypsy _____

9. tailgate _____

10. carpentry _____

D. Directions: Choose ten words of more than two syllables from any reading material. Write the words below. Use your skill in syllabicating words to divide each of the words and show how it is pronounced. Since they are real words, depend on your ears to find out if you have divided them correctly.

Word	*Divide*	*Pronounce*

1. _____

2. _____

3. _____

4. _____

5. _____

6. _____

7. _____

8. _____

9. _____

10. _____

CHAPTER 4

Word Clues in Context

It is hard to figure out the meanings of words when they stand alone. When the same words are used in phrases, sentences, or paragraphs, it is easier to figure out their meanings. For example, what does the word *ruler* mean when it stands alone? A ruler can be someone who governs. Or a ruler can be a marked strip of wood used for drawing lines. Even if you know both meanings for the word *ruler*, you have no way of knowing which one to choose. But, when *ruler* is used in a sentence, you can tell which meaning fits.

The king is a kind and gentle <u>ruler</u>.

Use a <u>ruler</u> to make lines on your paper.

The phrase, sentence, or paragraph in which a word is used is called **context.** For instance, in each of the two sentences above, the context is all the words in the sentence except for the word *ruler.* Context in these two sentences is shown in boxes below.

| The king is a kindly | ruler. |

| Use a | ruler | to make lines on your paper. |

As you found with *ruler*, context can give you clues to words that have more than one meaning. Context can also give clues to the meanings of unknown words as they are used in your reading. It is up to you to look for and use these clues in context.

In this chapter, you will learn how to

1. Look for and use clues in context for words with more than one meaning.
2. Look for and use three kinds of clues in context to help you figure out meanings of unknown words.

CLUES IN CONTEXT: WORDS WITH MORE THAN ONE MEANING

There are many words that have more than one meaning. The following two words, for example, can mean a number of things:

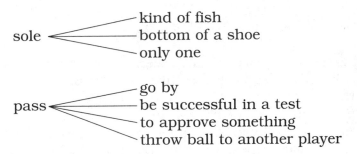

Many words with more than one meaning are words that you already know. As with the word *ruler*, you cannot figure out which meaning fits when the words stand alone. They must be used in phrases, sentences, or paragraphs. When words are used in context, the following steps will help you use clues to find their meanings:

1. *Use what you know about the other words in context to form a picture in your mind.*
2. *See which of the word's meanings fits into that picture.*
3. *Check to see if your meaning fits in context by using it in place of the unknown word.*

Read the following sample sentences. Notice how writers use clues in context to help you with words that have more than one meaning.

Sample A

The crook broke into the <u>safe</u> and took all the money.

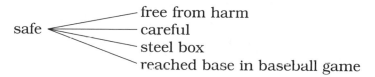

safe
- free from harm
- careful
- steel box
- reached base in baseball game

The word *safe* can have any of the meanings below the sentence. Use what you know about the other words in context to form a picture in your mind. Picture a crook taking money. What would the crook have to break into to get that money? Try *steel box* in place of *safe* to see if it fits in context.

The crook broke into the <u>steel box</u> and took all the money.

Sample B

Some trees <u>bear</u> fruit only every second year.

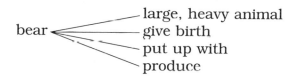

bear
- large, heavy animal
- give birth
- put up with
- produce

The word *bear* can have any of the meanings below the sentence. Use what you know about the other words in context to form a picture in your mind. Picture trees with fruit. These trees have fruit only every second year. They produce fruit every second year. Try *produce* in place of *bear* to see if it fits in context.

Some trees <u>produce</u> fruit only every second year.

Guided Practice 4–1: Words with More Than One Meaning

Directions: Read the following sentences. Look for clues in context to help you figure out the meaning of each underlined word. Be sure to follow the three steps listed below. Then choose the meaning of the word as it is used in context.

1. *Use what you know about the other words in context to form a picture in your mind.*

2. *See which of the word's meanings fits into that picture.*
3. *Check your meaning in context by using it in place of the word.*

1. The page worked very hard to learn everything he would need to know as a Knight of the Round Table.

   a. boy training to be a knight
   b. leaf out of a book
   c. youngster who carries messages
   d. try to find someone by calling the person's name

2. It may be easier to <u>track</u> an animal after a rain because paw prints will show up in wet ground.

   a. metal rails for a train to run on
   b. follow
   c. bring mud into a place
   d. a footprint

3. Roger always looks at the tag before buying anything to see if he can afford it.

   a. children's game
   b. metal point at end of a shoelace
   c. follow closely
   d. card that tells cost

4. If Sally does not take care of her business, sales will soon begin to slip, and she may have to close her shop.

   a. go down
   b. make a mistake
   c. move slowly
   d. put on easily

5. A careful speaker will always <u>check</u> facts before stating them in public.

   a. stop suddenly
   b. hold back
   c. make sure of
   d. statement of money owed for food in a restaurant

SKILL PRACTICE: CONTEXT CLUES—WORDS WITH MORE THAN ONE MEANING

A. Directions: Read each of the following sentences. Look for clues in context to help you choose the meaning of the underlined word. Use the same three steps you followed in the Guided Practice. Then choose the meaning of the underlined word as it is used in context.

1. If you <u>record</u> the money you spend during the year, it will be easier to fill out your income tax form.

    a. set down in writing
    b. a flat disk used on a phonograph
    c. put music, words, sounds on tapes
    d. known facts about a person

2. Allen is away from work too often; that is the <u>main</u> reason for his being fired.

    a. large pipe
    b. ocean
    c. most important
    d. largest

3. The <u>part</u> in the movie was a small one, but the actor became a star after playing it.

    a. less than the whole
    b. side in a disagreement
    c. dividing line in hair
    d. acting role

4. It is good manners to send a <u>note</u> of thanks after you receive a gift.

    a. sign in music
    b. short letter
    c. paper that says you will repay a loan
    d. pay attention to

5. She had not eaten for a long time; <u>still</u>, she would not touch food that was cooked in a dirty pot.

    a. yet
    b. posed photograph
    c. not moving
    d. quiet

6. The police officer usually covered the <u>beat</u> without any trouble.

    a. musical tempo
         c. mark time with drumsticks
    b. strike again and again
       d. regular route

7. When soldiers face an enemy, they often will show no <u>quarter</u>.

    a. one-fourth
            c. cut into four parts
    b. mercy
                d. kind of horse

8. It is sometimes cheaper to buy a <u>round</u>-trip ticket than two one-way tickets.

    a. shaped like a ball
        c. plump
    b. dance done in a circle
    d. return to starting point

9. The <u>fall</u> is a beautiful time of year; leaves of many colors make the trees look lovely.

    a. drop down from a higher place
        c. season between summer and winter
    b. amount that comes down
    d. do wrong

10. It is easy to break your <u>arm</u> if you are not careful when you ski down a dangerous slope.

    a. part of a person's body
       c. supply with weapons
    b. part of a chair
         d. gun, stick, sword

B. Directions: Read the following paragraphs. Look for context clues to the meanings of the underlined words. Then match each underlined word with its meaning. Be sure the meaning you choose makes sense in context.

1. The people who live on our <u>block</u>¹ bought a <u>block</u>² of tickets for the football game. But a <u>block</u>³ in traffic near the cement <u>block</u>⁴ stadium made them late for the game. They missed seeing the <u>block</u>⁵ by the home team's tackle—the best play of the game.

a. way of stopping a team's   d.   space in city or town____
   play   ____

b. large hollow building   e.   something preventing
   brick   ____   passage   ____

c. group   ____

2. When the small boy could not <u>lift</u>[1] the heavy box into the
<u>lift</u>[2] so that it could be taken to the second floor, a man gave him a <u>lift</u>[3].
It gave the boy a <u>lift</u>[4] to be helped by such a kind man. This man
also gave the boy a <u>lift</u>[5] home.

a. raise up ____   d. helping hand ____

b. ride   ____   e. good feeling   ____

c. elevator ____

3. After the long <u>run</u>[1] of the play, the actress decided to <u>run</u>[2] for
public office. She made speeches to all who would listen. One day
she found a <u>run</u>[3] in her stocking and had to <u>run</u>[4] into a store for a
new pair before she could make her speech. Even though she tried
hard, the actress did not win the election. The best she could do
was <u>run</u>[5] third.

a. rip   ____   d. finish   ____

b. go quickly   ____   e. be a candidate   ____

c. continuous number
   of performances   ____

4. The pitcher was able to <u>strike</u>[1] out every batter on the other team. One batter was angry enough to <u>strike</u>[2] that pitcher with his fist. Another batter yelled to the team manager, "Doesn't it <u>strike</u>[3] you as odd that he is able to get all of us? Something must be done about that pitcher or this team will go out on <u>strike</u>[4] before the clock can <u>strike</u>[5] again!"

a. tell the hour _____   d. walk out in protest _____

b. impress _____   e. hit _____

c. get rid of _____

CLUES IN CONTEXT—UNKNOWN WORDS

As you read, you probably will come across words you do not know. Even syllabicating and pronouncing the words may not help you with their meanings. One way to figure out their meanings is to look for and use clues in context. The meanings you get from these clues may not be as exact as those in the dictionary. But they will be close enough to help you understand what you are reading.

The following three steps tell how to figure out the meaning of a word you do not know.

1. *Use phonics and syllables to help you pronounce the word. Although you do not know the word in its written form, you may know it when you hear it. If so, stop with step 1. If you do not know the word when you pronounce it, go on to step 2.*

2. *Look in context for clues to word meaning. Three kinds of clues are often used in context: **definition, example,** and **experience.** They can help you figure out the meanings of unknown words. These clues may be found before or after a word. They may be in phrases, sentences, or paragraphs. If you know the ways a writer can help with word meanings, you will be able to use clues in context to figure out unknown words more easily.*

3. *Try your definition in place of the unknown word to see if it fits in context. It must make sense and also fit with the grammar of the context. If the phrase, sentence, or paragraph does not make sense with your meaning, go back and look at the context again. Repeat steps 2 and 3 until you find the word meaning that fits.*

Use the context clue Summary Sheet on page 128 as an aid to working with the three kinds of clues.

1. Definition

A writer may put the meaning of a word right into context. In other words, the writer has given you a direct clue to the **definition** of an unknown word. This direct clue can be given in two ways. First, the writer may tell you what a word means by using it in a sentence.

A lyre is a small harp.

If something is new, it is <u>recent</u>.

Second, the writer may use punctuation marks to show that a word meaning is being given. For instance, the writer may use commas, dashes, or parentheses to set the meaning off from the rest of the sentence.

The last <u>czar</u>, ruler of Russia, was killed in 1917.

Something voluntary—done by choice—is usually finished quickly and easily.

It is improbable (not likely) that the United States can take care of its energy problems without spending a great deal of money.

It is up to you to look for and use these definition clues in context.

Read the sample sentences to see how writers give definitions in context.

Sample A

The witness spoke so quickly that it was hard for the clerk to <u>transcribe</u>—write down—what he said.

In this sentence, you are clearly given the meaning of the word *transcribe:*

   write down

The writer has used dashes to set off the definition from the rest of the sentence.

Sample B

Don's aim in life is to become a <u>florist</u>, one who grows and sells flowers.

Again, the meaning of the word is clearly given in context:

   one who grows and sells flowers

Here the definition is set off from the rest of the sentence by a comma.

Guided Practice 4–2: Word Clues in Context—Definition

Directions: Read the following sentences. Apply the three steps that can help you figure out the meaning of each underlined word. They are printed for you below. Then circle or highlight the meaning of the underlined word as it appears in the sentence.

1. *Use phonics to help you pronounce the word.*

2. *Look in context for clues to word meaning. In each of these sentences, the clue in context will be a stated definition of the unknown word.*

3. *Try your meaning in place of the underlined word to see if it fits in context.*

1. Our laws tell us whether a child is legitimate (one who is born of parents who are legally married to each other) or not.

2. An egoist, a self-centered person, rarely worries about other people.

3. Too many people have the illusion—false idea—that money can buy happiness.

4. There, deep in the jungle, the hunters came upon a beautiful cascade—a small, steep waterfall.

5. The soldier kept his knife in its sheath (case) until the moment of attack.

2. Example

A writer may give indirect clues to an unknown word by using one or more **examples** of its meaning in context. A writer who uses examples gives you cases where the word fits. It is up to you to put the examples, or cases, together. Picture what the examples tell you. From this picture, you should be able to figure out the meaning of the unknown word and put that meaning into your own words. Then check to see if your meaning fits by using it in context in place of the unknown word.

Read the following samples to see how writers can use examples as clues in context.

Sample A

> Anna answered the ad for a <u>domestic</u>. This means she will have to dust, sweep, wash windows, and mop floors for the people who hire her.

The examples tell you the tasks Anna will have to do as a domestic. Picture these examples. They are the kinds of jobs usually done by a hired maid. Thus, a domestic is a maid. Try *maid* in place of *domestic* to see if it fits in context.

> Anna answered the ad for a <u>maid</u>. This means she will have to dust, sweep, wash windows, and mop floors for the people who hire her.

Yes, *maid* fits in context.

Sample B

> If you want your boss to think you are a <u>reliable</u> worker, always be on time and ready to do your job. Show that you can be counted on to do what is asked of you.

The examples tell you what a *reliable* worker is like. Picture the examples. They tell you that a reliable worker is one on whom the boss can depend. Thus, a reliable worker is dependable. Try *dependable* in place of *reliable* to see if it fits in context.

> If you want your boss to think you are a dependable worker, always be on time and ready to do your job. Show that you can be counted on to do what is asked of you.

Yes, *dependable* fits in context.

As you use example and experience clues to figure out unknown words in this chapter, you may find that your word meanings do not match exactly those of the writer of this book or exactly those in a dictionary. There may be some differences in wording. It is hard to get matching answers when you, the reader, puts meanings into your own words. As long as you have the same ideas and your meanings fit in context, mark your answers correct.

Guided Practice 4–3: Word Clues in Context—Example

Directions: Read each of the following sentences and paragraphs. Use the following three steps to figure out the meaning of each underlined word. These are the same three steps you used with definition clues.

1. *Use phonics to pronounce the unknown word.*

2. *Look in context for clues to word meaning. In each of these paragraphs, the clues will be examples of the unknown word.*

3. *Try your meaning in place of the underlined word to see if it fits in context.*

Remember, your words do not have to match those of the writer, but the ideas should be the same. The sentence should make sense with your meaning in place of the underlined word.

1. Jamie clearly <u>violated</u> the law. In addition to driving a stolen car without a driver's license, she went through at least six red traffic lights.

   violated: _____

2. Toby is a placid person. Very little bothers him; he never gets excited. Even when others are upset, he never gets angry.

   placid: _____

3. A good dressmaker will provide ample material in the seams and hem of a garment. Thus, the garment can be made larger if the wearer gains weight. The hem can be let down if styles change so that hemlines drop.

   ample: _____

4. The <u>veteran</u> wore his old uniform when he marched in the Fourth of July parade. The ribbons on his chest showed that he had fought in Europe during World War II and in Korea and Vietnam. Two silver bars pinned to his shoulders meant that he had been a captain.

   veteran: _____

5. Mr. Jackson's friends are amazed at his <u>liberal</u> view of spending money. He has a huge Christmas list of people for whom he always buys costly gifts. He often treats friends to lunch or dinner. And let's not forget that he is always ready to help anyone in need.

   liberal: _____

SKILL PRACTICE: WORDS IN CONTEXT—DEFINITION AND EXAMPLE

Directions: Read the following sentences and paragraphs. Apply the three steps you have learned to help you figure out the meaning of each underlined word. If the writer used a definition clue, circle or highlight that definition of the underlined word. If the writer used example clues, define the underlined word in your own words.

1. Every spring, birds make their nests under the <u>eaves</u>—the lower edge of the roof—of our house.

   eaves: _____

2. It is not unusual for large companies to <u>merge</u>. For example, Montgomery Ward and the Container Corporation of America became a new company called Marcor. Later, Marcor was bought by the Mobil Oil Company and became part of it.

   merge: _____

3. Sara's savings <u>dwindled</u> as she kept taking money out of the bank. Her bank balance went from $100 to $50 to $25 to zero in three months.

   dwindled: _____

4. The dodo bird has become <u>extinct</u>, no longer existing on Earth.

   extinct: _____

5. Don't use that package of butter for your baking. The strange taste and bad odor mean that it is probably <u>rancid</u>. It will surely ruin your cake.

   rancid: _____

6. Some married couples <u>bicker</u> (quarrel) about little things.

   bicker: _____

7. New cars may have a two-year <u>warranty</u>. This is a promise that anything wrong with the car will be repaired free of charge during that time.

   warranty: _____

8. That new house built by the shore is unique—one of a kind.

   unique: _____

9. Life can be better if members of a community live by principles. When there are some rules for how to behave, other rules for how to treat one another, and workable rules for solving problems, life in the community runs more smoothly.

   principles: _____

10. A well-balanced diet is <u>vital</u>—very necessary—for good health.

    vital: _____

11. Max has a phobia when it comes to snakes. He says it makes him ill just to look at a snake; the thought of touching a snake makes his flesh crawl. When someone once put a snake in Max's bed as a joke, he fainted.

    phobia: _____

12. Smoking may imperil your health. It has been found that smokers are more likely than nonsmokers to get lung cancer. Smokers are also more likely to have other lung diseases. Further, doctors are now saying that smoking may be one cause of heart attacks.

    imperil: _____

13. Why don't you acknowledge that you ruined my airplane model? Say that you added parts that don't belong. And say that you are the one who painted it the wrong color.

    acknowledge: _____

14. It is impossible to obtain the lumber you ordered before next week. The shipment is <u>en route</u>, on the way, from the sawmill to our lumberyard.

    en route: _____

15. When something is <u>unaccountable</u>, you cannot explain it.

    unaccountable: _____

3. Experience

Sometimes a writer may put one or more indirect clues in context that make you apply what you already know. The writer may tell about something that could have happened to you. Or the writer may tell something you have learned from other reading. In either case, you are expected to draw from your **experience** to figure out the meaning of an unknown word. Put that meaning into your own words. Then check to see if your meaning fits by using it in context in place of the unknown word.

Read the following sample paragraphs to see how writers use clues that make you apply your own experience.

Sample A

When you have close friends for a long time, you usually know how honest they are. Over the years, you have seen them behave in an honest way. You know that they can be trusted to repay loans. These are the only people you can <u>vouch</u> will pay back a bank loan. Yes, it is safe to sign the bank note with them.

This paragraph draws on experience of helping friends you know are honest. You are so sure they will repay a loan that you sign a bank note with them. You feel it is safe to promise that they will repay the loan. Use *guarantee* in place of *vouch*. It fits in context.

Sample B

The king's subjects are very unhappy with him. He spends so much time outside of the country that he does not know what is happening in his own land. Also, taxes are now so high that many of his subjects cannot afford to buy food. If the king is not careful, he will be deposed by his people.

This paragraph gives you a picture of a king who is doing a poor job of ruling his country. You know what happens to a king when his people are no longer happy with him. They may revolt, and then he will be removed from power. Try *removed from power* instead of *deposed*. It fits in context.

Guided Practice 4–4: Word Clues in Context—Experience

Directions: Read the following paragraphs. Apply the following three steps to figure out the meaning of each underlined word. These are the same steps you used with definition and example clues. Then write the meaning of the underlined word in your own words.

1. *Use phonics to help you pronounce the word.*

2. *Look in context for clues to word meaning. These clues will expect you to use your own experience.*

3. *Try your meaning in place of the unknown word to see if it fits in context. The sentence should make sense with your meaning in place of the underlined word.*

1. The two hikers had been lost in the mountains for nearly a week. Not having had much to eat for all that time, they were <u>ravenous</u>. They quickly ate everything placed before them by the rescue team that saved them.

   ravenous: _____

2. Isn't it strange that twin sisters can be so different from each other? Molly has always been selfish, never wanting to share anything. She has never been known to help anyone in need. Mary, on the other hand, is one of the most <u>charitable</u> people I know.

   charitable: _____

3. Mr. Bell is not <u>competent</u> to be president of such an important company. He does not know how to tell people what to do. Even worse, he does not insist that the company's product be as good as it once was. As a result, Mr. Bell cannot get his sales force excited about selling the product, and business is dropping. If he is not replaced by a better president, the company will surely go out of business.

   competent: _____

4. If a ship's captain is too cruel, his crew may stage a mutiny. A crew will take only so much cruelty before it turns on the captain and any other ship's officers who stand with him. When the crew takes over the ship, the officers may be killed. Or they may be sent away from the ship in small boats. The crew then runs the ship its own way.

   mutiny: _____

5. TV ads often exasperate viewers. Just as something exciting is about to happen, the program is cut off. Then, the next few minutes are used to sell toothpaste, soft drinks, or different kinds of pills. By the time the program begins again, viewers have lost track of what is happening in the story.

   exasperate: _____

As you work with example and experience clues to unknown words, you may sometimes find that the writer has given you context in which both kinds of clues will help you to define a word. In such cases, use either clue as an aid to defining words in context.

SKILL PRACTICE: WORD CLUES IN CONTEXT—EXPERIENCE

Directions: Read the following sentences and paragraphs. Apply the three steps you have learned to help you figure out the meaning of each underlined word. In this Skill Practice, all the clues in context make you use your own experience.

1. How hard it is to change the thinking of <u>narrow-minded</u> people! Being limited in their way of seeing things, they only half-listen to anything new or different. They have already decided that they have all the right answers. How sad! There is no way to reach them.

   narrow-minded: _____

2. The lawyer tried to tell the jury that the prisoner was not really a bad person. She spoke for a long time, telling sad stories about the prisoner's childhood. However, she could not <u>induce</u> that jury to declare the prisoner not guilty.

   induce: _____

3. Many homemakers used to save trading stamps. Then they would <u>redeem</u> these stamps for all kinds of products. They got things for the house. Or they got things for themselves. It was an easy way to get new items without using cash.

   redeem: _____

4. Many sunken ships sit at the bottom of the sea—a total loss. There are people now trying to salvage some of these ships. They hope to use new equipment to bring them to the surface. It will be costly, but they may do it.

   salvage: _____

5. The <u>transformation</u> from human to beast took place only when the moon was full. First, he became covered with hair. Then, his teeth became fangs. By the time the process was complete, the poor creature was an animal—a wolf.

   transformation: _____

6. Carl is much like a hero in a story. With his <u>venturesome</u> nature, he is not afraid of anything. He thinks he has to try everything. As a result, many exciting things have happened to Carl.

   venturesome: _____

7. During times of danger, the settlers would congregate in the fort. They felt safe behind its strong log walls. And they were sure that the soldiers in the fort were brave fighters who could hold off any enemy. Then, once the danger had passed, the settlers would go back to their own farms.

   congregate: _____

8. To protect the health of the prize-winning racehorse, the trainers kept his stall as sanitary as a hospital.

   sanitary: _____

9. The diamond in Terry's ring was <u>minute</u>; it was not much larger than the head of a pin.

   minute: _____

10. James <u>dominated</u> the conversation. When he joined the group, no one could speak for more than a moment or two. He kept interrupting as though only what he had to say was important.

    dominated: _____

11. If you are going to buy wall-to-wall carpeting, first measure the size of the room. That will help you compute how many yards of carpet you need. Then multiply that number by the price of carpet per yard to find out how much it will cost.

    compute: _____

12. Unlike Henry, who saves everything, Jenny <u>discards</u> things just to get them out of the house. She cannot stand clutter around her.

    discards: _____

13. Some people lead very dull lives. Their days never vary. They do the very same things every day.

    vary: _____

14. The colors in the desert sunset were so <u>vivid</u> that it hurt one's eyes to look directly at the it.

    vivid: _____

15. The army was small but <u>invincible</u>. Each soldier fought very hard. For months, the army held off enemy attacks. When the enemy finally saw that it could not win, its leaders asked for a truce.

    invincible: _____

SKILL PRACTICE: WORD CLUES IN CONTEXT—DEFINITION, EXAMPLE, AND EXPERIENCE

A. Directions: Read the following sentences and paragraphs. Apply the three steps you have learned to help you figure out the meaning of each underlined word. In this Skill Practice, look for context clues that are definitions, examples, or experiences. If the writer used a definition clue, circle or highlight that definition of the underlined word. If the writer used example or experience clues, define the underlined word in your own words. Remember that your meanings do not have to match those of this writer, but they must make sense in context.

1. The statue was carved out of ebony—a wood as black as ink.

   ebony: _____

2. Parents chastise children in different ways. When children don't behave, some parents scold or spank them. Others send their children to their rooms to think about what they have done wrong. Still others take away TV-watching time until the children behave properly.

   chastise: _____ _____

3. To help sell tickets for the rock concert, the manager paid for full-page ads in the local newspaper. She had the concert talked about on TV and radio. Posters were put up all over town, too. All this ballyhoo was meant to make fans aware that the group would appear at Concert Hall on Friday night.

   ballyhoo: _____

4. The owner of an old building may want to demolish it to make way for a new one. First, the old building is stripped bare of anything that is usable. Then, TNT charges are placed in a number of places in the building. All the charges are set to go off at the same time. As a result, the old building is flattened in only a few minutes.

   demolish: _____

5. Like a squirrel who collects nuts to be used later for food, Marcy <u>accumulates</u> things she thinks may one day be of use to her.

   accumulates: _____

6. The directions said to <u>omit</u> (leave out) any parts of the form that did not apply to the job seeker.

   omit: _____

7. No matter how many questions he was asked about his oil well, Stanley remained <u>mute</u>. He clenched his teeth and narrowed his lips to a stiff, straight line. Not one word came out of his mouth.

   mute: _____

8. How lucky for the crew of the sailboat to find that hidden cove! It proved to be a <u>haven</u> in the terrible storm. Many other pleasure boats were not so lucky; they sank in that sudden storm on the lake.

   haven: _____

9. The <u>lust</u> for gold has taken many people to faraway places. News of gold strikes in California, Alaska, South Africa, or Canada cause people to leave their homes and families. They then rush off to try their luck at finding that yellow metal.

   lust: _____

10. The firefighters were able to <u>douse</u> (put out) the fire in the hotel before it could cause much damage.

    douse: _____

11. Six people were called to the witness stand. Each was asked to give his or her own <u>version</u> of what had happened at the scene of the crime. Each one had a different tale to tell. No two witnesses could agree on any detail.

    version: _____

12. <u>Toxic</u> products can be found in many homes. They include bleach, lye, insect sprays, paint, and lighter fluid. Any of them can de deadly if swallowed.

    toxic: _____

13. When the boxer entered the ring, he looked ready for a good fight. By the second round, however, he began to look tired.

Halfway though the third round, he simply sat down to wait for the bell to ring. As a result of this act, the boxer was made to <u>forfeit</u> his title as Lightweight Champion of the World.

forfeit: _____

14. The <u>javelin</u>—a light spear—is used for throwing in track and field events.

javelin: _____

B. Directions: Choose five words from any reading material. Copy the paragraph with the word in it on a copy machine and attach the paragraphs to this Skill Practice. Underline the word you will define using context clues. Show your definition as you did in part A above.

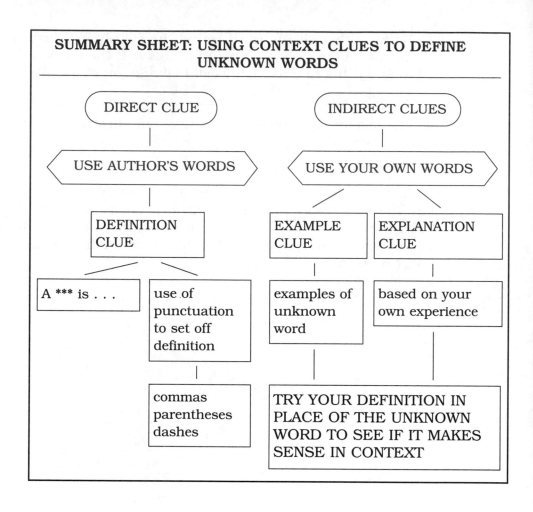

SUMMARY SHEET: USING CONTEXT CLUES TO DEFINE UNKNOWN WORDS

DIRECT CLUE

INDIRECT CLUES

USE AUTHOR'S WORDS

USE YOUR OWN WORDS

DEFINITION CLUE

EXAMPLE CLUE

EXPLANATION CLUE

A *** is . . .

use of punctuation to set off definition

examples of unknown word

based on your own experience

commas parentheses dashes

TRY YOUR DEFINITION IN PLACE OF THE UNKNOWN WORD TO SEE IF IT MAKES SENSE IN CONTEXT

CHAPTER 5

Word Structure

In Chapter Four, you learned how to find the meaning of a word by looking for clues in context. Another way to find out what a word means is to look for clues within the word itself. These clues can be found by looking at word structure—the way the parts of a word are put together. Many words are made up of parts: root words, prefixes, and suffixes. Each part has its own meaning. When you look at each part, you can get a good idea of what the whole word means. It is much like putting together pieces of a picture puzzle. Each piece adds something to the whole. At the end, you have a complete picture.

There are many different root words, prefixes, and suffixes. Only some often-used word parts are presented in this chapter. When you learn the meanings of these parts, you can begin to use them to work out some unknown words.

In this chapter, you will learn to look for clues to word meaning in

1. Root words.
2. Prefixes.
3. Suffixes.
4. Compound words.

There are three kinds of word parts: roots, prefixes, and suffixes. A **root** is the main part of a word. It carries the basic meaning of that word. A **prefix** is a part that is added to the front of a root. A **suffix** is a part that is added to the end of a root. Adding a prefix or suffix affects the root.

A root does not always have a prefix, suffix, or both added to it. You may find the following arrangements.

| root |

or

| prefix | + | root |

or

| prefix | + | root | + | suffix |

or

| root | + | suffix |

Roots can stand alone or they can have prefixes and/or suffixes added to them. For example,

act   (root)

or

re + act   =   react

or

re + act + ion = reaction

or

act + ion = action

VISIBLE CLUE 5 FOR DIVIDING WORDS INTO SYLLABLES

In Chapter Three, you learned four visible clues to use when dividing words into syllables. The fifth visible clue involves prefixes and suffixes. Prefixes and suffixes all include a vowel sound. Since a syllable must have a vowel sound in it, prefixes and suffixes form separate syllables. Look at the prefixes and suffixes presented in this chapter. You will find that they all have vowel sounds in them.

As you work in Chapter Five, you will learn a number of prefixes and suffixes. Look for them in long words and they will help you to see some syllables at the beginning or end of a word. In Chapter Three, you were advised to look for an **le** or **ed** at the end of a word and given clues for dividing these word endings quickly and easily. Now look for prefixes and suffixes in the same way.

Look at the Summary Sheet on page 132. It presents all five visible clues for dividing words into syllables.

ROOT WORDS

Many English words come from Latin or Greek root words. Sometimes, a number of words come from a single Latin or Greek root. Thus, if you learn the root, you often have the key to understanding an entire family of words. For example, the Greek root **ology** means **study of.** When you add prefixes to this root, you come out with a huge list of words that are commonly used in English. Here are samples of just a few of the words that have **ology** as a root.

anthropology—study of humankind
biology—study of plants and animals
dermatology—study of the skin
geology—study of the earth's crust
musicology—study of the history and forms of music
sociology—study of social relations, organization, change
zoology—study of animals and animal life

Since there are so many different root words, only some of the most often used are included in this chapter. However, even this small sample of roots and some words that come from them will give you an idea of the importance of Greek and Latin root words when using word structure as a way of working out the meanings of words in the English language.

1. Greek Root Words

auto   crat, cracy   graph   phon   tele

These Greek root words are shown below with samples of their use in English.

auto : self

automatic   autohypnosis   autopilot

crat, cracy : rule

democracy   aristocracy   technocrat

graph : write

paragraph   graphite   stenographer

phon : sound

phonics   xylophone   symphony

tele : at a distance

telescope   television   telephoto

Guided Practice 5–1: Greek Root Words

Directions: Some of the sample words with Greek roots shown above have been defined below. Use what you know about these roots to choose the word being defined. Make sure that the words you choose make sense in context.

1. A _____ is a musical instrument whose sound is pro-

   duced by hitting wooden bars with a small wooden hammer.

2. A country that is ruled by the wealthy is called an

   _____.

3. _____ is a system where letters stand for sounds.

4. A _____ is one who writes shorthand and later types what has been written.

5. A _____ allows you to watch things from afar.

6. If you put yourself into a trance, you are using _____.

7. To keep a plane going where it should, you can use _____ to keep it on a preset course and altitude.

8. _____ is the soft black form of carbon that is used in pencils.

2. Latin Root Words

aud   cred   dict   mort   spec

These Latin root words are shown below with samples of their use in English.

aud : hear

audience	audible	auditorium

cred : believe

creed	credit	incredible

dict : say

dictate	verdict	diction

mort : death

mortician	mortal	mortuary

spec : look

spectator	inspector	spectacles

Guided Practice 5–2: Latin Root Words

Directions: Some of the sample words with Latin roots shown on the previous page have been defined below. Use what you know about these roots to choose the word being defined.

1. A _____ is one who watches something without taking part.

2. If you have a secretary, you can _____ a letter rather than type it yourself.

3. All humans are _____ since they will all die.

4. If a sound is loud enough to hear, it is _____.

5. When you tell about your religious beliefs, you are telling about your _____.

6. An old-fashioned word for a pair of eyeglasses is _____.

7. People who sit together to hear and see something are called an _____.

8. A _____ is the person who will take care of funeral arrangements.

SKILL PRACTICE: ROOT WORDS

A. Directions: Use the words below that include Greek or Latin roots to complete the following sentences. (Check with the roots on pages 132–133 if you need help.)

verdict	Symphony	telescopic
incredible	mortuary	credit
auditorium	technocrat	decision
inspector		

1. A photographer can use a _____ lens to shoot pictures of wild animals without getting near them.

2. The Fifth _____, written by Beethoven, has remained a great favorite of music lovers.

3. Jon's story of his homework being eaten by aliens who landed in a UFO was _____.

4. The _____ was filled with people who had come to hear the famous general talk about his war experiences.

5. When a country has a leader who is a scientist or an engineer, that person is said to be a _____.

6. It was surprising to see how many of the dead woman's friends came to the ceremony at the _____.

7. When a leak was reported, the gas company sent out an _____ to check on the gas main.

8. It is wise to think carefully before you make an important

   _____.

9. People who pay their bills on time have a good _____ rating.

10. The foreman stood up to announce the jury's _____.

B. Directions: The underlined words include more than one Greek or Latin root word. Use what you know about root words to define these words.

> **Example:** When you answer the telephone, it lets you hear a voice from far away.

1. Graphology is _____.

2. Democracy is a form of government in which _____

   _____. (demos means people)

3. An autobiography is a book in which _____

   _____ .(bio means life)

4. A telegraph is a way of sending a _____.

5. When you ask for an autograph, you want the person to

   _____.

C. Directions: Write five sentences of your own using any of the words that include Greek and Latin root words which are found in this part of the chapter. Be sure the sentences show that you know the meaning of each word.

1. _____

2. _____

3. _____

4. _____

5. _____

PREFIXES

Prefixes are never used alone. They are always added to the fronts of root words. Because prefixes have one or more meanings of their own, they affect the root word. Therefore, prefixes change the meanings of root words.

The following prefixes are often used. Look at their meanings as well as some sample words that include them.

1. Prefixes That Always Mean **Not**

There are two prefixes that always mean *not*. Notice how they affect the meanings of root words they are added to.

non-
nonacid   — not an acid
nontaxable   — not taxable
nondrinker   — not a drinker

un-
uncoated   — not coated
unalike   — not alike
unfaded   — not faded

2. Prefixes That Have More Than One Meaning—
One Meaning Is **Not**

dis-

The prefix **dis** can mean *not*, or it can mean *lack of*. In either case, this prefix usually changes the root word so that it means the opposite.

distrust   — not trust (opposite of trust)
dislike   — not like (opposite of like)
dishonest   — not honest (opposite of honest)
disrespect — lack of respect (opposite of respect)
disunity   — lack of unity (opposite of unity)

Guided Practice 5–3: Prefixes non, un, dis

Directions: Look at the following words and think about what their roots mean. Write what the words mean with prefixes **non, un,** or **dis** added.

1. disobey _____

2. uncooked _____

3. disagree _____

4. nonactive _____

5. undated _____

in-

The prefix **in** has two meanings. It means *not* in the following sample words.

       inactive   — not active
       indirect   — not direct
       incomplete — not complete

The prefix **in** also means *in* or *into* in the following sample words.

       inlay   — to set a design or decoration in the surface
       insole   — sole inside of shoe or boot
       include — take in as part of a whole

im-

The prefix **in** often becomes **im** when it comes before **b, m,** and **p.** Like the prefix **in,** it has two meanings. The prefix **im** means not in the following sample words.

       impure   — not pure
       improper — not proper
       impossible — not possible

The prefix **im** means *in* or *into* in the following sample words.

impress — fix firmly in the mind
imbed — set into something (earth, mind, concrete)
implant — fix firmly into something

Guided Practice 5–4: Prefix in

Directions: Look at the following words. Think of what each word means. Mark an **x** next to each word in which the prefix **in** means *in* or *into*.

1. insane _____
2. insert _____
3. inward _____
4. inhuman _____
5. independent _____

6. instill _____
7. ingrown _____
8. inhabit _____
9. indecent _____
10. inborn _____

Guided Practice 5–5: Prefix im

Directions: Look at the following words. Put an **x** next to each word in which **im** means *not*.

1. imprint _____
2. immortal _____
3. impersonal _____
4. immigrant _____
5. impatient _____

6. imperfect _____
7. important _____
8. impractical _____
9. immoral _____
10. improve _____

3. Other Prefixes with More Than One Meaning

mis-

The prefix **mis** can mean *wrong* or *wrongly*, or *bad* or *badly*.

misspell — spell wrongly
misrule — rule badly
misinform — give wrong information

re-

The prefix **re** has two meanings. It means *anew* or *again* in the following sample words.

reborn — born anew
resale — sell again
recount — count again

The prefix **re** means *back* in the following sample words.

react — act back
refund — pay back money
return — come back

Guided Practice 5–6: Prefix re

Directions: Look at the following words. Think of what each word means. Put an **x** next to each word in which **re** means *again* or *anew*.

1. reawaken _____

2. refasten _____

3. reform _____

4. recapture _____

5. respect _____

6. readjust _____

7. rebuild _____

8. repay _____

9. reproduce _____

10. rerun _____

4. Prefixes with Opposite Meanings

anti-   pro-

The prefixes **anti** and **pro** can mean the opposite of each other when **anti** means against something, and **pro** means for something. Look at the word meanings next to the following sample words to see the effects of these prefixes.

antilabor — against labor
prolabor — for labor
antireligion — against religion
proreligion — for religion
antiwar — against war
prowar — for war

sub-   super-

The prefixes **sub** and **super** can also mean opposite things: **sub** can mean *under* or *below*, while **super** means *above, beyond,* or *over.* Look at these prefixes in the following sample words.

subhuman — below the level of human being
subnormal — below normal
subcompact car — below or smaller than a compact car
supermarket — more than just a market
supercharge — charged over and beyond the normal charge
superstar — more famous than usual movie or TV star

Use the Summary Sheet on page 148 to help you remember the prefixes covered in this part of Chapter Five.

5. Number Prefixes

When the following prefixes are added to words, they tell you the number of something. Look at the prefixes, their meanings, and the sample words.

Some of the sample words may be words you do not know. Pay special attention to the prefixes. You should then be able to tell the number part of the word.

Prefix	Meaning	Sample Word
uni-, mono-	one, single	*uniform*—all the same, *1* kind
		monorail—railway with only *1* track
bi-	two, twice	*bicycle*—*2*-wheeled
tri-	three, every third	*trio*—group of *3* who play or sing together
quadr-, tetra-	four	*quadrangle*—figure with *4* sides
		tetragram—a word with *4* letters
penta-, quin-	five	*pentagon*—figure with *5* sides
		quintet—group of *5* who play or sing together
sex-, hexa-	six	*sextet*—group of *6* who play or sing together
		hexagon—figure with *6* sides
sept-	seven	*septilateral*—having *7* sides
oct-	eight	*octagon*—figure with *8* sides
nov-, non-	nine	*novena*—prayers or services on *9* days
		nonagon—figure with *9* sides
dec-	ten	*decimal*—going by *tens*
cent-	one hundred	*century*—*100* years
milli-, kilo-	one thousand	*milligram*—unit of weight = to *1/1000* of a gram
		kilogram—unit of weight = to *1000* grams
hemi-, semi	half	*hemisphere*—half of a globe
		semicircle—half of a circle
multi-	many	*multiply*—increase in numbers

Note the prefixes **sept, oct, nov,** and **dec,** which are used in September, October, November, and December. These prefixes do not match the number order of the months. For example, the prefix **sept** means seven, but September is the ninth month. The old Roman year began in March, thus making September the seventh month. About two thousand years ago, the Romans changed this, beginning the year as we now know it with January. The names of months already in use were kept. But the months September, October, November, and December became out of order, no longer matching their prefixes.

SKILL PRACTICE: PREFIXES

A. Directions: Put an **x** next to any word that has a prefix meaning *not*.

1. incapable   _____
2. nonstop   _____
3. unasked   _____
4. misbehave   _____
5. improbable   _____
6. disband   _____
7. ingrain   _____

8. anti-Greek _____
9. imprison   _____
10. displeased _____
11. refined   _____
12. inside   _____
13. submarine _____
14. unexcited _____

B. Directions: Circle the word that finishes each of the following sentences.

1. No matter how hard they looked for him, the prisoner remained _____.
   (recaptured   uncaptured)

2. I went to the wrong house because I was _____
   (uninformed

   _____ about the address.
   misinformed)

3. George was so upset at the results of the tennis game that he asked his partner for a _____.
   (rematch   mismatch)

4. When the mayor took his wife on a business trip, he _____ public funds.
   (reused   misused)

5. If the citizens of another country say, "Yankee, go home!" you know they are _____.
   (anti-American   pro-American)

6. After the old table was _____, it looked brand new.
   (unfinished   refinished)

7. Sometimes it is best to leave nasty things _____.
   (unstated   restated)

8. If you don't get the job now, _____ the next time there is an opening.
   (reapply   misapply)

9. It was hard to _____ the country after the Civil War.
   (reunite   disunite)

10. Alice and Harry liked the auto club's services so much that they have _____ each year.
    (unjoined   rejoined)

11. It took _____ strength to lift the fallen tree.
    (subhuman   superhuman)

12. Anything lost on the trip will have to be _____ when you return.
    (replaced   misplaced)

C. Directions: Fill in the blank in each of the following sentences with a number. You may not know some of the underlined words. Use their prefixes and context to help you figure them out.

1. An octopus is a sea animal that has _____ legs.

2. The septuagenarian will retire from her job because she is

   _____ years old.

3. A <u>decathlon</u> is a sports meet that has _____ different

   kinds of events.

4. In 1976, the United States celebrated the <u>bicentennial</u>

   because the country was _____ years old.

5. Pictures of Neptune usually show him carrying a <u>trident</u>—a

   spear that has _____ points.

6. Having quintuplets, _____ children at one time, can be a

   shock to any family.

7. People who are paid biweekly get their salaries every _____

   weeks.

8. Monogamy is a marriage of _____ husband and _____

   wife.

9. A figure with _____ sides and _____ angles may be

   called a quadrangle or a tetragon.

10. When the choir sang in <u>unison</u>, it sounded like _____

    person singing.

SUMMARY SHEET: PREFIXES

PREFIXES THAT ALWAYS MEAN NOT	PREFIXES THAT HAVE MORE THAN ONE MEANING—ONE MEANING IS NOT	OTHER PREFIXES WITH MORE THAN ONE MEANING	PREFIXES WITH OPPOSITE MEANINGS
non- (nonacid)	**dis-** not (dislike—not like)	**mis-** wrong, wrongly (misspell—spell wrong)	**anti-** against something (antilabor—against labor)
un- (uncoated)	lack of (disrespect—lack of respect)	bad, badly (misrule—rule badly)	**pro-** for something (prolabor—for labor)
	in- not (inactive—not active)	**re-** anew, again (resale—sell again)	**sub-** under, below (subhuman, below level of being human)
	in (inhabit—live in)	back (refund—pay money back)	**super-** above, beyond, over (superhuman—above what can be expected from a human being)
	(in becomes im before b, m, p)		
	im- not (impure—not pure)		
	in (impress—fix firmly in the mind)		

148

SUFFIXES

Suffixes, like prefixes, are never used alone. They are always added to the ends of root words. And like prefixes, they have meanings of their own. Unlike prefixes, however, suffixes do not usually change the meanings of roots. The main effect of suffixes is that they show, and sometimes change, the parts of speech of words. For example, the root *home* is a noun. If the suffixes **y** or **less** are added, *home* becomes an adjective.

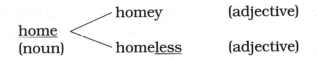

The root *home* does not change its meaning when suffixes are added to it. By itself, *home* means a place where one lives. *Homey* is still talking about a place where one lives. But now, the word means like a home. *Homeless* is also talking about a place where one lives. Now, however, the word means without a place to live.

You cannot work with suffixes without knowing about parts of speech. You should know that words are divided into classes, or parts of speech, according to how they are used in sentences. Four of these parts of speech can accept suffixes. They are

1. **Nouns** are the names of persons, place, things, ideas, or events (examples: teacher, judge, New York, apples, peace, party).

2. **Verbs** tell about action or being (examples: walk, run, stay, freeze, enter, bring).

3. **Adjectives** describe nouns (examples: green apples, funny man, happy children, <u>fat</u> bear).

4. **Adverbs** describe verbs or adjectives (examples: ran quickly, slept <u>well</u>, spoke sweetly, felt badly).

Like the prefixes you learned earlier in this chapter, certain suffixes have been chosen for study because they are often used. In this chapter, you will learn about four different kinds of suffixes: **noun suffixes, adjective suffixes, verb suffixes,** and **adverb suffixes.** These suffixes are named according to the parts of speech formed when the suffixes are added. Most of the suffixes you will learn form nouns and adjectives.

Noun Suffixes

-ance   -ion

-ment

-ence   -tion

These suffixes are usually added to root words that are verbs. The new words formed are nouns. Each of these suffixes has more than one meaning. But they all have one meaning in common, which is presented here. All these noun suffixes can mean *state of being something*.

The following sample nouns have been formed by adding the suffixes **ance, ence, ion, tion,** or **ment** to verbs.

Verb		Suffix	Noun	Meaning
exist	+	**ence**	existence	state of existing
repent	+	**ance**	repentance	state of repenting
agree	+	**ment**	agreement	state of agreeing
recite	+	**ation**	recitation	state of reciting
attract	+	**ion**	attraction	state of attracting

Notice that the final **e** in *recite* is dropped and **a** is added before **tion** in this case.

-er   -or

These two suffixes are also added to verbs to form nouns. They mean *a person or thing that does something*. The following sample nouns have been formed by adding the suffixes **er** or **or** to verbs.

Verb		Suffix	Noun	Meaning
act	+	**or**	actor	one who acts
bake	+	**er**	baker	one who bakes

Notice that in *bake* + **er**, there is only one **e**. Some words drop the final **e** when suffixes are added.

-ness

When the suffix **ness** is added to adjectives, nouns are formed. This suffix can mean *condition of being something*. The following words are samples of how the suffix **ness** is used.

Adjective		Suffix	Noun	Meaning
sore	+	**ness**	soreness	condition of being sore
frank	+	**ness**	frankness	condition of being frank
happy	+	**ness**	happiness	condition of being happy

Note the change in the spelling of *happy* with the addition of the suffix. In words that end in **y**, the **y** is sometimes changes to **i** when suffixes are added. Other examples of this change are

nasty	+	ness	nastiness
gloomy	+	ness	gloominess

-hood   -ship

These suffixes are added to nouns. Although they do not change the part of speech of the root, they do affect its meaning.

Both suffixes can mean *state of being something*. The following sample words have been formed by adding one of these two suffixes to nouns. Notice that the new words are also nouns.

Noun		Suffix	New Noun	Meaning
child	+	**hood**	childhood	state of being a child
leader	+	**ship**	leadership	state of being a leader

Guided Practice 5–7: Noun Suffixes

A. Directions: Write the nouns formed by adding the suffix **ance, ence, ion, tion,** or **ment** to the following words. Then write their meanings.

Verb		Suffix	Noun	Meaning
1. employ	+	ment	_____	_____
2. confess	+	ion	_____	_____
3. avoid	+	ance	_____	_____
4. depend	+	ence	_____	_____
5. adopt	+	ion	_____	_____

B. Directions: Write the nouns formed by adding the suffix **er** or **or** to the following verbs. Then write their meanings.

Verb		Suffix	Noun	Meaning
1. object	+	or	_____	_____
2. govern	+	or	_____	_____
3. talk	+	er	_____	_____

C. Directions: Write the nouns formed by adding the suffix **ness** to the following adjectives. Then write their meanings.

Adjective		Suffix	Noun	Meaning
1. weak	+	ness	_____	_____
2. dark	+	ness	_____	_____
3. plain	+	ness	_____	_____

D. Directions: Write the new nouns formed by adding the suffix **hood** or **ship** to the following nouns. Then write their meanings.

Noun		Suffix	New Noun	Meaning
1. saint	+	hood	_____	_____
2. citizen	+	ship	_____	_____

2. Verb Suffixes

-en   -fy   -ize

All three of these suffixes are added to adjectives. The words formed by adding these suffixes are verbs. Some of these suffixes have more than one meaning. However, they all have one meaning in common: *cause to be something.* The following sample verbs are formed by adding the suffixes **en**, **fy**, or **ize** to adjectives.

Adjective	Suffix	Verb	Meaning
weak	+ **en**	weaken	cause to be weak
simple	+ **fy**	simplify	cause to be simple
legal	+ **ize**	legalize	cause to be legal

Note the change in the spelling of *simple* when the suffix is added. In words that end in an **e**, the **e** is sometimes changed to **i** when the suffix **fy** is added.

Guided Practice 5–8: Verb Suffixes

Directions: Write the verbs formed by adding the suffix **en**, **fy**, or **ize** to the following adjectives. Then write their meanings.

Adjective	Suffix	Verb	Meaning
1. false	+ **fy**	_____	_____
2. tender	+ **ize**	_____	_____
3. short	+ **en**	_____	_____
4. solid	+ **ify**	_____	_____

Note that **false** and **solid** both need **ify**, rather than just **fy**, to form the new words.

3. Adjective Suffixes

-ful   -ous   -y

These three suffixes are added to nouns. The words formed by adding **ful, ous,** or **y** are adjectives. They have one common meaning: *full of something.* The following sample adjectives have been formed by adding **ful, ous,** or **y** to nouns.

Noun		Suffix	Adjective	Meaning
fruit	+	**ful**	fruitful	full of fruit
danger	+	**ous**	dangerous	full of danger
smoke	+	**y**	smokey	full of smoke

-ish

The suffix **ish** is added to nouns. The words formed are adjectives. This suffix means *somewhat like something.* The following sample adjectives have been formed by adding **ish** to nouns.

Noun		Suffix	Adjective	Meaning
red + d	+	**ish**	reddish	somewhat like red
fool	+	**ish**	foolish	somewhat like a fool

-ly

The suffix **ly** is added to nouns. The words formed by adding this suffix are adjectives. The suffix **ly** means *like something.* The following sample adjectives have been formed by adding **ly** to nouns.

Noun		Suffix	Adjective	Meaning
ghost	+	**ly**	ghostly	like a ghost
friend	+	**ly**	friendly	like a friend

-less

The suffix **less** can be added to nouns. Words formed by adding **less** are adjectives. This suffix means *without something*. The following sample adjectives have been formed by adding **less** to nouns.

Noun		Suffix	Adjective	Meaning
meat	+	**less**	meatless	without meat
top	+	**less**	topless	without a top

-able   -ible

The suffixes **able** and **ible** are added to verbs. Words formed by adding these two suffixes are adjectives. The two suffixes mean *able to be something.* The following sample adjectives are formed by adding **able** or **ible** to verbs.

Verb		Suffix	Adjective	Meaning
adopt	+	**able**	adoptable	able to be adopted
market	+	**able**	marketable	able to be marketed
reverse	+	**ible**	reversible	able to be reversed

Note that the final **e** is dropped in *reverse* before adding the suffix **ible**.

Guided Practice 5–9: Adjective Suffixes

A. Directions: Write the adjectives formed by adding the suffix **ful, ous,** or **y** to the following nouns. Then write their meanings.

Noun		Suffix	Adjective	Meaning
1. power	+	**ful**	_____	_____
2. joy	+	**ous**	_____	_____
3. wind	+	**y**	_____	_____

B. Directions: Write the adjectives formed by adding the suffix **ish** to the following nouns. Then write their meanings.

Noun		Suffix	Adjective	Meaning
1. boy	+	ish	_____	_____
2. sweet	+	ish	_____	_____

C. Directions: Write the adjectives formed by adding the suffix **ly** to the following nouns. Then write their meanings.

Noun		Suffix	Adjective	Meaning
1. sister	+	ly	_____	_____
2. coward	+	ly	_____	_____

D. Directions: Write the adjectives formed by adding the suffix **less** to the following words. Then write their meanings.

Noun		Suffix	Adjective	Meaning
1. faith	+	less	_____	_____
2. fault	+	less	_____	_____

E. Directions: Write the adjectives formed by adding the suffix **able** or **ible** to the following verbs. Then write their meanings.

Noun		Suffix	Adjective	Meaning
1. read	+	able	_____	_____
2. predict	+	able	_____	_____
3. reduce	+	ible	_____	_____

4. Adverb Suffix

-ly

The suffix **ly** is added to adjectives to form adverbs. This suffix means *in a certain manner.* The following sample abverbs have been formed by adding **ly** to adjectives.

Adjective		Suffix	Adverb	Meaning
safe	+	ly	safely	in a safe manner
kind	+	ly	kindly	in a kind manner

Guided Practice 5–10: Adverb Suffix

Directions: Write the adverbs formed by adding the suffix **ly** to the following adjectives. Then write their meanings.

Adjective	Suffix	Adverb	Meaning
1. dear	+ ly	_____	_____
2. grand	+ ly	_____	_____

Use the Summary Sheet on page 162 to help you master what you have learned about suffixes.

Name _____

SKILL PRACTICE: SUFFIXES

A. Directions: Read the following sentences. Circle or highlight each word that has a suffix covered in this chapter.

1. The penniless designer was hopeful that her fashionable clothing would be worn by stoutish women.

2. Once inside the shadowy cell, the convict made a confession that he had a weakness when it came to the invention of fearful crimes.

3. Needless to say, parentless children are more adoptable by childless couples during early childhood.

4. Lester's written story showed that he had a good education, an active imagination, and fairly good penmanship.

5. In all likelihood, the partnership rules will see to it that the workers' investment in the company is made fairly and equally.

6. It is unbelievable how many careless fires are caused by forgetful people who leave filthy, greasy rags around the house.

7. Maud's friends lost their sorrowful feelings and suddenly began to act more cheerful when they learned that her muscle soreness surely was curable.

8. The overly cloudy sky caused a fearful darkness and chilly dampness.

9. The head of production wearily gave directions to stop the skillful weavers' action against the company.

10. The continuous noise made the renters nervous enough to demand that the faultless landlord make the noisemakers live more quietly.

B. Directions: Write the words formed when the following suffixes are added to the underlined words.

-ance   -er   -ly   -ize

1. cause to be <u>slender</u>   slender   _____

2. state of avoiding   avoid   _____

3. in an <u>excited</u> manner   excited   _____

4. one who jumps   jump   _____

5. cause to be <u>modern</u>   modern   _____

6. one who pushes   push   _____

7. state of being annoyed   annoy   _____

8. state of <u>performing</u>   perform   _____

9. in a <u>false</u> manner   false   _____

10. in a <u>sad</u> manner   sad   _____

C. Directions: Write the words formed when the following suffixes are added to the underlined words.

-ous   -tion/ion   -hood   -ness

1. state of forming   form   _____
   (add **a** before suffix)

2. full of <u>thunder</u>   thunder   _____

3. condition of being <u>bald</u>   bald   _____

4. state of locating   locat   _____

5. state of being complete   complet   _____
   (**e** dropped before suffix)

6. state of being a knight   knight   _____

7. state of examining   examin   _____
   (add **a** before suffix)

8. condition of being pleasant   pleasant   _____

9. condition of being <u>bold</u>   bold   _____

10. condition of being a <u>father</u> father   _____

SUMMARY SHEET: SUFFIXES

NOUN SUFFIXES	VERB SUFFIXES	ADJECTIVE SUFFIXES	ADVERB SUFFIXES
state of being ___	cause to be ___	full of ___	in a ___ manner
-ence (exceptence)	**-en** (weaken)	**-ful** (fruitful)	**-ly** (safely)
-ance (avoidance)	**-fy** (simplify)	**-ous** (dangerous)	
-ment (agreement)	**-ize** (legalize)	**-y** (smokey)	
-tion (recitation)			
-ion (confession)		somewhat like ___	
		ish (foolish)	
person or thing that does ___			
		like a ___	
		-ly (ghostly)	
-or (actor)			
-er (writer)		without ___	
		-less (meatless)	
condition of being ___			
-ness (soreness)		able to be ___	
		-able (adoptable)	
state of being ___		**-ible** (reversible)	
-hood (childhood)			
-ship (leadership)			

SUMMARY SHEET: FIVE VISIBLE CLUES FOR DIVIDING WORDS INTO SYLLABLES

CLUE 1

VC/CV

vowel in middle of syllable

- short vowel
- vowel +r
- ə

CLUE 2

V/CV   VC/V

vowel at end of syllable

- long vowel

CLUE 3

le at the end of a word

- separate syllable after **ck**
- əl sound
- forms syllable with consonant before **le**

CLUE 4

ed at the end of a word

- separate syllable after **d** or **t**

CLUE 5

separate syllables

- prefixes
- suffixes

COMPOUND WORDS

Sometimes two roots are joined together to form a single word. The words that result from this joining are called **compound words.** For example, the following pairs of words form compound words:

hill   +   side   hillside
steam   +   ship   steamship

The meaning of a compound word is usually the combined meaning of the words that form it. For example,

hillside   —   side of a hill
steamship   —   ship moved by steam

Guided Practice 5–11: Compound Words

Directions: Write what you think each of the following compound words means.

1. madman   _____

2. overstock   _____

3. nutcracker   _____

4. homebody   _____

5. rainfall   _____

6. horseshoe   _____

7. foxhound   _____

8. thumbnail   _____

9. washcloth   _____

10. headband   _____

Name _____

SKILL PRACTICE: COMPOUND WORDS

A. Directions: Use the following words to form compound words that will finish the sentences.

war	box	kick	night
ice	off	sea	feather
rust	shirts	tail	men
sick	weight	proof	pony
writers	path	ghost	folk

1. It was so hot that Ella pulled her long hair back into a

    _____.

2. If you are late for a football game, you may miss the

    _____.

3. During rough weather, passengers on ships may become

    _____.

4. A boxer who weighs between 116 and 126 pounds is called a

    _____.

5. In days gone by, food was kept cold in an _____.

6. In those same old days, men slept in _____.

7. People who cannot write their own books may use

    _____.

8. If you don't want metal outside chairs to be ruined by damp-

    ness, you should _____ them.

9. Pioneer women usually worked in the home while their

_____ worked in the fields.

10. When Indians became angry with tribes other than their own,

they often went on the _____.

B. Directions: Make compound words by adding to the following words.

1. sun _____   5. _____house

2. _____ ball   6. over_____

3. farm_____   7. sea_____

4. head_____   8. door_____

C. Directions: Each of the following phrases describes a compound word. Put the compound words in the correct squares of the puzzle. The first one has been done for you.

1. Pain in the head
2. Where dog lives outside
3. Seen in old-time Western movies
4. Used for wrapping food
5. Place to pay money to ride on a road
6. Must get things done before this
7. Light shines from top of this to help ships
8. Game played with pigskin ball
9. Working extra hours, to be paid for this
10. One of these and you wake up screaming
11. Children's game played by jumping over others
12. Window in a ship
13. One to whom you send a Valentine
14. Cowboys do this to cattle
15. When workers are paid

CHAPTER **6**

The Dictionary

The dictionary is an important tool to help build your vocabulary. It is the tool to use if context or word structure cannot help you with word meaning. It is also the tool to use to find out more about a word whose meaning you already know. But, like all tools, the dictionary is of value only when you know how to use it. Learn to use the dictionary with ease. Then you may form the habit of using it very often. It can become so very important to you that you won't read unless you have one within easy reach.

In this chapter you will learn skills to help you

1. Choose a dictionary that is right for you.
2. Use alphabetical order.
3. Use a dictionary with ease.

There are three steps to forming the dictionary habit. The first step is to have a dictionary that is right for you. The second step is to learn how to use it with ease. The third step is to use this tool as much as you can. The more you use the dictionary, the easier it is to find what you need in it.

Since the first step is to have a dictionary that is right for you, it is important to know how to choose one. You may already own a dictionary. Or you may now be planning to buy one. In either case, use the following four tests to see if a dictionary is right for you:

1. *The print is clear and easy to read. Open the dictionary to any page. Check to see if the words stand out clearly. They should not seem to fade into the page. The words should also look separate—not blended into each other.*
2. *The words are large enough to read without strain. Read two or three pages. The words should be easy to see. Your eyes should not feel tired or strained.*
3. *The word meanings are easy to understand. If you are trying to decide between dictionaries, look up the same word in each. Choose the dictionary that explains the word in language you can understand.*
4. *The dictionary is up to date. Check the date on the back of the title page. It will tell you when the dictionary was printed. Choose one that has been brought up to date. It should have words that have recently become part of the English language and new meanings for words already in use.*

Choosing a dictionary is not something to be done only once. As your needs change, you will probably want to buy a new one. Or you may want a more up-to-date dictionary in the future. Whatever the reason, be sure that you choose one that passes all four tests.

After you choose a dictionary, take time to look at what is in it. Check the front part of the dictionary. You may find special directions there. They will tell you how to use your dictionary. Not all dictionaries are exactly alike. It is very important to find out about your own dictionary. This will make it much easier to use.

A dictionary often tells about things other than words. When you check the front and back parts of your dictionary, you may find, for example, lists of U.S. presidents and vice presidents, states of the United States, or nations of the world. It is good to know the kinds of facts that are there if you need them.

Now that you know how to choose a dictionary, the next important step is to learn how to use it with ease.

ALPHABETICAL ORDER

Dictionaries are always arranged in alphabetical order. Therefore, you must be able to work with the alphabet if you are to find words quickly. If you have to go through the alphabet from the beginning to know where a letter fits, it will take you too long to use the dictionary. Now is the time to learn the order of the letters in the English language if you don't already know it.

a b c d e f g h i j k l m
n o p q r s t u v w x y z

In addition to learning the letters of the alphabet, you should group them in your mind. Think of the alphabet in terms of three groups of letters. Think of letters at the front, letters in the middle, and letters at the end. Learn which letters fall into each group. This will help you find words in the dictionary more quickly. For instance, if the word you want begins with **b**, look toward the front of the dictionary. If the word begins with **m**, look toward the middle. Or, if the word begins with **s**, look toward the back of the dictionary.

Guided Practice 6–1: Alphabetical Order

A. Directions: Read the following groups of letters. Fill in the blanks with the missing letters. Try not to look back at the alphabet.

1. w x __ z   6. f g __ __ j

2. b c __ __ f   7. m __ __ p

3. s t __ __ w   8. j k __ __ __ o

4. p __ __ s   9. a b c __ __ f

5. h __ __ k   10. v w __ __ __

B. Directions: Now see how quickly you can write the letter that comes before or after each of the following letters. Do not look back at the alphabet.

1. before **g** _____   6. before **k** _____
2. after **x** _____   7. before **d** _____
3. after **p** _____   8. after **t** _____
4. before **i** _____   9. after **u** _____
5. after **m** _____   10. before **z** _____

If you had a hard time with Guided Practice 6–1, go back and work with the alphabet until you learn it.

Words in alphabetical order are placed by the order in which their letters appear in the alphabet. Look at the following two sample lists of words placed in alphabetical order according to their **first** letters.

	Sample A			*Sample B*	
	bomb	**(b)**		party	**(p)**
	foe	**(f)**		quite	**(q)**
	given	**(g)**		sound	**(s)**
	runner	**(r)**		very	**(v)**
	white	**(w)**		zero	**(z)**

Guided Practice 6–2: Alphabetical Order—First Letters

Directions: Write the words in List 1a in alphabetical order according to their first letter. Check your answers on page 396. If you need extra practice, work with List 1b. If not, go on to List 2a and write these words in alphabetical order according to their first letters. Check your answers on page 396. If you need extra practice with a longer list, work with list 2b.

List 1a		*List 1b*	
offer	1. _____	really	1. _____
band	2. _____	absent	2. _____
heart	3. _____	comet	3. _____
many	4. _____	friend	4. _____
supper	5. _____	water	5. _____

	List 2a			List 2b
dozen	1. _____		nation	1. _____
artist	2. _____		east	2. _____
wrapper	3. _____		pillow	3. _____
effect	4. _____		junk	4. _____
test	5. _____		bark	5. _____
Sunday	6. _____		untidy	6. _____
life	7. _____		model	7. _____
marsh	8. _____		quick	8. _____
cork	9. _____		open	9. _____
flame	10. _____		X-ray	10. _____

Sometimes more than one word in a list may begin with the same letter. Then you must place those words in alphabetical order according to their **second** letters. Look at the following sample list of words placed in alphabetical order according to their second letters.

	Sample A		Sample B
happy	(a)	pats	(a)
hear	(e)	pencil	(e)
hit	(i)	plow	(l)
hope	(o)	prince	(r)
hymn	(y)	punk	(u)

Guided Practice 6–3: Alphabetical Order—Second Letters

Directions: Write the words in List 3a in alphabetical order according to their second letters. Check your answers on page 396.

If you need extra practice, work with List 3b. If not, go on to List 4a and write these words in alphabetical order according to their second letters. Check your answers on page 396. If you need extra practice with a longer list, work with List 4b.

List 3a		*List 3b*	
actor	1, _____	woman	1. _____
ask	2. _____	wake	2. _____
ankle	3. _____	wind	3. _____
able	4. _____	well	4. _____
apart	5. _____	write	5. _____

List 4a		*List 4b*	
slump	1. _____	chop	1. _____
scene	2. _____	comb	2. _____
sap	3. _____	clean	3. _____
some	4. _____	Czech	4. _____
sift	5. _____	case	5. _____
Sunday	6. _____	city	6. _____
smack	7. _____	cramp	7. _____
spar	8. _____	cut	8. _____
step	9. _____	certain	9. _____
shame	10. _____	cycle	10. _____

Sometimes words have the same two letters at the beginning. Then those words are placed in alphabetical order according to their **third** letters. Look at the following sample lists.

Sample A		Sample B	
draft	(a)	imagine	(a)
dread	(e)	imbed	(b)
drip	(i)	imitate	(i)
dropper	(o)	immediate	(m)
dry	(y)	impolite	(p)

Guided Practice 6–4: Alphabetical Order—Third Letters

Directions: Write the words in List 5a in alphabetical order according to their third letters. Check your answers on page 396. If you need extra practice, work with List 5b. If not, go on to List 6a and write those words in alphabetical order according to their third letters. Check your answers on page 397. If you need extra practice with a longer list, work with List 6b.

	List 5a			*List 5b*	
rumble	1. _____		eagle	1. _____	
rust	2. _____		eaves	2. _____	
rug	3. _____		each	3. _____	
rule	4. _____		eat	4. _____	
rude	5. _____		ear	5. _____	

	List 6a		List 6b
happen	1. _____	mitten	1. _____
hard	2. _____	mirror	2. _____
hair	3. _____	mice	3. _____
haste	4. _____	mix	4. _____
habit	5. _____	mince	5. _____
have	6. _____	Mike	6. _____
hammer	7. _____	mistake	7. _____
hack	8. _____	mild	8. _____
hag	9. _____	middle	9. _____
hand	10. _____	might	10. _____

Sometimes more than just the first two letters of different words are alike. These words are placed in alphabetical order according to the **first letters that are different**. Note which letters are used to put the words in alphabetical order in the following lists.

Sample A		Sample B	
counter		sound	
counteract	(a)	sounded	(d)
counterclaim	(c)	sounder	(r)
counterman	(m)	sounding	(i)
counterspy	(s)	soundless	(l)

(Notice that in Sample B, *sounded* and *sounder* were alike up until their last letters, **d** and **r**.)

Guided Practice 6-5: Alphabetical Order—First Letters That Are Different

Directions: Write the words in List 7a in alphabetical order according to the first letters that are different. Check your answers on page 397. If you need extra practice, work with List 7b. If not, go on to list 8a and write those words in alphabetical order according to the first letters that arc different. Check your answers on page 397. If you need extra practice with a longer list, work with List 8b.

List 7a		*List 7b*	
teary	1. _____	passage	1. _____
tear	2. _____	passable	2. _____
tearless	3. _____	passing	3. _____
tearful	4. _____	passed	4. _____
tearing	5. _____	passer-by	5. _____

List 8a		*List 8b*	
leafy	1. _____	forgiveness	1. _____
lead	2. _____	forget	2. _____
leafless	3. _____	forgive	3. _____
leads	4. _____	forgets	4. _____
leadership	5. _____	forgiving	5. _____
leaf	6. _____	forgetful	6. _____
leading	7. _____	forgave	7. _____
lead-in	8. _____	forgivingly	8. _____
lead-off	9. _____	forgiven	9. _____
leader	10. _____	forgiver	10. _____

SKILL PRACTICE: ALPHABETICAL ORDER

A. Directions: Circle any word in each of the following rows that is out of alphabetical order. Draw an arrow to show where it belongs. A sample has been done for you.

Sample

earache   elf   equal   error   ermine

1. quaint   quake   quilt   quite   quiet

2. operate   open   other   outlaw   outline

3. jockey   jelly   jerk   jet   job

4. board   boat   boot   boast   border

5. yours   yard   yesterday yet   young

6. lack   laugh   lock   life   look

7. fold   fox   fret   free   from

8. trade   treat   trap   tree   trip

9. under   unhappy unplug   until   untie

10. zest   zero   zip   zoo   zoom

B. Directions: Fill in the blanks in each of the following lists. Use any word that fits according to the alphabetical order of **first** letters. The first blank has been done for you. The word *giant* has been written in. But note that any word that begins with **g** will fit just as well.

1. dress
   Easter
   freeze

   giant
   _____

   hurry
   _____

   Jack
   _____

   lunch
   money
   _____

2. party
   quarter
   race
   _____

   upset
   _____

   xylophone
   yell
   _____

3. lodge
   mister
   _____

   October
   _____

   quiz
   _____

   trout
   umbrella

HOW TO USE THE DICTIONARY

1. Guide Words

Two guide words are found at the top of each dictionary page. They are there to help you find the word you are looking for. The first guide word is the first word on that page. The second guide word is the last word on the same page. If the word you need comes between the two guide words according to alphabetical order, it is found on that page.

The following words are from a sample dictionary page whose guide words are **drum** and **duck**. Note how the words in the middle fit between *drum* and *duck* according to alphabetical order.

drum	drunk	**duck**
drum	dry	**duck**
drum	dub	**duck**

Guided Practice 6–6: Guide Words

Directions: Read each of the following pairs of underlined guide words. Circle or highlight the word between the guide words if it fits there according to alphabetical order.

1.	<u>fat</u>	father	<u>favor</u>
2.	pang	part	paper
3.	revamp	revolt	<u>revive</u>
4.	stagger	stain	stamp
5.	gold	gone	good
6.	<u>cram</u>	cradle	crazy
7.	<u>mantle</u>	marble	margarine
8.	pinwheel	pipe	pitch
9.	<u>backhand</u>	baby	baffling
10.	carhop	carpet	carry

2. Dictionary Entries*

Each term in the dictionary is called an entry word. All entry words are arranged in alphabetical order. Words are printed in heavy, dark (boldface) type so that they are easy to find. There are different kinds of entry words. They include one word, several words, prefix, suffix, letter of the alphabet, abbreviation, and name of a person or place.

Here are some samples of entry words as they appear on a dictionary page.

one word: **form**
several words: **mirror image**
an abbreviation: **TA** *abbr.* Teaching assistant
name of a person: **Joan of Arc**
name of a place: **Blue Ridge**
a prefix: **mono-**
a suffix: **-ous**

Note that the prefix has a dash after it, showing that it must be attached to the front of a word. The suffix has a dash in front of it, showing that it must be attached to the end of a word.

The dictionary gives you a great deal of information about a word. This information is found following the entry word. For example, look at what you can learn about the term *giraffe* from its entry.

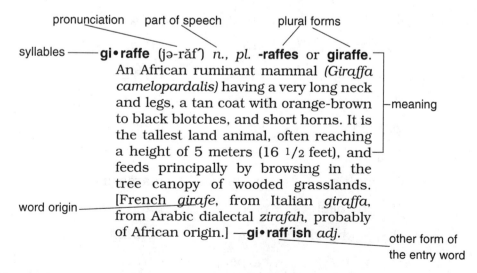

3. Syllables

Each entry word is divided into syllables. This division may be shown in different ways. Sometimes a dictionary entry word shows syllables by placing dots between them. Other dictionaries show syllables in an entry word by leaving small spaces between them.

Guided Practice 6–7: Syllables

Directions: Look at the following entry words. Write the number of syllables in each entry word.

1. gal • ler • ry   _____
2. fore • run • ner   _____
3. ir • re • sis • ti • ble   _____
4. tab • er • na • cle   _____
5. ta • ble • ware   _____

4. Spelling

The entry word shows how a word is spelled. If a word can be spelled in more than one way, different correct spellings are given. For example, note two spellings of the word *forgo* in an entry; **for • go** also **fore • go.**

Most nouns show that they are plural by the use of **s** or **es.** Other nouns, however, change their spelling when they become plural. This change of spelling is shown in the dictionary entry. Notice the use of **pl** in this sample entry before the plural form of *louse.*

> **louse** (lous) *n.* **1.** *pl.* **lice** (lis). Any of numerous small, flat-bodied, wingless biting or sucking insect of the orders Mallophaga or Anoplura, many of which are external parasites on various animals, including human beings. **2.** *pl.* **lous • es.** *Slang.* A mean or despicable person. —**louse** *tr.v.* **loused, lous • ing, lous • es.** *Slang.* To bungle: *loused the project; louse up a deal.* [Middle English, from Old English *lus.* See **lus-** in Appendix.]

Guided Practice 6–8: Plural Forms of Words

Directions: Look at each of these entries. Write the plural form of each entry word.

1. **ta • ble • spoon • ful**   (tabəl´-spoon-fōol´) *n., pl.* **-fuls.** *Abbr.* **T., tbs., tbsp.** The amount that a tablespoon can hold.

   plural of *tablespoonful:* _____

2. **plat • y • pus**   (plătĭ´-pəs) *n., pl.* **-pus • es.** A semi-aquatic egg-laying mammal *(Ornithorhynchus anatinus)* of Australia and Tasmania, having a broad flat tail, webbed feet, and a snout resembling a duck's bill. Also called *duckbill, duck-billed platypus.* [New Latin, from Greek *platupous,* flat-footed : *platu-,* platy- + *pous,* foot; see **ped-** in Appendix.]

   plural of *platypus:* _____

3. **bug • gy**[1]   (bŭg´e) *n., pl.* **-gies. 1.** A small, light, one-horse carriage usually having four wheels in the United States and two wheels in Great Britain. **2.** A baby carriage. **3.** *Informal.* An automobile. **4.** *Chiefly Southern U.S.* A shopping cart, especially for groceries. [Origin unknown.]

   plural of *buggy:* _____

4. **cac • tus**   (kăk´təs) *n., pl.* **ti** (-tī´) or **-tus • es. 1.** Any of various succulent, spiny, usually leafless plants native mostly to arid regions of the New World, having variously colored, often showy flowers with numerous stamens and petals. **2.** Any of several similar plants. [Latin, cardoon, from Greek *kaktos.*]

   plural of *cactus:* _____

5. **ox**   (ŏks) *n., pl.* **ox • en** (ŏk´sən). **1.** An adult castrated bull of the genus *Bos,* especially *B. taurus,* used chiefly as a draft animal. **2.** A bovine mammal. [Middle English, from Old English *oxa.*]

   plural of *ox:* _____

5. Pronunciation

The **pronunciation** of a word is the way it is said aloud. In the dictionary, pronunciation of an entry word is usually found right after it. Look at any of the sample entries in this chapter. Note that pronunciation of the word is set off by parentheses ( ). Watch for words that have more than one pronunciation. Sometimes, only the part that is different is shown as a second pronunciation rather than the whole word. For example, look at *crayon* in Guided Practice 6–11 on page 190.

You have already worked with word pronunciation in this book. In Part One, you used phonics to pronounce unknown words. You learned the sounds that letters of the alphabet stand for. You also learned to use the marks for long and short vowels. Pronunciation in a dictionary is much the same. You use sounds that letters stand for both when they are used alone and when they have marks with them. Many of these sounds will be familiar to you.

A full key to pronunciation is usually found in the front of a dictionary. Smaller copies of this key are usually found on the bottom or sides of pages within the dictionary to make it easy for you to pronounce words on these pages. The sounds and marks shown in pronunciation keys are used in sample words. When you do not know how to pronounce a letter in a word, look at the key and find the same letter in a sample word. Say the sample word and listen to the sound of that letter. Then say the same sound in the entry word you are trying to pronounce.

If you look at pronunciation keys in several dictionaries, you will find that they are not all exactly the same. Different letters and marks are sometimes used for the same sounds. But you should not have a problem with this. When you know how to use a pronunciation key, you can use one in any dictionary. Just be sure to check the pronunciation key carefully if you change dictionaries.

Look at the short pronunciation key provided here. Notice that the letters and their marks are given with sample words. Say each sample word and listen for the sound of the letter or letters described.

ă	pat	oi	boy
a	pay	ou	out
âr	care	o͝o	took
ä	father	oo	boot
ĕ	pet	ŭ	cut
e	be	ûr	urge
ĭ	pit	th	thin
i	pie	*th*	this
îr	pier	hw	which
ŏ	pot	zh	vision
o	toe	ə	about, item
ô	paw	♦	regionalism

Stress marks: ´ *(primary);* ῾ *(secondary),*
as in **dictionary** *(dĭ k´ shə-nĕr´e)*

Note that this dictionary pronunciation key also presents the way to use stress marks. These will be explained later in this chapter.

Guided Practice 6–9: Pronunciation

Directions: Look at the following sample words. Use the pronunciation key above to help you say each word. Then write the entry word for each pronunciation. You will find entry words in the list to the right.

Pronunciation		*Entry Word*
1. blous	_____	crowd
2. blŭnt	_____	teen
3. tem	_____	blotch
4. ten	_____	herb
5. plez	_____	crawl
6. krôl	_____	team
7. blûr	_____	blouse

8. blŏch _____ blunt

9. ûrb, hûrb _____ please

10. kroud _____ blur

Pronunciation syllables do not always match those of the entry word. For example, in the entry word *owlish*, the syllables are divided between **owl** and **ish**. However, the pronunciation syllables show that the word is pronounced **ou lish**. The entry word syllables are divided according to the way the word is written. If you want to say a word, be sure to use the pronunciation syllables as your guide.

A stress mark (also called an accent mark) ´ placed after a syllable tells you that the syllable should be stressed when you pronounce the word. When a syllable is accented, it is said with more stress than the rest of the word.

Knowing how to use stress marks can help you with word meanings. Some words have different pronunciations for different meanings. For example, the word *minute* has two different meanings. Each meaning is pronounced in a different way. Use the stress marks to help you pronounce the word *minute*.

minute

| mĭn´ĭt | — | 60 seconds |
| mi-noot´ | — | very tiny |

Guided Practice 6–10: Stress Marks

Directions: Say the following words. Use the pronunciation key examined earlier for letters or marks you do not know. Circle the part of the word that you stressed.

1. pŏp´yə-lər
2. rôr´ĭng
3. tə-boo´
4. fôr-ĕv´ər
5. plĕzh´ər

In some cases, a word may have two stress marks. The mark you already know is called the **primary stress**. It is printed in heavy print. The primary stress mark shows that the syllable before it is said with much stress. The other mark is called a **secondary stress** mark. It is printed in regular print. The secondary mark shows that the syllable before it is said with some stress, but not with as much stress as is used for the primary stress. Examples of the two stress marks are found in the following words. Practice saying these words. The marks will help you know how to stress syllables in entry words.

ta • ble • top   (ta´bəl-tŏp´)   **blow-dry**   (blo´dri´)
pop • u • late   (pŏp´yə-lat´)   **road • side** (rod´sid´)

Some words are pronounced in more than one way. The dictionary may show different ways to pronounce the same word by putting the pronunciations next to each other within the parentheses. For example,

tomato can be pronounced (tə ma´to, te mä´to)

rodeo can be pronounced (ro´de-o, ro-da´o).

6. Parts of Speech

The part of speech of an entry word is given to tell you how the word is used in a sentence. Sometimes and entry word can have more than one meaning. Then, parts of speech are given for each meaning.

The following are common parts of speech that you will find in the dictionary, along with their abbreviations.

noun	—	n.
pronoun	—	pron.
verb	—	vb.
adjective	—	adj.
adverb	—	adv.
conjunction	—	conj.
preposition	—	prep.
interjection	—	interj.

7. Word Origin

There are many words that have come to the English language from other languages. The **origin,** where the word came from, is usually set off by brackets [ ] in the dictionary entry. This is done only for words that have come from languages other than modern English. The following entries show samples of word origin information. That information has been underlined for you. Notice that a word is sometimes traced back to more than one language.

for • lorn (fər-lôrn´, fôr-) *adj.* **1.a.** Appearing sad or lonely because deserted or abandoned. **b.** Forsaken or deprived: *forlorn of all hope.* **2.** Wretched or pitiful in appearance or condition: *forlorn roadside shacks.* **3.** Nearly hopeless; desperate. See Synonyms at **despondent.** [Middle English *forloren, past participle of forlesen, to abandon, from Old English forleosan.* See **leu-** in Appendix.] —**for • lorn´ly** *adv.* **for • lorn´ness** *n.*

pleas • ant (plĕz´ent) *adj.* **-er, -est. 1.** Giving or affording pleasure or enjoyment; agreeable: *a pleasant scene; pleasant sensation.* **2.** Pleasing in manner, behavior, or appearance. See Synonyms at **amiable. 3.** Fair and comfortable: *pleasant weather.* **4.** Merry; lively. [Middle English *plesaunt, from Old French plaisant, present participle of plasir, to please, from Latin placere.*

Guided Practice 6–11: Word Origins

Directions: Look at the following entries. Write the origin of each entry word.

1. **gin • ger • bread** (jĭn´jər-brĕd´) *n.* **1.a.** A dark molasses cake flavored with ginger. **b.** A soft molasses and ginger cookie cut in various shapes, sometimes elaborately decorated. **2.a.** Elaborate ornamentation. **b.** Superfluous or tasteless embellishment, especially in architecture. [Middle English *gingebred,* a stiff pudding, preserved ginger, alteration (influenced by *bred, bread,* bread; see BREAD) of Old French *gingembrat,* from Medieval Latin **gingibratum, from gingiber,* ginger. See GINGER.] —**gin´ger • bread´** —**gin´ger • bread´y** *adj.*

origin of *gingerbread:* _____ _____

2. **tab • let**   (tăb′lĭt) *n.* **1.** A slab or plaque, as of stone or ivory, with a surface that is intended for or bears an inscription. **2.a.** A thin sheet or leaf, used as a writing surface. **b.** A set of such leaves fastened together, along one edge. **3.** A small flat pellet of medication to be taken orally. **4.** A small flat cake of a prepared substance, such as soap. **—tablet** *tr.v.* **-let • ed, -let • ing, -lets. 1.** To inscribe on a tablet. **2.** To form into a tablet. [Middle English *tablette,* from Old French *tablete,* diminutive of *table,* table. See TABLE.}

origin of *tablet:* _____

3. **cray • on**   (kraŏn′, -en) *n.* **1.** A stick of colored wax, charcoal, or chalk, used for drawing. **2.** A drawing made with one of these sticks. **—crayon** *tr.v.* **-oned, -on • ing, -ons.** To draw, color, or decorate with a stick of colored wax, charcoal, or chalk. [French, diminutive of *craie,* chalk, from Latin *cre t̄a.*] **—cray′on • ist** (-ə-nĭst) *n.*

origin of *crayon:* _____

8. Word Meaning

The meaning of an entry word is found after its pronunciation. If there are a number of meanings in an entry, you should not just choose the first one. It may not be the one used most often. Or it may not be the one you need. Also, it may not match the way you are using the word. The meaning you choose must match the part of speech.

Sometimes the meanings of a word are not all put in the same entry. They may be put into more than one entry. In that case, the entry word is followed by a small number. For example, look below at two entries for the word *tab.* Notice the small number after each entry word. Whenever you see an entry word followed by a small number, always look for other entries for the same word.

tab[1]   (tăb) *n.* **1.** A projection, flap, or short strip attached to an object to facilitate opening, handling, or identification. **2.** A small, usually decorative flap or tongue on a garment. **3.** A small auxiliary airfoil that is attached to a larger one and that helps stabilize an aircraft. **4.** A pull-tab. **—tab** *tr.v.* **tabbed, tab • bing, tabs.** To supply with a tab or tabs. [Origin unknown.]

tab² (tăb) *n.* **1.** *Informal.* A bill or check, such as one for a meal in a restaurant. **2.** A tabulator on a typewriter. **—*idiom.* keep tabs on.** *Informal.* To observe carefully: *Let's keep tabs on expenditures.* [Short for TABLET or TABULATION. Sense 2, short for TABULATOR.]

You must read all the meanings in an entry carefully. See which one fits your needs. This is easier to do if the word you want is in context. You can then try each meaning to see if it fits your context. This is the same thing you did in Chapter Four when you used word clues in context for words that had more than one meaning.

Look at the entry for *blowup.* It shows three meanings:

blow • up (blō´ŭp´) *n.* **1.** An explosion. **2.** An outburst of temper. **3.** A photographic enlargement.

You must use clues in context to know which meaning to choose. Look at the clues in context in each of the following three sentences. Note which meaning of *blowup* fits.

1. The gas leak caused a <u>blowup</u> in the house. (meaning 1: explosion)
2. The <u>blowup</u> of the picture showed all the small details. (meaning 3: enlargement of photograph)
3. A person with a bad temper will often have a <u>blowup</u> over small things. (meaning 2: outburst of anger)

Guided Practice 6–12: Word Meanings

Directions: Read the following sentences. Use any clues given in the dictionary to help you choose the right meaning and the right part of speech. Then check your meaning in the context of the sentence.

1. Some people believe that a rainy day can bring on a bad case of the <u>blues</u>.

blues (blooz) *pl.n. (used with a sing. or pl. verb)* **1.** A state of depression or melancholy: *The blues has finally gotten me today. I really have the blues today.* **2.** *Music.* A style of music evolved from southern Black American secular songs and usually distinguished by slow tempo and flatted thirds and

sevenths. [Short for BLUE DEVILS.] —**blues´man** *n.* —**blues´y**
adj.

part of speech: _____

meaning number: _____

2. "Don't hog the sofa," said Peggy. "I want to sit there, too."

hog (hôg, hŏg) *n.* **1.a.** Any of various mammals of the family
Suidae, which includes the domesticated pig as well as wild
species, such as the boar and the wart hog. **b.** A domesticated pig, especially one weighing over 54 kilograms (120
pounds). **2.a.** A self-indulgent, gluttonous, or filth person. **b.**
One that uses too much of something. **3.** Also **hogg. a.** *Chiefly*
British. A young sheep before it has been shorn. **b.** The wool
from this type of sheet. **4.** *Slang.* A big, heavy motorcycle. —
hog *v.* **hogged, hog • ging, hogs.** —*tr.* **1.** *Informal.* To take
more that one's share of: *Don't hog the couch.* **2.** To cause (the
back) to arch like that of a hog. **3.** To cut (a horse's mane)
short and bristly. **4.** To

part of speech: _____

meaning number: _____

3. My nephew likes to monkey with the television set.

mon • key (mŭng´ke) *n., pl.* **-keys. 1.** Any of various long-tailed,
medium-sized members of the order Primates, including the
macaques, baboons, guenons, capuchins, marmosets, and
tamarins and excluding the anthropoid apes and the
prosimians. **2.** One that behaves in a way suggestive of a
monkey, as a mischievous child or a mimic. **3.** The iron block
of a pile driver. **4.** *Slang.* A person who is mocked, duped, or
made to appear a fool: *They made a monkey out of him.* **5.**
Slang. Drug addiction: *have a monkey on one's back.* —**mon-**
key *v.* **-keyed, -key • ing, -keys.** —*intr. Informal.* **1.** To play, fiddle, trifle, or tamper with something. **2.** To behave in a mischievous or apish manner: *Stop monkeying around! —tr.* To
imitate or mimic; ape. [Origin unknown.]

part of speech: _____

meaning number: _____

4. Flora has just adopted a tabby that has four cute kittens.

tab • by (tăb´e) *n., pl.* **-bies. 1.** A rich watered silk. **2.** A fabric of plain weave. **3.a.** A domestic cat with a striped or brindled coat of a gray or tawny color. **b.** A domestic cat, especially a female. **4.** A spinster. **5.** A prying woman; a gossip. **6.** *South Atlantic U.S.* A mixture of oyster shells, lime, sand, and water used as a building material. **—tabby** *adj.* **1.** Having light and dark striped markings: *a tabby cat.* **2.** Made of or resembling watered silk. [French *tabis,* from Old French *atabis,* from Medieval Latin *attabi,* from Arabic ʻ*attabi,* after *al-ʼAttabiya,* a suburb of Baghdad, Iraq.]

part of speech: _____

meaning number: _____

5. The <u>gallant</u> warrior, who fought to the end, was the only one

left after the battle.

gal • lant (găl´ənt) *adj.* **1.** Smartly or boldly stylish; dashing: *a gallant feathered hat; cut a gallant figure at the coronation.* **2.a.** Unflinching in battle or action; valiant: *put up a gallant resistance to the attackers.* **b.** Nobly or selflessly resolute: *made a gallant attempt to save his friend's reputation.* **3.** Stately; majestic. **4.** (gə-lănt´, -länt´) **a.** Courteously attentive especially to women; chivalrous. **b.** Flirtatious; amorous. **— gallant** (gə-lănt´, -länt´, găl´ənt) *n.* **1.** A fashionable young man. **2.a.** A man courteously attentive to women. **b.** A woman's lover; a paramour. **—gallant** (gə-lănt´, -länt´) *v.* **-lant • ed, -lant • ing, -lants.** *—tr.* To woo or pay court to (a lady). — *intr.* To play the gallant. [Middle English *galaunt,* from Old French *galant,* present participle of *galer,* to rejoice, of Germanic origin. See **wel-**[1] in Appendix.] **—gal´lant • ly** *adv.*

part of speech: _____

meaning number _____

Most dictionaries help the reader understand word meanings by providing two aids. First, phrases or sentences are given. They show how different meanings fit in context. This is most helpful when an entry word has a number of meanings. Second, pictures are provided. They help explain entry words. Pictures may include photographs, drawings, maps, and charts. Be aware of both kinds of aids. Look for them. Get in the habit of using them and you will find it easier to understand dictionary meanings.

Most dictionaries also give information in an entry that will help you to use the entry word correctly. For example, you may be told if the word is slang. Then you know when it is proper to use that word. In addition, there may be information that tells where the entry word is used. For instance, some word meanings are connected to scientific or health fields. Other word meanings may be identified because they are used in sports or games. Look at the two dictionary entries below. They give examples of how you can know where the special meaning of a word is used.

The word **shield** has special meanings in physics (meaning 3b), electronics (meaning 3c), zoology (meaning 4), and geology (meaning 6).

> **shield** (sheld) *n.* **1.** A broad piece of armor made of rigid material and strapped to the arm of carried in the hand for protections against hurled or thirsted weapons. **2.** A person or thing that provides protection. **3.** A protective device or structure, as: **a.** A steel sheet attached to an artillery piece to protect gunners from small-arms fire and shrapnel. **b.** *Physics.* A wall or housing of concrete or lead built around a nuclear reactor to prevent the escape of radiation. **c.** *Electronics.* A structure or arrangement of metal plates or mesh designed to protect a piece of electronic equipment from electrostatic or magnetic interference. **d.** A pad word, as at the armpits, to protect a garment from perspiration. **4.** *Zoology.* A protective plate or similar hard outer covering; a scute or scutellum. **5.** Something that resembles a shield, as: **a.** An escutcheon. **b.** A decorative emblem that often serves to identify an organization or a government. **c.** A police officer's badge. **6.** *Geology.* A large lowland area, the geologic nucleus of a continent, whose bedrock consists of igneous and metamorphic rocks that are usually Precambrian in age: *the Canadian Shield.* — **shield** *v.* **shield • ed, shield • ing, shields.** —*tr.* **1.** To protect or defend with or as if with a shield; guard. See Synonyms at **defende. 2.** To cover up; conceal. —*intr.* To act or serve as a shield or safeguard. [Middle English *sheld*, from Old English *scield.* —**shield´er** *n.*

When you examine the two entries for the word **tee**, you find that this word has special meanings in sports and games as well as in sports alone. There is also a slang meaning for tee.

> **tee**[1] (te) *n.* **1.** The letter *t.* **2.** Something shaped like a T. **3.** *Sports & Games.* A mark aimed at in certain games, such as curling or quoits. —*idiom.* **to a tee.** Perfectly; exactly: *a plan that suits me to a tee.*
>
> **tee**[2] (te) *n. Sports.* **1.** A small peg with a concave top for holding a golf ball for an initial drive. **2.** The designated area of each golf hole from which a player makes his or her first stroke. —**tee** *tr.v.* **teed, tee • ing, tees.** *Sports.* To place (a golf ball) on a tee. Often used with *up.* —*phrasal verb.* **tee off. 1.** *Sports.* To drive a golf ball from the tee. **2.** *Slang.* To start or begin: *They teed off the fundraising campaign with a dinner.* **3.** *Slang.* To make or become angry or disgusted: *The impertinent remarks teed the speaker off. He was teed off because it rained all weekend.* [Back-formation from obsolete Scots *teaz* (taken as a pl.).]

To help you understand a word meaning, sometimes the dictionary entry information also includes a synonym of the entry word. This synonym is a word that means the same or almost the same as the entry word. For example, the entry below includes two synonyms for the entry word **crave**. The synonyms are found after the first and third meanings of crave.

> **crave** (krav) *v.* **craved, crav • ing, craves.** —*tr.* **1.** To have an intense desire for. See Synonyms at **desire. 2.** To need urgently; require. **3.** To beg earnestly for; implore. See Synonyms at **beg.** —*intr.* To have an eager or intense desire. [Middle English *craven*, from Old English *crafian*, to beg.] —**crav´er** *n.* —**crav´ing • ly** *adv.*

SAMPLE DICTIONARY PAGE

---

cross vault   *n.* A vaulting formed by the intersection of two or more simple vaults. Also called *cross vaulting.*

cross vine   *n.* See **bignonia.**

cross • walk   (krôs′wôk′, krŏs′-) *n.* A path marked off for pedestrians crossing a street.

cross • way   (krôs′wa′, krŏs′-) *n.* A crossroad.

cross • ways   (krôs′wāz, krŏs′-) *adv.* Variant of **crosswise.**

cross • wind   (krôs′wĭnd′, krŏs′-) *n.* A wind blowing at right angles to a given direction, as to an aircraft's line of flight.

cross • wise   (krôs′wĭz′, krŏ˘s′-) also **cross • ways** (-wāz′) *–adv.* So as to be or lie in a cross direction; across: *placed the kindling crosswise to the rest of the wood. –adj.* Crossing: *a crosswise piece.*

cross • word puzzle   (krôs′wûrd′, krŏs′-) *n.* A puzzle in which an arrangement of numbered squares is to be filled with words running both across and down in answer to correspondingly numbered clues.

crotch   (krŏch) *n* **1.** The angle or region of the angle formed by the junction of two parts or members, such as two branches, limbs, or legs. **2.** The fork of a pole or other support. [Possibly alteration of CRUTCH and partly from *croche,* crook, crosier (from Old French *croche,* hook, shepherd's crook, feminine of *croc,* hook).] **—crotched** (krŏcht) *adj.*

crotch • et   (krŏch′ĭt) *n.* **1.** An odd, whimsical, or stubborn notion. **2.** *Music.* See **quarter note. 3.** *Obsolete.* A small hook or hooklike structure. [Middle English *crochet,* from Old French. See CROCHET.]

crotch • et •y   (krŏch′ĭ-te) *adj.* Capriciously stubborn or eccentric; perverse. **—crotch′et • I • ness** *n.*

Croth • ers   (krŭth′erz), **Rachel.** 1878–1958. American playwright, director, and producer whose plays, including *Susan and God*

(1937), often concern women's issues.

cro • ton   (krot′n) *n.* **1.** Any of various plants of the genus *Croton,* which includes the sources of cascarilla bark and croton oil. **2.** An Old World tropical evergreen shrub *(Codiaeum variegatum)* widely cultivated as a houseplant for its glossy, multicolored foliage. [New Latin *Croton,* genus name, from Greek *kroton,* castor oil plant.]

Cro • ton bug   (krōt′n) *n.* See **German cockroach.** [After the *Croton* River of southeast New York.]

cro • ton • ic acid   (kro-tŏn′ĭk) *n.* An organic acid, $C_4H_6O_2$, used in the preparation of pharmaceuticals and resins. [From New Latin *Croton,* plant genus. See CROTON.]

croton oil   *n.* A brownish-yellow oil obtained from the seeds of a tropical Asian shrub or small tree *(Croton tiglium)* and having a cathartic action too violent for human use.

crot • in   (krŏt′n) *n.* **1.** A pungent cheese made of goat's milk and formed into small disks. **2.** A disk of this cheese. [French, from Old French *crotin,* animal dropping, diminutive of *crotte,* dung, probably of Germanic origin.]

crouch   (krouch) *v.* **crouched, crouch • ing, crouch • es.** *—intr.* **1.a.** To stoop, especially with the knees bent: *They crouched over the grate with a flashlight, searching for the lost gem.* **b.** To press the entire body close to the ground with the limbs bent: *a cat crouching near its prey.* **2.** To bend servilely or timidly; cringe. *—tr.* To bend (the head or knee, for example) low, as in fear or humility. **—crouch** *n.* The act or posture of bending low or crouching. [Middle English *crouchen,* probably from Old North French **crouchir,* to become bent, variant of Old French *crochir,* from *croche,* hook. See CROCHET.]

croup[1]   (kro͞op) *n.* A pathological condition of the larynx, especially in infants and children, that is characterized by respiratory difficulty and a hoarse, brassy cough. [From dialectal *croup*, to croak.] — **croup´ous** (kro͞o´pǝs), **croup´y** *adj.*

croup[2] (kro͞op) *n.* The rump of a beast of burden, especially a horse. [Middle English *croupe*, from Old French, of Germanic origin.]

crou • pi • er (kro͞o´pe-ǝr, -pe-ā´) *n.* An attendant at a gaming table who collects and pays bets. [French, one who rides behind another on a horse (obsolete), croupier, from *croupe*, rump, croup, from Old French. See CROUP[2].]

crouse (kro͞os) *adj.* *Scots.* Lively, vivacious. [Middle English *crous*, fierce, bold, perhaps from Middle Flemish *cruus*, curly, bold.]

Crouse (krous), **Russel.** 1893–1966. American playwright whose works include several collaborations, such as *State of the Union,* for which he shared a Pulitzer Prize (1946), and the musical *Call Me Madam* (1950).

crous • tade (kro͞o-städ´) *n.* A molded or hollowed bowllike crust, as of pastry, rice, or bread, used as a serving container for another food. [French, from Provençal *croustado,* from Latin *crustatus,* past participle of *crustare,* to encrust, from *crusta,* crust. See CRUST.]

crou • ton (kro͞o´tŏn´, kro͞o-tŏn´) *n.* A small crisp piece of toasted or fried bread. [French *croûton,* diminutive of *croûte,* crust, from Old French *crouste,* from Latin *crusta.* See **kreus-** in Appendix.]

crow[1] (kro) *n.* 1. Any of several large, glossy, black birds of the genus *Corvus,* having a characteristic raucous call, especially *C. brachyrhynchos* of North America. 2. A crowbar. —*idiom.* **as the crow flies.** In a straight line. [Middle English *croue,* from Old English *crawe.* See **gere-**[2] in Appendix.]

crow[2] (kro) *intr.v.* **crowed, crow • ing, crows.** 1. To utter the shrill cry characteristic of a cock or rooster. 2. To exult loudly, as over another's defeat; boast. See Synonyms at **boast**[1]. 3. To make a sound expressive of pleasure or well-being, characteristic of an

infant. —**crow** *n.* 1. The shrill cry of a cock. 2. An inarticulate sound expressive of pleasure or delight. [Middle English *crouen,* from Old English *crawan.* See **gere-**[2] in Appendix.]

Crow[1] (kro) *n., pl.* **Crow** or **Crows.** 1.a. A Native American people formerly inhabiting an area of the northern Great Plains between the Platte and the Yellowstone rivers, now located in southeast Montana. The Crow became nomadic buffalo hunters after migrating west from the Missouri River in North Dakota in the 18th century. b. A member of this people. 2. The Siouan language of the Crow. Also called *Absaroke.*

Crow[2] (kro) *n.* See **Corvus.**

crow • bar (kro´bär´) *n.* A straight bar of iron or steel, with the working end shaped like a chisel and often slightly bent and forked, used as a lever. —**crowbar** *tr.v.* **-barred, -bar • ring, -bars.** To extract, remove, or insert forcibly: "[The newsmagazines] *can crowbar stories in as late as Sunday and still be out on Monday"* (Edwin Diamond). [From the resemblance of its forked end to a crow's foot or beak.]

crow • ber • ry (kro´ber´e) *n.* 1. A low-growing evergreen shrub *(Empetrum nigrum)* native to cool regions of the Northern Hemisphere and having tiny leaves, small pinkish or purplish flowers, and black, berrylike fruits. 2. The fruit of this plant.

crow blackbird *n.* See **grackle** (sense 1).

crowd[1] (kroud) *n.* 1. A large number of persons gathered together; a throng. 2. The common people; the populace. 3. A group of people united by a common characteristic, as age, interest, or vocation: *the over-30 crowd.* 4. A group of people attending a public function; an audience: *The play drew a small but appreciative crowd.* 5. A large number of things positioned or considered together. –**crowd** *v.* **crowd • ed, crowd • ing, crowds.** —*intr.* 1. To congregate in a restricted area; throng: *The children crowded around the TV.* 2. To advance by pressing or shoving: *A bevy of reporters crowded toward the candidate.* —*tr.* 1. To force by or as if by pressing or shoving: *Police crowded the spectators back to the viewing stand. Urban sprawl crowded the small farmers out of the immediate area.* **2.** To draw or stand near to: *The batter crowded the plate.* **3.** To press, cram, or force tightly together: *crowded the clothes into the closet.* **4.** To fill or occupy to overflowing: *Books crowded the shelves.* **5.** *Informal.* To put pressure on, as to pay a debt. —*idiom.* **crowd (on) sail.** *Nautical.* To spread a large amount of sail to increase speed. [From Middle English *crowden,* to crowd, from Old English *crudan,* to hasten.] —**crowd´er** *n.*

SYNONYMS: *crowd, crush, flock, horde, mob, press, throng.* The central meaning shared by these nouns is "a large group of people gathered close to one another": *a crowd of well-wishers; a crush of autograph seekers; a flock of schoolchildren; a horde of demonstrators; a mob of hard-rock enthusiasts; a press of shoppers; throngs of tourists.*

---

crowd[2] (kroud, krōd) *n.* **1.** *Music.* An ancient Celtic stringed instrument that was bowed or plucked. Also called *crwth.* **2.** *Chiefly British.* A fiddle. [Middle English *croud,* from Welsh *crwth,* hump, crowd.]

crow • die or **crow • dy** (krōo´de, krō´-, krōod´e) *n., pl.* **dies.** *Scots.* **1.** A soft cheese made from curds. **2.** Porridge; gruel. [Origin unknown.]

crowd pleas • er also **crowd-pleas • er** or **crowd • pleas • er** (kroud´ple´zər) *n.* *Informal.* A person, spectacle, work, or idea that appeals to popular taste: *"an ambitious exhibit that is neither an easy crowd pleaser not a rehash of old ideas, but an original look at German expression-*

ist sculpture" (Mark Stevens).

crowd-pleas • ing or **crowd • pleas • ing** (kroud´ple´zĭng) *adj.* *Informal.* Having characteristics that satisfy popular taste: *a crowd-pleasing musical comedy.*

crow • dy (krōo´de, krō´-, krōod´e) *n.* Variant of **crowdie.**

crow • foot (krō´fŏot´) *n.* **1.** *pl.* **-foots.** **a.** Any of numerous plants of the genus *Ranunculus* that have palmately cleft or divided leaves, such as the buttercups. **b.** Any of several other plants having leaves or other parts somewhat resembling a bird's foot. **2.** *pl.* **-feet** (-fet´) An iron ball with four spikes arranged so that one always points upwards, used to delay the advance of mounted troops and infantry; a caltrop. **3.** *pl.* **-feet.** *Nautical.* A set of small lines passed through holes of a batten or fitting to help support the backbone of an awning.

Crow • ley (krou´le) A city of southern Louisiana west of Lafayette. It is the trade and shipping center of a rice-growing region. Population, 16,036.

crown (kroun) *n. Abbr.* **cr. 1.** An ornamental circlet or head covering, often made of precious metal set with jewels and worn as a symbol of sovereignty. **2.** Often **Crown. a.** The power, position, or empire of a monarch or of a state governed by constitutional monarchy. **b.** The monarch as head of state. **3.** A distinction or reward for achievement, especially a title signifying championship in a sport. **4.** Something resembling a diadem in shape. **5.a.** A coin stamped with a crown or crowned head on one side. **b.** A silver coin formerly used in Great Britain and worth five shillings. **c.** Any one of several coins, such as the koruna, the krona, or the krone, having a name that means "crown."

Name _____

SKILL PRACTICE: USING THE DICTIONARY

A. Directions: Use the Sample Dictionary Page beginning on page 196 to complete the following exercises.

1. Write the guide words for the Sample Dictionary Page.

   _____ —

2. Write the number of syllables shown in each of the following entry words.

   crowbar   _____

   crown   _____

   crowberry   _____

   crosswise   _____

   Crowley   _____

3. Name the languages from which each of the following words comes.

   crow[1]   _____

   crotchet   _____

   crouton   _____

   crowd[2]   _____

   croton   _____

4. Write the part(s) of speech for each of the following entry words.

crow^2 _____

crowd^1 _____

crossways _____

crosswise _____

crotchety _____

5. Write the entry words for a:

place _____

person _____

tool _____

6. Name a cheese made from goat's milk and formed into small disks.

_____

7. Write the number of meanings given for each of the following entry words.

crowfoot _____

crown _____

crouch _____

crowd^2 _____

crowdie _____

8. Name the American playwright who wrote the musical *Call Me Madam.*

_____

9. Name the entry that has seven synonyms given with it.

_____

10. Write the entry words presented with numbers to show that they have more than one entry.

_____

_____

_____

B. Directions: Write the meaning of the underlined word in each of the following sentences. You will find the word meanings on the Sample Dictionary Page. It there is more than one meaning, choose the one that best fits the context. Keep your meanings brief. Use only as much information as you need.

1. Only a poor sport will <u>crow</u> when he or she wins a game.

crow: _____

2. Fitting the right words into a <u>crossword</u> puzzle can be difficult to do.

crossword puzzle: _____

3. The <u>crow</u> flew away when I tried to capture it.

crow: _____

4. Always cross the street in the <u>crosswalk</u>.

crosswalk: _____

5. The <u>Crow</u> lived in an area of the northern Great Plains.

crow: _____

6. I saw Queen Elizabeth's <u>crown</u> when I visited the Tower of London.

crown: _____

7. The gambler couldn't win because the croupier drew all the winning cards.

croupier: _____

8. The over-60 <u>crowd</u> probably remembers World War II.

crowd: _____

9. We have a crowberry growing in our garden.

crowberry: _____

10. The slave would always <u>crouch</u> when scolded by his master.

crouch: _____

C. Directions: Choose five words from any reading material. Look them up in a dictionary. Fill in the information below for each word. The sentence will be yours using the word.

1. word:

   pronunciation:

   meaning:

   sentence:

2. word:

   pronunciation:

   meaning:

   sentence:

3. word:

   pronunciation:

   meaning:

   sentence:

4. word:

   pronunciation:

   meaning:

   sentence:

5. word:

   pronunciation:

   meaning:

   sentence:

CHAPTER 7

Personal Vocabulary System

Applying clues in context or word structure and using a dictionary are good ways to find word meanings. However, even if you have a word's meaning, you may find that you don't remember it well enough to use again. This is not unusual. In fact, many people figure out or look up the same words over and over again. The problem is that they have not really worked with the word. They have not learned it. The word has not become part of their personal vocabulary.

You are about to learn a system, a way, that will help you build a large personal vocabulary. It will take work on your part, but it will be worth it. You will learn many words. They will be yours to use whenever you need them. If you are really serious about improving your vocabulary, the **Personal Vocabulary System (PVS)** is for you.

In this chapter you will learn how to master new words so that you can

1. Understand them when you hear them spoken by someone else.
2. Use them properly when you speak.
3. Recognize and understand them in print.
4. Use them properly when you write.

Let's start by taking a quick look at vocabulary. You do not have just one vocabulary. Unless there is a serious problem with your hearing or speech, you really have four vocabularies. These vocabularies may be a bit different from each other. They may not be the same size. You may be stronger in one vocabulary and weaker in another. But the four vocabularies are related to each other. Together they affect how well you can handle the English language.

Your four vocabularies did not begin and grow at the same time. A **listening vocabulary** came first. As a very young child, you began to recognize sounds spoken to you. As you matched these word sounds to things or actions, you understood what they meant. Then you began to react to words. However, you could not yet answer in words. But you knew what was being said to you. If you can, watch a young child react to hearing the word "no" if it has been used many times. You will see a sample of early listening vocabulary. In fact, a recent research study has shown that babies as young as eight months old can recognize words that have been read to them. Over the years, you have learned many words that you can understand when you hear them. This is your listening vocabulary.

The second vocabulary developed was your **speaking vocabulary.** You began by making sounds. Then came parts of words. Finally, you began to use a growing number of words. This has grown into your speaking vocabulary—all the words you use in speech. If you are like most people, your speaking vocabulary is not as large as your listening vocabulary. There are many words you hear and understand but do not use when you speak.

When you started going to school, you began to develop your third vocabulary. You learned to recognize written words, their sounds, and their meanings. Your **reading vocabulary** began to grow. Like your listening vocabulary, your reading vocabulary is probably larger than your speaking vocabulary. You can read and understand someone else's words in written form. But you may not use many of these words when you speak.

Along with a reading vocabulary, you developed a **writing vocabulary.** You learned how to write letters of the alphabet and how to spell words. Your writing vocabulary is probably the smallest of the four vocabularies. Unless you feel comfortable with words and know how to spell them, you probably will not use them in writing. Therefore, you probably use in writing only a limited number of the words you know.

PVS will help you build up all four vocabularies. It is not just a reading vocabulary system. As the steps of PVS are explained, you will see how they help all four of your vocabularies to grow.

The only supplies you need for PVS are a dictionary, a pen or pencil, and a supply of 3 × 5 cards. (It does not matter if the cards are lined or unlined.) Always keep a good supply of cards on hand to use as you need them.

There are two parts of PVS. In the first part, you record all you need to know about a word on a 3 × 5 card. In the second part, you learn the word. Both parts will be explained shortly.

PVS begins when you meet a word you want to learn. This word can be in your reading or in what someone else is saying to you. If it is in your reading, use your skills with clues in context, word structure, and the dictionary to help with word meaning. If the word is spoken to you, try to hear clues in context to help with word meaning. If this doesn't work, jot the word down the way you think it might be spelled and check it out later. You are now ready for the first part of PVS.

FILLING OUT CARDS

The following six steps are used to write down on cards what you need to know about a word.

1. *Write the word you want to learn in the middle of a 3 × 5 card. Be sure the spelling is correct. (For spoken words, check the dictionary spelling before you write down the word.)*
2. *Write the context for the word below it. Context can be a phrase or a sentence. Take context from what you are reading if the word comes from there. When the word is a spoken one, try to write down the phrase or sentence in which the speaker used the word. Remember how important context is. It gives clues to which meaning of a word is being used.*
3. *Write the dictionary pronunciation for the word in the upper right-hand corner of the card. Copy the letters and marks very carefully. Be sure to show the spoken syllables.*

At this point, you have finished the front of the card. It should have the following information about the word you want to learn.

Front

```
┌─────────────────────────────────────────────────────┐
│                                                      │
│                                      dictionary      │
│                                      pronunciation   │
│                                                      │
│                         word                         │
│                                                      │
│                        context                       │
│                                                      │
│                                                      │
│                                                      │
└─────────────────────────────────────────────────────┘
```

Now you are ready to turn to the back of the card. The last three steps are done on that side.

4. *Write the dictionary meaning of the word. There may be more than one meaning for your word. Check the context the word came from to make sure you choose the right meaning. The meaning must fit into the context.*

5. *Write the word's part of speech in the upper right-hand corner. If an entry has a number of definitions and parts of speech, you must select what matches the way the word has been used in context. Knowing whether the word is a **noun** (name of a person, place, or thing), a **verb** (an action word), an **adjective** (a word that describes a noun or pronoun), or an **adverb** (a word that describes verbs, adjectives, and other adverbs), will help you to use the word correctly in speaking or writing.*

6. *Write a sentence of your own for the word. Use the dictionary meaning. Make sure that your sentence tells the meaning of the word. If your sentence is so general that it can fit any number of words, it is not a good sentence. For example, if the new word is* content, *you must tell something about it. If your sentence reads "He was* <u>content</u>," *it is a poor sentence. Think of how many words you can use in place of the word* content *in that context. You learn nothing about the meaning of* content. *A sentence such as "He as so* <u>content</u> *with his life that he smiled much of the time" is better. It gives a clue to the meaning of* content: pleased.

The back of the card should have the following information about the word you want to learn.

Back

```
                                          part of
                                          speech


        dictionary definition

        your own sentence


```

You have now finished the first part of PVS.

Look at the two sides of the sample card shown here. Notice how the six steps have been done. The word to be learned on the sample is *invalid*. This word has two dictionary meanings, so it is important to stick to the one that is needed. The word, context, pronunciation, meaning, and sentence must all match.

Front

```
                                          in´və lid


              invalid

          (accident made Josie
            an invalid for life)


```

> noun
>
> person who is weak
> because of sickness or injury
>
> The invalid has been in bed so long
> that she can't stand up without help.

Check the sentence by putting the definition in place of the word. "The person who is weak because of sickness or injury has been in bed so long that she can't stand up without help." Yes, it fits. The sentence is a good one.

Look back at the information you have written on your 3 × 5 card. Be sure that all the information about the word goes together. That means that the pronunciation, definition, and your sentence all relate to the way the word was used in context. In other words, your 3 × 5 card is really a package of related information.

Guided Practice 7–1: PVS

Directions: The following paragraph has words you may not know. These words have been underlined. Use the six steps of PVS to fill out the blank cards that follow the paragraph. These cards are slightly smaller than 3 × 5, but you should be able to write all you need on them. Don't forget to use your dictionary skills. See dictionary entries for the four words on the following pages in Chapter Six:

craved
teed off } on page 195

crowd } on Sample Dictionary Page
croutons } beginning on page 196

Also, be sure to check your sentences to make sure that they are good ones because they show you know what the word means and how to use it properly.

The chef at the restaurant grumbled to herself as she prepared food for the crowd. She was teed off by the many people who had come to eat without advance notice. They all craved her famous onion soup topped off with croutons.

After you have finished using PVS for all four underlined words, check your cards on pages 399 to 402 at the back of the book. Then return to this paragraphs and read it again. If you did a good job of mastering the four new words, it should now be easy for you to understand the paragraph.

1.

Front

Back

2.

Front

Back

3.

Front

Back

4.

Front

Back

LEARNING THE WORDS

Now you are ready for the second part of PVS. In this part, you learn the new words so that they become yours. You will not be able to do the following steps with the cards you just filled in for Guided Practice. You need real 3 × 5 cards. But you will be able to do the steps in Skill Practice at the end of this chapter.

The following steps will help you learn the meaning of new words. Read the steps and picture what you will do in each.

1. *Look at the front of the card and pronounce the word.*

2. *Say the word's meaning.*

3. *Check the back of the card to see if the meaning you said is correct.*

4. *Make two piles of cards. Put all the cards with word meanings you know in one pile. Put cards with word meanings you do not know in the other pile.*

5. *Go over the cards in the "don't know" pile until you do know the meaning of each of these words.*

6. *Review all the cards at least once a week. Relearn any words you may have forgotten.*

If you learn words by following these steps of PVS, you will be using a very flexible system. Unlike trying to learn lists of words, you do not go over and over words you already know. You only work with those you need for as long as you need. You can watch the pile of words you know grow higher. It will make you feel good to watch the other pile go down. As you can see, PVS saves you time and energy. You spend time and energy only where they are needed, only on words you do not know.

Earlier in the chapter, you learned about your four vocabularies. PVS helps you to add to all four vocabularies. Let's see how this happens. When you pronounce a word and its meaning aloud, you say it and hear it. Thus, you add the word to your listening and speaking vocabularies. You will be able to recognize the word when someone else says it and you will be able to say it, too. When you see the word several times, you learn its written form. It then becomes part of your reading vocabulary. When you write the word several times (as a word and in a sentence), you learn how to spell it. The word becomes part of your writing vocabulary. You are able to use the word in all four vocabularies. You have really mastered that word! It has indeed become part of your personal vocabulary.

As you card pile grows, you will find it most helpful to buy a file box and a set of alphabet cards. When you have learned a word, file it in the box according to alphabetical order. You have then begun to develop your own personal dictionary. And, best of all, this dictionary is made up of words you do not have to look up over and over again. They are your words!

Name _____

SKILL PRACTICE: PERSONAL VOCABULARY SYSTEM

A. Directions: Read the following newspaper story. Use PVS to make out cards and learn the underlined words. Use your own 3 × 5 cards. When you finish, you will have the first ten cards of your personal vocabulary.

Sheriff's Sgt. Dan Rhyne used to <u>scoff</u>[1] at <u>witchcraft</u>[2], but not anymore.

He took it so lightly that while investigating[3] a prowler call at a 100-year-old house last month, he laughingly and irreverently[4] walked through a witches' circle found in an upstairs room of the house, which some people in Topeka, Kansas, claim is used for <u>occult</u>[5] <u>ceremonies</u>[6].

Two car accidents and 30 stitches later, Rhyne is not laughing. He is not even smirking[7].

"I did not believe in witches, but now I'm beginning to wonder," he said Thursday, referring to the strange run of bad luck he has had since he smugly[8] walked through the circle used during witchcraft <u>rites</u>[9].

The morning after he investigated the prowler call, Rhyne was sitting in his patrol car parked against a curb when another car crossed three lanes of traffic and hit him. He suffered minor back injuries and the damage to his car cost $3,800 to repair.

Three days later, he fell from a bench in his garage and cut his right hand. It took 15 stitches to patch it up.

And three days after that, he returned to the house only to find another bad <u>omen</u>[10]—two dead squirrels had been placed in the middle of the circle.

Four days later, Rhyne reached around a corner in his basement to turn off a light. He cut his right hand on a screw and had to go to the hospital—for another 15 stitches to close the gash.

Finally, about two weeks later, someone crashed into his newly repaired car.

"I'm just kind of wondering what's going to be next," he said.

Check your 3 × 5 cards. Make sure that you have matching information on each card. For example, does all of your information for words 3 and 7 end in **ing**? Also, is all of your information for words 6 and 9 plural? You can't change the form of the word as it appears in context, but you can fix your information so it fits that form.

B. Directions: Choose five words from any reading material. Make out 3 × 5 cards using the Personal Vocabulary System. Staple or clip the cards to this Skill Practice.

CHAPTER 8

Main Ideas in Paragraphs

A paragraph is a group of sentences that begins on a new line with an indented first word. These sentences are usually related to each other because they tell about the same subject. This subject is called the **main idea** of the paragraph. Finding the main idea helps you understand and remember what a paragraph is generally about. It gives you a broad idea of what the writer is trying to tell you. The main idea also acts as the base for related details which present more detailed information about the same idea. Together, the main idea and supporting details give the reader a package of related information—information that goes together because it tells about the same thing.

In this chapter, you will learn how to

1. Find stated main ideas in paragraphs.
2. Work with implied main ideas in paragraphs.
3. Check to see if the main idea is correct.

The first step in locating the main idea of any paragraph is to read the paragraph carefully. Then ask two important questions to help you locate that main idea:

1. *Who or what is the paragraph about?*
2. *What does the writer really want you to know about that "who" or "what"?*

The answer to the first question will give you a very general idea of what the paragraph is about. It may be about a person, place, thing, or event that is mentioned over and over again. The answer to this question is the paragraph's **topic**. This paragraph topic can usually be said in just one or two words. Question 2 makes you look at the sentences to find out what the writer *really* wants you to know about that topic. The answer to this second question is the **main idea** of the paragraph.

STATED MAIN IDEAS IN PARAGRAPHS

When you ask the second question to locate the main idea of a paragraph, answer it in a sentence using your own words. Base your answer on what you think the author wants you to know about the topic of the paragraph. Now look in the paragraph. Has the writer written a sentence that sounds much like your own answer to the second question? If so, the writer has stated the main idea for you in a topic sentence. You need only to identify it within the paragraph. A main idea that is found directly in the paragraph is called a **stated main idea.**

The stated main idea may appear in different parts of a paragraph.

1.

Main Idea
Related Sentences

The stated main idea may be located in the first or second sentence of a paragraph.

John worked hard around the house. He dusted and cleaned all the rooms. He usually washed and dried the dishes. John also made sure that the trash was put out into the alley once a week.

2.

Related Sentences
Main Idea

The stated main idea may be located at the end of a paragraph.

Sandy now weighs 15 pounds more than she did last year. Her clothing is much too tight for her. She cannot wear her best jeans because they do not button at the waist. Sandy is getting heavier than she wants to be.

3.

Related Sentences
Main Idea
Related Sentences

The stated main idea may be located in the middle of a paragraph.

Walking, jogging, and running have become forms of exercise for people who want to stay healthy. There are different ways people show that they care about their health. They eat good food and don't smoke or drink. And they get lots of rest, too.

No matter where a stated main idea is found, it can be underlined or highlighted. The writer has given that main idea to you in the paragraph.

You can check to see if your stated main idea is correct. Think of the answer to question 2 as an umbrella statement—one that covers the whole paragraph. Then see if each sentence tells something about that main idea. Write the main idea in a full sentence. The details can be written as full sentences or as phrases that contain the major ideas of the details. All or most of the sentences should fit under the umbrella statement because they give you information about that statement. If they do fit, you have located the main idea of the paragraph.

To help you understand the idea of an umbrella statement, imagine this paragraph. The umbrella statement is: "A deck of playing cards has four suits." The other sentences in the paragraph should give you information about those four suits. Perhaps they name and describe each suit.

The following two sample paragraphs will show you how to use the two questions you have learned to locate stated main ideas and how to use an umbrella statement to check that main idea.

Sample A

Toys can be very harmful to children. For instance, some metal toys may have sharp edges that can cause bad cuts. Or plastic toys may have small pieces that children can bite off and swallow. Also, the paint on some toys might have lead in it; these toys are not safe because children might put them in their mouths.

Who or what is the paragraph about?
toys
What does the writer really want you to know about toys?
Children's toys may not be safe.
(Your own words might be slightly different but the idea must be the same.)

Is there a sentence that has the same idea as this answer to the second question? Even though the words do not match, the first sentence has the same idea. Thus, the first sentence is probably the stated main idea of this paragraph. Now you can check to be sure the stated main idea is correct by using it as an umbrella statement. Then see if the other sentences in the paragraph fit under the umbrella by giving information about toys being harmful for children. They do, so the main idea is correct.

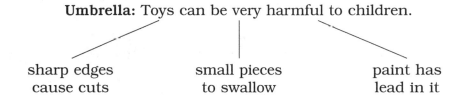

Umbrella: Toys can be very harmful to children.

| sharp edges | small pieces | paint has |
| cause cuts | to swallow | lead in it |

Sample B

Cabbage is high in vitamins A, B_1, B_2, and C. It is very low in calories, with only 24 calories per cup raw and 30 calories per cup when cooked. Cabbage can be used to make many tasty low-calorie dishes. Thus, cabbage is a good food for people on diets.

Who or what is the paragraph about?
cabbage
What does the writer really want you to know about cabbage?
People on diets should eat cabbage.
(Your own words might have been slightly different but the idea must be the same.)

Is there a sentence that has the same idea as this answer to the second question? Even though the words do not match, the last sentence has the same idea. Thus, the last sentence is the stated main idea of this paragraph. Now you can check to be sure the stated main idea is correct by using it as an umbrella statement. Then see if the other sentences in the paragraph fit under the umbrella by giving information about why people on diets should eat cabbage. If they do, the main idea is correct.

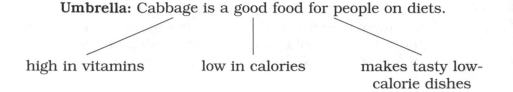

Umbrella: Cabbage is a good food for people on diets.

high in vitamins   low in calories   makes tasty low-calorie dishes

Yes, the stated main idea is correct because each of the sentences is related to it. Each sentence tells why cabbage is a good food for people on diets.

Guided Practice 8–1: Stated Main Ideas—A

Directions: Read each of the following paragraphs carefully. Ask the two questions to help you locate the stated main idea. Remember to say the answer to the second question in your own words and then look for the same idea in a sentence in the paragraph. Underline or highlight the stated main idea. Then check to see if your main idea is correct by first using it as an umbrella statement and then seeing if the other sentences fit under that umbrella.

1. Seth was a salesperson until he changed jobs at age 50. Betty was 51 years old when she left teaching to become a writer. Many people have made midlife job changes. For example, Sam was 54 when he left his job on the newspaper to become a housepainter. Then Jack, who is the same age, also left the newspaper to join him.

Who or what is the paragraph about?

_____

What does the writer really want you to know about that "who" or "what"?

(in your own words)

_____

Underline or highlight and then check the stated main idea:

Umbrella: _____

/ | | \

_____ _____ _____ _____

2. Avoid feeling helpless in electric power failures by knowing what to do. First, be prepared by keeping candles in the house. Second, have at least one flashlight with batteries that work. Third, turn off almost all lights and anything that uses electric power. Last, keep one or two lights as they were when the electric power went out so you will be able to tell when it is back again.

Who or what is the paragraph about?

_____

What does the writer really want you to know about that "who" or "what"?

(in your own words)

_____

Underline or highlight and then check the stated main idea:

Umbrella: _____

/ | | \

_____ _____ _____ _____

_____ _____ _____ _____

3. The daytime temperature was usually 110°F in the shade. And the over-100°F temperatures went on day after day with no relief in sight. Each day brought a cloudless sky with no chance that rain would bring a break in the heat. Surely, it was the hottest summer ever seen in that part of the country.

Who or what is the paragraph about?

_____

*What does the writer really want you to know about that "who"
or "what"?*
                    (in your own words)

_____

Underline and then check the stated main idea:

Umbrella: _____

```
        /              |              \
   _____    _____      _____

   _____    _____      _____
```

4. A crude chopping tool, made from a rock the size of a man's
   fist, was used as an all-purpose tool. The hand axe, shaped
   like a pick, had a fairly sharp point and was used to dig roots
   out of the ground. As you can see, Stone Age people used simple tools to meet their needs. Other simple tools were the borer,
   used to punch holes in animal skins, and the sidescraper,
   used for dressing hides.

   Who or what is the paragraph about?

   _____

   *What does the writer really want you to know about that "who"
   or "what"?*
                    (in your own words)

   _____

   Underline and then check the stated main idea:

Umbrella: _____

```
      /          |              |            \
  _____  _____    _____    _____

  _____  _____    _____    _____
```

5. Today, fewer farmers are able to grow more food because of new kinds of farm machinery. Many young people who grow up on farms take jobs in the cities instead of becoming farmers. Some farmers sell their land so that houses can be built. They then go into other kinds of work. Thus, there are fewer farmers today than there were 50 years ago.

Who or what is the paragraph about?

_____

What does the writer really want you to know about that "who" or "what"?

(in your own words)

_____

Underline or highlight and then check the stated main idea:

Umbrella: _____

Seeing if the sentences fit under an umbrella statement is a good way to check a stated main idea. But writing down the umbrella statement and sentences can take time. Once you know what to do, it is easier and quicker to make an umbrella statement and check the sentences in your mind. Picture the stated main idea. Then picture each of the sentences. Ask yourself if most of the sentences fit under that umbrella. If they do, you have the right stated main idea. If they do not fit, try another umbrella statement. Check to see if all, or most, of the sentences fit under that umbrella. With practice, you will soon find that this check takes only a few minutes.

Guided Practice 8–2: Stated Main Ideas—B

Directions: Locate and underline or highlight the main idea in exactly the same way you did in Guided Practice 8–1. In this practice, check the stated main idea in your mind rather than writing it out.

1. The prices of new houses are so high that many people are fixing up their homes instead of moving. Houses are being repaired and repainted to look like new. Bathrooms and kitchens are being redone. Also, carpets and tile floors are being replaced. As a result of their efforts, homeowners will feel like they have new houses.

   Who or what is the paragraph about?

   _____

   What does the writer really want you to know about that "who" or "what"?
   (in your own words)

   _____

2. Taking a small calculator with you when you go shopping can be very helpful. If you add up the prices of items as you put them in the shopping cart, you will know exactly what you are spending. This will make is easier for you to stay within your budget. And, you won't be surprised when the clerk totals your bill at the checkout counter.

   Who or what is the paragraph about?

   _____

   What does the writer really want you to know about that "who" or "what"?
   (in your own words)

   _____

3. There are many places in Arizona where hunters can find game. There are also streams and lakes full of fish to catch. Forest trails are there for hikers to enjoy. And mountain climbers have a number of mountains from which to choose. Yes, Arizona has much to offer those who enjoy the outdoors.

Who or what is the paragraph about?

_____

What does the writer really want you to know about that "who" or "what"?

(in your own words)

_____

4. Avoid hilltops, open spaces, and high ground in a storm. Also, stay away from wire fences and metal poles. Every year, people all over the United States die from being struck by lightning. There are a number of other ways to avoid being struck by lightning if you are caught in a storm. If possible, go into a building or car. Do not stand near the tallest thing around. And if *you* are the tallest thing around, like down flat on the ground until the storm is over.

Who or what is the paragraph about?

_____

What does the writer really want you to know about that "who" or "what"?

(in your own words)

_____

5. People have certain advantages over animals. First, they are able to make more different sounds so that they are able to speak. Second, the thumb gives a person the power to grasp things. Third, a person's combined senses are greater than those of animals. Finally, people live longer than most animals

so they have a better chance to use what they learn. In fact, more people are living longer today. This is because of better diet, health care, and living conditions.

Who or what is the paragraph about?

_____

What does the writer really want you to know about that "who" or "what"?

(in your own words)

_____

SKILL PRACTICE: STATED MAIN IDEAS IN PARAGRAPHS

Directions: Use the two questions you have learned to help you find stated main ideas. Underline or highlight the stated main idea in each of the following paragraphs. Check the main ideas in your mind.

1. Famous athletes can earn a lot of money doing things that are not related to sports. For example, some athletes sell shaving cream on TV. Others make statements about how good some products are so that people will buy them. Finally, famous athletes are also paid to wear certain brands of clothing in public.

2. Always pull weeds as they pop up. Water your plants before they begin to look like they need it. Also, use plant food as directed on the bottle. There are a number of good ways to avoid problems in your garden. Thin out plants so there is plenty of space for them to grow. And, if needed, spray to kill plant-eating insects.

3. High in calories, alcoholic beverages are fattening without providing nutritional benefits. Heavy drinkers can suffer appetite loss which can lead to health problems caused by poor nutrition. Other health problems, such as liver disease and some types of cancer, can result from heavy drinking. Studies have shown that babies can be born with serious birth defects when women use alcohol during pregnancy. Alcohol certainly can have an effect on one's well-being.

4. You can use music to change your mood or the mood of others. The trick is to do it slowly. If you are in a bad mood, begin with blue songs. Then slowly change the music to happier, more cheerful songs. If you or someone else is highly disturbed and nervous, start out with exciting music. Then slowly move toward calmer music.

5. If your car has been sitting out in the rain or cold for a few days, it may be hard to start. There are several reasons why it may be hard to start your car at times. If the battery is "dead," the car will not start until the battery has been recharged. Or

there may be a short in the electrical system. Finally, you may be out of gas.

6. About 25,000 B.C. people started using bait on a bone fastened to a line. This was called a fishing gorge. Fish would take the bait, and the gorge would become stuck in the fish's mouth. Later, people learned to carve fishing hooks from the bones and horns of animals. People have indeed been fishing for a long time.

7. More and more Americans live in a number of different places during their lives. City dwellers often move from city to city or from one section of a city to another with little regret for the place they leave. Newlyweds tend to move from the small apartment they rented right after marriage to a house with a yard when they have children. Many people leave the cities and move out to the suburbs when they can afford it. When their children have grown and left home, parents move back into a small apartment or they may leave the area entirely to retire in a warm climate.

8. Like all mammals, a cow gives milk because she has a calf to feed. Since milk is such an important food, the cow has been developed to give more than just milk for her calf. Now she feeds her calf and gives enough milk and dairy products to meet the needs of 19 people. Today's cow is truly a great milk producer.

9. Filing any lawsuit is a serious matter. It will take your time and attention. You may even have to appear in court. It surely will cost you money for a lawyer. And, if you lose the case, you probably will have to pay court costs, too. Win or lose, you will make enemies of those you sue.

10. The manatee, or sea cow, is in danger of disappearing. Hunters made huge cuts in the sea cow population in the eighteenth and nineteenth centuries. And now, we are harming the manatees with motor boats and fishing tackle instead of harpoons. These tame, slow-moving beasts are easy targets for senseless attacks with weapons ranging from guns to boat prows. Today, only 700 to 1000 manatees still swim the Earth.

IMPLIED MAIN IDEAS IN PARAGRAPHS

All the paragraphs presented so far in this chapter have had stated main ideas. All you needed to do was to locate that main idea as it appears in the paragraph. However, this does not always happen. Sometimes a writer may not come right out and state the main idea anywhere in the paragraph. For instance, a brief paragraph might describe the following scene.

> Snow is on the ground. Icicles hang from bare branches. Lakes are frozen. And it is so cold—below zero.

The writer has given you the information you need to picture a winter scene. There is no need to state that it is winter. Thus, when a main idea is not stated directly, you must use clues in the paragraph to help you come up with a main idea. A main idea that is not stated directly is called an **implied main idea.**

To find an implied main idea, ask the same questions you use to locate the stated main idea.

1. *Who or what is the paragraph about?*
2. *What does the author really want you to know about that "who" or "what"?*

As with stated main ideas, the answer to the first question will give you the topic—a general idea of what the paragraph is about. Again, you ask the second question and put the answer into a sentence of your own. However, when you look for a sentence in the paragraph that comes close to matching your answer to the second question, you will not find one. There isn't any sentence to underline or highlight. Instead, the writer has provided you with details that are clues to the main idea. In such a case, you must become the writer and come up with a main idea in your own words. Use your own sentence that answered the second question as the implied main idea of the paragraph.

You can check to see if your implied main idea is correct by using it as an umbrella statement. Write the main idea as a full sentence. The details under the implied main idea can be written as full sentences or as phrases. Now see if all, or most, of the sentences in the paragraph fit under that umbrella by giving detailed information about the implied main idea.

The following two sample paragraphs will show you how the two questions you have learned are used to find implied main ideas.

Sample A

> First, make sure the sleeves of these shirts are unrolled. Second, check all pockets to make sure they are empty. Third, use a special cleaner on soiled collars and cuffs. Finally, wash these shirts in a machine set on the gentle cycle.

Who or what is the paragraph about?
shirts

What does the writer really want you to know about shirts?
There are four steps to follow when washing shirts.

Check the implied main idea:

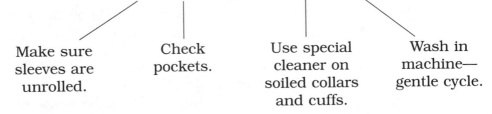

Umbrella: There are four steps to follow when washing shirts.

| Make sure sleeves are unrolled. | Check pockets. | Use special cleaner on soiled collars and cuffs. | Wash in machine— gentle cycle. |

Yes, the implied main idea is correct. Each of the sentences gives a step in washing shirts.

Sample B

> When shopping for potatoes, look for those that are firm, well shaped, and smooth. They should have few eyes. The potatoes should be free from large cuts and bruises. They should also be free of decay. Also check the color of the potatoes. Make sure they are the usual brown color, not green. Green potatoes have a bitter taste. They may even act as a poison to some people.

Who or what is the paragraph about?
    potatoes
What does the writer really want you to know about potatoes?
    There are things to look for when you shop for potatoes.

Check the implied main idea:

Umbrella: There are things to look for when you shop for potatoes.

| firm, well shaped, smooth | few eyes | free from large cuts and bruises | free of decay | usual brown color |

Yes, the implied main idea is correct. Most, but not all, of the sentences tell you things to look for when you shop for potatoes. Thus, they fit under the umbrella.

Your answers to the second question in Samples A and B may not be exactly like those given. Remember that you are using your own words. The important thing is that the sentences in the paragraph fit under the main idea umbrella.

Guided Practice 8–3: Implied Main Ideas—A

Directions: Read each of the following paragraphs. Ask the two questions you have learned to find the implied main idea. Then check your implied main idea by using it as an umbrella statement. See if the sentences fit under that umbrella.

1. If you smell gas, check any pilot lights in the house. Stove burners may have been turned on but left unlit. If you cannot find where the gas is coming from, it may be a gas leak. Call the gas company. Open all windows. Turn off the main gas shutoff valve that is near the gas meter.

Who or what is the paragraph about?

_____

*What does the writer really want you to know about that "who"
or "what"?*

_____

Check the implied main idea:

Umbrella: _____

2. Always swim with a friend who has done "rough-water swimming" before. Stay in the area marked for swimming. Wear a
   brightly colored cap for safety and warmth. Stay close to shore
   unless a boat goes along with you. Don't underrate the dangers
   of open water, its current, tides, creatures, and boat traffic.
   And don't overrate your fitness and your being able to stand
   the cold.

   Who or what is the paragraph about?

   _____

   *What does the writer really want you to know about that "who"
   or "what"?*

   _____

   Check the implied main idea:

Umbrella: _____

3. Some people yell and scream when they are angry; others kick furniture. Still others hit walls or doors as hard as they can with their fists. Or some people show their anger by slamming doors with as much noise as possible.

Who or what is the paragraph about?

_____

What does the writer really want you to know about that "who" or "what"?

_____

Check the implied main idea:

Umbrella: _____

___   ___   ___   ___

___   ___   ___   ___

4. The town was once crowded, but now the people have all gone away. Once busy shops are empty. Their shelves are dusty and bare. The town was once noisy and laughter could be heard; it is now very quiet. Only the sound of the wind can be heard as it blows through the empty streets and houses.

Who or what is the paragraph about?

_____

What does the writer really want you to know about that "who" or "what"?

_____

Check the implied main idea:

Umbrella: _____

___/___ | _____ | _____ | _____ ___

_____   _____   _____   _____   _____

_____   _____   _____   _____   _____

5. The airplane ride will be exciting, so sit back and enjoy it. Be sure to choose a hotel where the rooms are pretty as well as clean so you can be happy there. Try to eat new foods instead of what you usually eat. Chat with people you do not know; they will soon become your friends. Finally, visit places of interest you have never seen before.

Who or what is the paragraph about?

_____

What does the writer really want you to know about that "who" or "what"?

_____

Check the implied main idea:

Umbrella: _____

_____   _____   _____   _____

_____   _____   _____   _____

_____   _____

_____   _____

You have learned that writing an umbrella statement and sentences that fit under it is a good way to check an implied main idea. Now make that umbrella statement and the paragraph's sentences in your mind. Don't write anything down. Picture an umbrella statement using the main idea in your sentence. Then see if all, or most, of the sentences fit under it. If they do, you have the correct implied main idea. If the sentences do not fit, change the umbrella statement until they do. With practice, you will soon find that it takes only a few minutes to check an implied main idea in your mind.

Guided Practice 8–4: Implied Main Ideas—B

Directions: Read each of the following paragraphs. Write the implied main idea after using the two questions you have learned. Check this main idea in your mind.

1. The workday begins at 8:00. It is now 8:15 and Jim is still not at his desk. He says that he leaves his house early enough to make it to work on time, but he rarely arrives before 9:00. As a result, Jim doesn't always make it to meetings held first thing in the morning. His boss is unhappy with Jim because he does not like workers to come in late.

   Who or what is the paragraph about?

   _____

   What does the writer really want you to know about that "who" or "what"?

   _____

2. The woman was tall, slim, and well built. She carried herself well and had beautiful posture. Her hair was cut into a beautiful crown of gray curls. Although her smooth face made it hard for anyone to guess her age, she probably was in her early fifties. Her clothing seemed to be chosen for a woman of that age.

   Who or what is the paragraph about?

   _____

   What does the writer really want you to know about that "who" or "what"?

   _____

3. Mike is a freshman in college. He is also trying to earn the money he needs to live on. As a result, he works 40 hours a week at a gasoline station. But this work must be done at night because Mike is a full-time college student. Mike also tries to make time for things he enjoys doing that are not related to college or work. He likes to ski in winter and play golf in summer. However, he is finding less and less time for these pleasures.

Who or what is the paragraph about?

_____

What does the writer really want you to know about that "who" or "what"?

_____

4. If you think someone is having a heart attack, send for a doctor or an ambulance right away. Meanwhile, place the person in a comfortable position. Keep the person warm. Then try to keep the person calm by saying that help is on the way. Finally, stay until medical help arrives.

Who or what is the paragraph about?

_____

What does the writer really want you to know about that "who" or "what"?

_____

5. The office was beautiful. Very modern furniture had been ordered just for her. She sat at her new desk with papers piled up in front of her, but she did not begin to work. Instead, she stared off into space. Then, her fingers began to tap a drum-like beat on the arms of her chair. With her legs crossed, the one on top started to swing to and fro in time to the drumming. She yawned and thought of today as just another boring day to get through.

Who or what is the paragraph about?

_____

*What does the writer really want you to know about that
"who" or "what"?*

_____

Use the Summary Sheet on page 251 to help you remember
how to work with main ideas in paragraphs.

Name _____

SKILL PRACTICE: IMPLIED MAIN IDEAS IN PARAGRAPHS

Directions: Use the two questions you have learned to work out the implied main idea of each paragraph. Check the main idea in your mind. Then write the implied main idea in your own words in a full sentence under the paragraph.

1. Catsup is made from fresh, red, ripe tomatoes with added sugar, salt, onions, spices, and vinegar. The tomatoes are chopped into a pulp. They are strained to remove the seeds. Then they are pumped into cook tanks where spices and seasonings are added. The catsup is then cooked until it is rich and thick.

    Implied main idea: _____

    _____

    _____

2. In New York City, there are museums to tour. It is exciting that there are so many shows to see. Shoppers will find just about anything in New York that they want to buy. Restaurants serve every kind of food you can imagine. Most exciting of all is the boat ride to the Statue of Liberty in New York Harbor.

    Implied main idea: _____

    _____

    _____

3. When you're warned of a fire in the building, feel the door with the back of your hand before leaving the room. If the door is hot, don't open it. If it is cool, open it slowly and check the hall for smoke. If there is no smoke, go to the nearest stairway

and leave the building. If there is smoke in the stairway, use another one. Never use the elevator in a fire.

Implied main idea: _____

_____

_____

4.   If the radiator/heater hoses in your car are quite hard or very soft when squeezed, replace them. If you are in doubt about whether or not to replace them, remove the hose clamps and look inside the hose with a flashlight. If the coil spring in the lower radiator hose is rusted or damaged, replace it. Without a strong spring, the hose can cave in under the suction made by the coolant pump at high speeds.

Implied main idea: _____

_____

_____

5.   Of all the wandering stars called planets by ancient peoples, Saturn is the faintest and moves most slowly. As long as 2500 years ago, people recognized that Saturn marked the outer limits of the visible solar system. Its beautiful rings give Saturn a very special appearance. Even after faint rings were discovered around Jupiter and Uranus in the 1970s, Saturn has kept its special place in our imaginations as *the* ringed planet. Saturn is the second-largest planet in our solar system.

Implied main idea: _____

_____

_____

6.   If you are moving into a new home, read about your heater in the manual that comes with it. Ask questions of the com-

pany that put the heater in. If you are moving into an older home, it may be harder to find out about your heater. Ask the people who last lived in the house. Or try to find the name of the company that has worked on the heater and ask what you need to know.

Implied main idea: _____

_____

_____

7.   Sunglass lenses in bright colors and soft shadow may look pretty. But they give little protection from the sun's glare. Lenses that fade from dark at the top to light at the bottom do not help you to see. The most effective sunshades are greenish grays, grays, or browns. Lenses of other tints may upset the way you see colors. When you put on a sun lens, the world should appear in its true colors, just not as bright.

Implied main idea: _____

_____

_____

8.   Cross-country skiers enjoy being alone in forests and fields as they glide on their way. They enjoy the silence and the beauty of the countryside. Downhill skiers enjoy these things, too. But they get more kick from the plunge down a steep trail, showing their skills by mastering whatever springs up on the path. They really enjoy the thrill of going at great speeds.

Implied main idea: _____

_____

_____

9.   The Sears Tower in Chicago, which is the largest private office building in the world, contains 4.5 million gross square

feet of space and a total height of 1707 feet. Opened in 1973, the Sears Tower took three years and as many as 1600 people to build. The Tower's framework consists of 76,000 tons of steel. The building, which contains enough concrete to build a five-mile-long eight-lane highway, has more than 16,000 bronze-tinted windows and 28 acres of a special black aluminum skin.

Implied main idea: _____

_____

_____

10.   Positive stress can help you concentrate better and to do well. Many people do, in fact, perform better when they are under some pressure. Then, when they have completed the task, they are able to relax. Negative stress, on the other hand, doesn't disappear. One remains tense under constant stress. Negative stress can be harmful to your health. It has been know to trigger some serious physical conditions.

Implied main idea: _____

_____

_____

SKILL PRACTICE: STATED AND IMPLIED MAIN IDEAS IN PARAGRAPHS

A. Directions: In this Skill Practice, you will find both stated and implied main ideas. Use the two questions you have learned to work out the main idea of each paragraph. If the main idea is stated, underline or highlight it in the paragraph. If the main idea is implied, write it in your own words in a full sentence below the paragraph. Check each main idea in your mind.

1. There are new kinds of food being developed that may help solve world hunger problems. For example, there is a new kind of fast-growing grain. There are new foods from the sea, such as krill and seaweed. There are also milklike drinks. Some of these are made from soybeans. They are rich in protein but have no sugar.

   Main idea (if implied): _____

   _____

2. Jogging is a good way to exercise. It is an ongoing activity, so you can do it every day. You do not jog to beat anyone else. And there are other advantages of jogging. You don't need any unusual skills to do it. After learning some basic rules, almost anyone can jog well. Jogging can be enjoyed without special equipment, and it can be enjoyed anywhere. Finally, jogging can be done alone, with a friend, or with a group of fellow joggers.

   Main idea (if implied): _____

   _____

3. You'll often see hikers in shorts and tennis shoes. Year-round, however, it's wise to wear long pants for protection against stickers, stings, and scrapes. Long-sleeve shirts, sunglasses, and lotion help keep off the sun. Sturdy hiking boots

protect your feet from stickers and heat. In winter months, a wool cap, warm top, and gloves are protection against chill winds.

Main idea (if implied): _____

_____

4. Does the FBI have a file on you? How are local nursing homes being run? What kinds of studies have been done on certain drugs? On what ship did your grandparents arrive in America? The answer to these and many other questions can be found in the files of U.S. government agencies. In 1966, the U.S. Congress decided that government records should be open to the people, and they therefore passed the Freedom of Information Act. Now, except for nine special kinds of information, all government records are open. You need only to ask for information from the right agency and it will be sent to you. Americans have the right to look at government records to find out almost anything they want to know.

Main idea (if implied): _____

_____

5. Most people who grow parsley use if for cooking. It gives a good flavor to fish, stews, or soups. Some gardeners, however, use it for edging flower and vegetable beds. A few people have also found that parsley can be used instead of ferns and other greenery in flower arrangements. It makes cut flowers in vases look very pretty. Parsley has more than a single use.

Main idea (if implied): _____

_____

6. Sparkling wine that's too warm or shaken up will pop its cork. It will gush from the bottle when opened. To avoid this, buy your wine a few days before the party so that the wine can rest. The best temperature for pouring wine is between 40°F

and 45°F. A few hours on the bottom shelf of your refrigerator will be enough. If your refrigerator can't hold all the wine, chill the bottles by putting them in a large tub filled with ice for a few hours. Turn the bottles once in a while so that they chill evenly.

Main idea (if implied): _____

_____

7. The marijuana produced today is from five to twenty times stronger than what was available as recently as ten years ago. Regular use by young people has been known to result in a condition in which there is a lack of motivation and a loss of goals. Research shows that severe mental and emotional damage can occur when marijuana contains 2 percent THC, a substance that affects the way one's mind works. Since the early 1980s, most marijuana has contained from 4 to 6 percent THC, two or three times the amount that can cause serious damage.

Main idea (if implied): _____

_____

8. Music is used in stores to encourage shoppers to buy more. It is used in fast-food eating places to make you eat faster and leave quicker. In banks, music is piped in to give you a feeling of cheerfulness and confidence. Indeed, music is used in many ways to affect people's feelings and actions. It is used in factories to speed up the workers and increase the amount of work produced. It is used in hospitals to make the sick feel better. And, at sporting events, music is used to make players try harder.

Main idea (if implied): _____

_____

9. After a night's sleep, air your sleeping bag to let body mois-

ture escape. When it's time to clean your synthetic bag, wash it by hand in soap and warm water or in a machine on the gentle cycle. Rinse and drip or tumble dry on the no-heat setting. Never dry-clean synthetic bags. Take your down bag to a cleaner who knows about down products. Neither a synthetic bag nor a down bag should be kept in its storage cover. Instead, hang it in your closet or in another loose manner. Most important, never store a bag when it's wet.

Main idea (if implied): _____

_____

10.   As for the old saying, if you've seen one snowflake you've seen them all—baloney! The snow in New York is most like the snow I've skied on in recent trips to Aspen, Colorado, or Park City, Utah. When snow falls in the East, it is usually due to one part moist Gulf air to one part cold Canadian air. The result is a moist snowfall with large wet flakes that are easily packed down. Western snow is not much different. The real change comes from the eastern slopes of the Rocky Mountains. The air there is much cooler and stays colder longer. There isn't as much moisture carried over the mountains. What does get over is frozen harder, faster, and more completely than it is on either coast. It becomes crystals with smaller, more powdery, sometimes granular flakes. Snow type depends on how much moisture there is and the temperature of the air.

Main idea (if implied): _____

_____

B. Directions: Select four paragraphs from any reading material. Copy the paragraphs on a copying machine and attach them to this Skill Practice. Use what you know about implied and stated main ideas to show the main ideas as you did in part A above. Try to find paragraphs that have implied as well as stated main ideas.

SUMMARY SHEET: MAIN IDEAS IN PARAGRAPHS

Read the paragraph carefully.

Ask the two questions to help you find the main idea of the paragraph.

1. Who or what is the paragraph about? ⟶ topic

2. What does the writer really want you to know about that who or what (topic)?

Put the answer to this question in your own words.
Look in the paragraph to see if there is a sentence that sounds
like what you have said in your own words.

YES. There is a sentence that sounds like your answer to the second question. The paragraph has a stated main idea. The stated main idea may be found anywhere in the paragraph.

beginning   end   middle

NO. There isn't any sentence that sounds like your answer to the second question. Use your own words, in a complete sentence as the main idea. You now have an implied main idea.

Check your main idea by using it as an umbrella statement. If you have the correct main idea, all or most of the sentences in the paragraph should give you specific information about that main idea.

CHAPTER 9

Details in Paragraphs

Finding the main idea is a good first step in understanding a paragraph. But it is not enough. The main idea gives only a broad idea of what the paragraph is about. It does not tell the writer's full message. To understand the full message, an effective reader must be able to do two things. First, the reader must find out the main idea of the paragraph. Second, the reader must know *how* details within that paragraph relate to it's main idea.

In Chapter Eight, you learned about stated and implied main ideas. You also found that all, or most, of the sentences in a paragraph usually support the stated or implied main idea by providing specific information about it. The sentences that provide specific supporting information about the main idea are called **related details.** The combination of main ideas and related details form a solid package of information. With the elimination of unrelated details, the block of related information becomes easier to understand and remember. The effective reader forms these blocks of related information.

There are a number of different kinds of related details. In this book, two often-used kinds of related details have been chosen for study and practice. They will give you a good start on learning how details can support a main idea. You will find that writers often support a main idea with related details that are **examples** of the main idea or **reasons** for it.

Not every paragraph contains each of these two kinds of related details. Sometimes a writer may use only one kind of related detail to support the main idea. Or the writer may choose to use both examples and reasons in the same paragraph. The way a writer uses related details to support main ideas often depends on an author's writing style.

In addition to related details, writers sometimes use two kinds of details that do not provide information about the main idea. The writer may repeat information in the main idea in a **restatement** that does not say anything new about the main idea. Or the writer may include information that is interesting but not related to the main idea at all.

In this chapter, you will learn to identify details that are

1. Related to the main idea because they provide
   a. examples of it.
   b. reasons for it.
2. Unrelated to the main idea because they
   a. restate the main idea without providing new information.
   b. do not support the main idea at all.

DETAIL: EXAMPLE

A writer may support a main idea by giving an example of it. For instance, the main idea of a paragraph may be that Maria bakes many fruit pies for her family. Each sentence that tells about a kind of fruit pie Maria bakes is a related detail that supports the main idea. Each of the related details is an example of the main idea.

> **Main idea:** Maria bakes many fruit pies for her family.
> **For example:** She bakes apple pies.
> **For example:** She bakes cherry pies.
> **For example:** She bakes peach pies.
> **For example:** She bakes blueberry pies.

Sometimes a writer may help the reader know that examples of the main idea are being given. Terms such as *for example* and *for instance* are clues to such related details. Look for these clues as you relate details to the main idea.

The following two sample paragraphs show how writers use examples to support both stated and implied main ideas. Note how you can check to see if you have correctly identified an example by inserting "for example" or "for instance" between the main idea and the detail. When you put the main idea, "for example," and a detail together in this way, it should make sense. If it doesn't, the detail is not an example.

In the first paragraph, full sentences have been used as a check to see how details support the main idea. In the second paragraph, words have been used as a check to see how details support the main idea. You can use words, phrases, or sentences as you check on how details support main ideas.

Sample A

> <u>Some birds are able to find food in deserts</u>. Cactus wrens, for instance, eat desert insects. Sparrow hawks are able to feed on grasshoppers and small mammals. Roadrunners eat insects but also add lizards and snakes to their diet.

The stated main idea of the paragraph is underlined for you. Each of the other sentences is an example of that main idea. Each example tells of a different kind of bird that is able to find food in deserts.

Stated main idea:	Some birds are able to find food in deserts.
For example:	Cactus wrens eat desert insects.
For example:	Sparrow hawks feed on grasshoppers and small mammals.
For example:	Roadrunners eat insects, lizards, and snakes.

Sample B

> Some people use coal to heat their homes. Others use gas heaters. Still other use oil as fuel. A few people have gone back to heating their homes with wood used in stoves and fireplaces.

In Paragraph B, the main idea is implied. You must first put the main idea into your own sentence. Then relate the sentences in the paragraph to that main idea. Details that are examples relate to an implied main idea just as they do to a stated main idea. In this paragraph, each example of the main idea tells of a different kind of fuel people use to heat their homes.

Implied main idea: People use different kinds of fuel to heat their homes.

For example: coal
For example: gas
For example: oil
For example: wood

In the Guided Practices and Skill Practices in this chapter, the sentences in paragraphs have been numbered to make it easier to complete these practices. When you are told to check your answers, apply what you know about each kind of detail and how it relates to a main idea.

Guided Practice 9–1: Detail: Example—A

Directions: The main idea of each of the following paragraphs has been underlined or written for you. Write **E** next to the number of each sentence that is an **example** of that main idea. Check your answers by using an umbrella statement.

1. (1) Robert's golf game is getting better. (2) For example, he now knows which clubs to use. (3) He is also able to hit the ball more often. (4) When Robert hits the balls, it now goes very far. (5) Sometimes he even beats other players. (6) As a result, Robert is getting to be known as a good golfer.

    Stated main idea: Robert's golf game is getting better.

    1. _MI_   3. _____   5. _____
    2. _____   4. _____   6. _____

2. (1) Flowers are starting to bloom. (2) The trees are now green again. (3) Birds are making nests in their branches. (4) It is getting warmer. (5) And people are beginning to shed their

heavy clothing. (6) There are many signs that spring is here at last. (7) Therefore, summer (my favorite season of the year) is not far behind.

Stated main idea: There are many signs that spring is here at last.

1. _____   3. _____   5. _____   7. _____
2. _____   4. _____   6. _MI_

3.   (1) Ride on the bus instead of driving your car. (2) You'll probably meet some nice people. (3) Share rides with other people. (4) You may have to get up earlier, but it will be worth it. (5) Also, walk when you don't have far to go. (6) It's good for your health. (7) Finally, check your car to make sure it doesn't use extra gasoline. (8) Remember: waste not, want not.

Implied main idea: There are ways to save gasoline.

1. _____   3. _____   5. _____   7. _____
2. _____   4. _____   6. _____

4.   (1) The Blake family did not catch any fish. (2) Meanwhile, they were bitten by flies as they sat in the boat. (3) Then, a sudden storm came up and rain soaked them. (4) The worst thing that happened was when a huge blast of wind tipped the boat over. (5) The Blakes almost didn't make it to shore alive!

Implied main idea: Bad things happened on the Blake family's fishing trip.

1. _____   3. _____   5. _____
2. _____   4. _____

5.   (1) To be a good salesperson, you must speak clearly and correctly. (2) Don't be afraid to talk to strangers. (3) Make the buyer feel that you are interested in their problems. (4) Know your product so that you can talk about it. (5) Also, know when to stop talking and write up the order. (6) Finally, leave buyers feeling that you want to deal with them again. (7) They will want to buy from you the next time they need what you are selling.

Implied main idea: There are ways to be a good salesperson.

1. _____   3. _____   5. _____   7. _____
2. _____   4. _____   6. _____

Guided Practice 9–2: Detail: Example—B

Directions: For each of the following paragraphs, write **MI** next to the number of the sentence where it is stated. If the main idea is implied, write it in a sentence. Write **E** next to the number of each sentence that is an **example** of that main idea. Check your answers by using an umbrella statement.

1. (1) Once, horses could be seen in the streets of every town or city. (2) They were as common as the auto is today. (3) But times have changed; the horse has been replaced. (4) However, the horse is still widely used in sports. (5) For example, horse racing is popular in many states. (6) Rodeos are fun to watch and often draw large crowds. (7) There is a growing interest in polo, which started in the East and is now spreading across the country.

Main idea (if implied): _____

_____

1. _____   3. _____   5. _____   7. _____
2. _____   4. _____   6. _____

2. (1) Do you think of brick as being used mainly to build houses? (2) This may be true in parts of the United States where bricks are the most used building material. (3) But brick can also be used in a number of ways in and around the home. (4) For instance, good-looking fireplaces can be built of brick. (5) Walls or room dividers can be made of brick. (6) Outside, brick makes long-lasting patios, walls, or tree wells.

Main idea (if implied): _____

_____

1. _____   3. _____   5. _____
2. _____   4. _____   6. _____

3. (1) Think about the kind of business you want to open. (2) Get all the facts you can about this business. (3) Be sure you are clear in your own mind as to what products or services the business will offer. (4) Visit businesses of this kind to get a good idea of how they are run. (5) Check to see if the business products or services are needed in the community.

Main idea (if implied): _____

_____

1. _____   3. _____   5. _____
2. _____   4. _____

4. (1) Proper lighting above the bathroom sink is needed for grooming and shaving. (2) It is hard to do a good job of these if your face is only dimly seen in the mirror. (3) In a large bathroom, good overhead lighting is most important. (4) Otherwise, parts of the room will be dark. (5) If the bathroom includes a shower, a second overhead light in or near the stall can be most helpful. (6) A night light should always be set up just inside the bathroom door. (7) If the night light is turned on each evening, your bathroom becomes a safer place.

Main idea (if implied): _____

_____

1. _____   3. _____   5. _____   7. _____
2. _____   4. _____   6. _____

5. (1) Cook your food in one-fourth the time it takes in a regular oven. (2) Save on energy bills. (3) Keep your kitchen cooler in summer. (4) Save on cleanup time by cooking and serving in the same dish. (5) Sound too good to be true? (6) These are just some of the advantages of cooking in a microwave oven.

Main idea (if implied): _____

_____

1. ____   3. ____   5. ____
2. ____   4. ____   6. ____

DETAIL: REASON

Sometimes a writer may support a main idea by giving **reasons** for it. These related details explain the main idea. They answer the question "*Why?*" This question is not usually found in the paragraph. You must ask the "Why?" to see if details give reasons for the main idea. For instance, the main idea following is still that Maria bakes many fruits pies for her family. Now, however, each related detail tells a reason **why** Maria bakes many fruit pies.

Main idea:	Maria bakes many fruit pies for her family.
Reason (Why?):	Her family likes fruit pies.
Reason (Why?):	They can be served as tasty desserts.
Reason (Why?):	They are easy to bake.

The following two sample paragraphs show how writers use details that are reasons to support both stated and implied main ideas. Note how you can check to see if you have correctly identified a detail that is a reason by inserting the question "why?" between the main idea and the detail. When you put the main idea, "why?," and the detail together in this way, the detail should answer that question. If it doesn't, the detail is not a reason that supports the main idea. In both paragraphs, phrases have been used to check if the details are reasons that support the main idea.

Sample Paragraph A

Many people came to America during the nineteenth century. Some of them were looking for a better life. Others wanted to live in a place where they would be free to pray to God in their own way. Still others came mainly for the adventure of living in a new land.

Stated main idea:	Many people came to America during the nineteenth century.
Reason (Why?):	better life
Reason (Why?):	free to pray to God in own way
Reason (Why?):	adventure

Each of these details supports the stated main idea by helping to explain it. They are all reasons **why** people came to America during the nineteenth century.

Sample Paragraph B

> Bedsheets cost less than rolls of wallpaper. They add softness and warmth to any room. There are many beautiful printed bedsheets to choose from. And you will find sheets easier to put on the walls than wallpaper.

In Paragraph B, the main idea is implied. Remember, you must first put the main idea into a sentence in your own words. Then relate each of the sentences to that main idea.

Each detail in the paragraph is related to the implied main idea by telling **why** bedsheets make a good covering for walls.

Implied main idea:	Bedsheets make a good covering for walls.
Reason (Why?):	cost less than wallpaper
Reason (Why?):	add softness and warmth
Reason (Why?):	many beautiful prints to choose from
Reason (Why?):	easier to hang than wallpaper

Guided Practice 9–3: Detail: Reason—A

Directions: The stated or implied main idea of each of the following paragraphs has been found for you. Write **R** next to the number of each sentence that is a **reason** for the main idea. Check your answers by using an umbrella statement.

1. (1) After 100 years, the Statue of Liberty's torch leaked and was badly rusted. (2) Her face was discolored due to air pollu-

tion. (3) Many of the rivets in the statue were rusted because of the salt air. (4) The iron ribs within the statue needed to be replaced. (5) In addition, the interior of the statue needed to be cleaned and repainted.

Implied main idea: The Statue of Liberty needed repair.

1. _____   3. _____   5. _____
2. _____   4. _____

2.   (1) The workers have gone out on strike against the factory. (2) They claim that they are not paid enough for what they do. (3) Workers who do the same jobs in other factories earn much more money. (4) They are also angry about the way their bosses treat them. (5) The workers feel cheated because they are not able to have two coffee breaks each day. (6) Finally, there is a question as to the safety of the factory; workers say there have been too many accidents that could have been avoided.

Stated main idea: The workers have gone out on strike against the factory.

1. _____   3. _____   5. _____
2. _____   4. _____   6. _____

3.   (1) I don't think I'll ever forget the summer I was ten years old. (2) There I was, born and raised in a large eastern city, spending the summer on a farm in Kansas. (3) It was my first time away from home and family; I was scared. (4) Life on the farm took some getting used to; it was just too quiet for one bred on street noises. (5) Also, living so close to animals was hard to take at first. (6) The only other animals I'd ever seen were on visits to the zoo. (7) Most of all, there was my surprise and delight at finding out where milk, eggs, and vegetables really came from. (8) There I was, ten years old, still thinking they came from the corner grocery store.

Stated main idea: I don't think I'll ever forget the summer I was ten years old.

| 1. ____ | 3. ____ | 5. ____ | 7. ____ |
| 2. ____ | 4. ____ | 6. ____ | 8. ____ |

4. (1) General Robert E. Lee raised a large army to fight for the South during the Civil War. (2) The men who were led by Lee loved him both as a person and as a great leader and fought bravely under his command. (3) Lee was able to lead his army to victory in a number of battles. (4) When the war was lost, General Lee was the one who made peace with the North. (5) After the war, Lee left the army and later became the president of a college in the South.

Implied main idea: General Robert E. Lee was important to the South during the Civil War.

| 1. ____ | 3. ____ | 5. ____ |
| 2. ____ | 4. ____ | |

5. (1) Credit is a most useful thing to have. (2) It lets you charge a meal or things you buy. (3) It allows you to pay for something in a number of payments while you are enjoying it. (4) With credit, you can take out a loan when you need it. (5) It is, therefore, very important for you to keep a good credit rating.

Stated main idea: Credit is a most useful thing to have.

| 1. ____ | 3. ____ | 5. ____ |
| 2. ____ | 4. ____ | |

Guided Practice 9–4: Detail: Reason—B

Directions: For each of the following paragraphs, write **MI** next to the number of the sentence where it is stated. If the main idea is implied, write it in a sentence. Write **R** next to the number of each sentence that is a **reason** for the main idea. Check your answers by using an umbrella statement.

1. (1) Exchanging homes with someone is a simple idea, but a good one. (2) You agree to let someone use your home while you stay in theirs—without charge. (3) A home away from

home saves you hotel and restaurant bills. (4) There are hotels in many cities that are costly to stay in. (5) Exchanging homes makes it easier to travel with children. (6) Generally, it lessens the strain of living out of a suitcase.

Main idea (if implied): _____

_____

1. _____ 3. _____ 5. _____
2. _____ 4. _____ 6. _____

2. (1) Far away from the cares of city life, you begin to feel at ease. (2) You become so relaxed that problems that seemed large become small and unimportant. (3) Food made over an open fire tastes better than that prepared by famous cooks. (4) The meals are simple and filling. (5) Somehow, sleep is better in a sleeping bag under the stars. (6) Then you wake up each morning feeling great and ready for whatever the new day might bring.

Main idea (if implied): _____

_____

1. _____ 3. _____ 5. _____
2. _____ 4. _____ 6. _____

3. (1) People come to the sunbelt of the United States in hope of finding a more relaxed pace of living. (2) Pressures of living in other parts of the country are left behind. (3) They come to enjoy plenty of sunshine. (4) No one seems unhappy at leaving rain and snow. (5) They look forward to spending more time outdoors. (6) Good weather lends itself to this. (7) Finally, they hope to find cheaper living costs. (8) If nothing else, it costs less to heat a home where the weather is warmer and the winter is shorter.

Main idea (if implied): _____

_____

1. _____	3. _____	5. _____	7. _____
2. _____	4. _____	6. _____	8. _____

4. (1) You may be better off working for someone else rather than being boss in your own business. (2) First, your working hours are probably shorter. (3) Think of all the times you have left work while your boss stays behind to finish extra things. (4) Second, you don't have to worry about meeting a payroll. (5) If business is good or bad, you still get your paycheck. (6) Third, you are not the one to take care of major problems. (7) They are turned over to the boss. (8) And finally, you may be happier when someone else is in charge. (9) Not everyone is a leader. (10) Some people are happier as followers.

Main idea (if implied): _____

_____

1. _____	3. _____	5. _____	7. _____	9. _____
2. _____	4. _____	6. _____	8. _____	10. _____

5. (1) Every year, thousands of visitors come to Sunset Crater National Monument in northern Arizona. (2) It is here that Sunset Crater, a volcano, erupted about 900 years ago. (3) The monument area has been left exactly as it was after the volcano erupted. (4) Visitors come to walk over the Lava Flow Nature Trail. (5) This trail is laid out through lava beds. (6) Walking the trail, visitors can feel as though they have gone back in time—away from the twentieth century to the long ago day when lava flowed from Sunset Crater.

Main idea (if implied): _____

_____

1. _____	3. _____	5. _____
2. _____	4. _____	6. _____

Sometimes the same related detail can be both an example and a reason. It depends on how the reader sees it. The most important thing, however, is that this detail *does* support the main idea. The following paragraph shows how a related detail can be both example and reason.

> People all over the world wear hats to cover their heads. In cold places, people need hats to keep their heads warm. Hats protect people from the sun in very warm places. Some people wear hats because they think hats look good on them. Others wear hats as part of a costume or uniform.

Stated main idea: People around the world wear hats to cover their heads.

Examples of people around the world wearing hats

Reasons why people around the world wear hats

in cold places—keep heads warm
in warm places—protect from sun to look good
as part of a costume or uniform

Name _____

SKILL PRACTICE: DETAILS—EXAMPLE AND REASON

A. Directions: Read each main idea and the details below it. If the detail is an example of the main idea, put an **E** on the line next to it. If the detail is a reason for the main idea, put an **R** on the line next to it.

1. **Main idea:** Redwood lumber is one of the best woods for building.
   a. Redwood lumber is strong and lasts a long time. _____
   b. Redwood lumber can be used for houses. _____
   c. Termites and other insects do not harm it. _____
   d. Redwood lumber is weatherproof. _____
   e. Redwood lumber does not rot outdoors. _____

2. **Main idea:** Airlifts can be used to bring food and supplies to people.
   a. Rail lines and roads may be closed down. _____
   b. Airlifts can be used to bring food to people stranded after heavy snowstorms. _____
   c. One famous airlift brought food and fuel to the people of West Berlin in 1948. _____
   d. Mountain climbers may arrange for food and supplies to be dropped to them by airlift. _____
   e. Airlifts may save the lives of people who cannot get food or supplies any other way. _____

3. **Main idea:** Iceburg lettuce has become America's favorite for use in salads.
   a. It can easily be prepared in different ways. _____
   b. Iceburg lettuce is low in calories. _____
   c. Cool, crisp iceburg lettuce has a light flavor. _____
   d. During the growing season, its cost is usually quite low. _____
   e. Iceburg lettuce is often used in tossed green salads. _____

4. **Main idea:** Bring different kinds of clothing with you if you plan on staying in Hong Kong for awhile.
   a. There are two seasons with different kinds of weather. _____
   b. Heavy clothing is needed for the winter. _____
   c. Lightweight summer clothing is worn the rest of the year. _____
   d. A good supply of informal evening clothing is needed because of the active social life in Hong Kong. _____
   e. You may not be able to buy exactly what you need or want in Hon Kong. _____

5. **Main idea:** Backpackers take pride in being able to travel light.
   a. They cut towels in half and saw toothbrushes in half to save ounces. _____
   b. Every ounce that can be left out means the backpack will be that much lighter. _____
   c. They measure just the right amount of food and put it in plastic bags. _____
   d. It is easier to cover rough ground with less to carry. _____
   e. They carry scouring pads with built-in soap so they don't need a soap dish or a dish cloth. _____

B. Directions: Read each paragraph. Locate the main idea. If the main idea is **stated,** write **MI** next to the sentence number under the paragraph. If the main idea is **implied,** write it in a full sentence in your own words under the paragraph. Then look at the numbered details. Tell if each detail is an **example (E)** or **reason (R).** Write your answer on the lines under the paragraph. Here is a sample of what to do:

(1) Sharks are feared by many people. (2) People are so afraid of sharks that they will not swim in the ocean. (3) This fear has been caused by stories of shark attacks on swimmers. (4) Attack scenes in the movie *Jaws* were so real that they have also made people afraid of sharks.

Main idea (if implied): _____

_____

Sentence 1: _MI_   Sentence 3: _R_

Sentence 2: _E_   Sentence 4: _R_

1.   (1) For most people, clothing fills the need to be warm and comfortable. (2) But if chosen wisely, clothing can also make one look better. (3) Clothing can also make someone feel part of a group. (4) In addition, clothing can satisfy a person's need to look different.

Main idea (if implied): _____

_____

Sentence 1: _____   Sentence 3: _____

Sentence 2: _____   Sentence 4: _____

2.   (1) Although skiing is fun, it can also be a costly sport. (2) You will need special equipment such as skis, bindings, poles, and boots. (3) Since skiing must be done in places that have the right conditions, it will probably cost you money to get to the skiing area. (4) Once there, you will need to pay for a place to stay. (5) Finally, if you've never skied before, it is most likely that you will have to spend money on lessons.

Main idea (if implied): _____

_____

Sentence 1: _____   Sentence 4: _____

Sentence 2: _____   Sentence 5: _____

Sentence 3: _____

3.   (1) Above-ground swimming pools are low cost compared to built-in pools. (2) Since aboveground pools don't count as improvements added to your home, there is no tax on them. (3) If you decide to move, you can take an above-ground swim-

ming pool with you. (4) There is the safety feature of the pool being about four feet higher than the ground. (5) In recent times, above-ground home swimming pools have become very popular.

Main idea (if implied): _____

_____

Sentence 1: ____	**Sentence 4:** ____
Sentence 2: ____	**Sentence 5:** ____
Sentence 3: ____	

DETAIL: RESTATEMENT

As you have learned earlier in this chapter, details that are examples or reasons give you more information about the main idea. The third kind of detail covered in this chapter, **restatement**, does not add to what you already know about the main idea. Instead, different words may be used to tell the main idea. The main idea and restatement are both saying the same, or almost the same, thing. The restatement usually does not say anything totally new. The writer may use a restatement to help you understand the main idea by rewording it. Or the writer may use a restatement to pull together what has already been said in the paragraph.

Related details that are examples or reasons support either stated or implied main ideas. Restatements can only appear with stated main ideas.

The main idea—Maria bakes many fruit pies for her family, for example—is stated. It can then have a restatement in the paragraph.

> **Stated main idea:** Maria bakes many fruit pies for her family.
>
> **Restatement:** Maria is the family's fruit pie baker.
>
> **Restatement:** The family's fruit pies are baked by Maria.

In both cases, the restatement is saying just about the same thing as the stated main idea. It does not provide new information about Maria baking pies for her family.

Read the following two sample paragraphs. They show how writers use restatements in paragraphs.

Sample A

Many Americans enjoy watching baseball games. Some enjoy going to the baseball park to watch the game. They like the excitement of being where the action is. Other baseball fans follow the game on television. These fans root for their favorite players and teams just as if they were in the park. Yes, great numbers of Americans are baseball fans.

Stated main idea:	Many Americans enjoy watching baseball games.
Restatement:	Yes, great numbers of Americans are baseball fans.

When you read the main idea and the restatement, you find that they both say just about the same thing: many Americans enjoy watching baseball games.

Sample B

> One small mammal, the bat, is able to fly. Its large wings make the bat very good at flying. It is able to go very far and has been seen hundreds of miles out at sea. Although it can twist and turn in the air better than most birds, the bat is not a bird. The bat is a flying mammal.

Stated main idea:	The small mammal, the bat, is able to fly.
Restatement:	The bat is a flying mammal.

Again, both the main idea and the restatement tell just about the same thing: the bat is a mammal that can fly.

Guided Practice 9–5: Detail: Restatement—A

Directions: The stated main idea of each of the following paragraphs has been located for you. Underline or highlight the detail that is a restatement of the main idea in each paragraph.

1. Tim enjoys mountain climbing. He always feels like he has done something great when he gets to the top of a mountain. Once up there, he likes to breathe the cool, crisp air and feel far away from the rest of the world. What joy climbing a mountain is for Tim!

Stated main idea: Tim enjoys mountain climbing.

2.   Some people can be called TV addicts. They stare at cartoons or Westerns or soap operas. It's all the same to them. They don't care if a show is good or bad. As long as it's on TV, they will watch it. TV addicts would rather sit glued in front of the set than do anything else. In other words, some people are hooked on TV.

Stated main idea: Some people can be called TV addicts.

3.   Take care to look well groomed when you go for a job interview. For example, your shoes should be shined. And your clothes should be neat and clean. Make sure you go to an interview looking your best. Finally, be certain that the clothes you wear are proper for the job you want to get.

Stated main idea: Take care to look well groomed when you go for a job interview.

4.   You are going to move! That statement will ring true for most Americans. It will be unusual for you to stay at your present address for the rest of your life. About one in five persons moves each year. The average person moves once every five years. Put another way, it is unlikely that you will stay where you are now living.

Stated main idea: You are going to move!

5.   It is important that you know what to do when your car goes into a skid. When the car skids, the back end usually fishtails or turns in one direction. If your car has the usual rear-wheel drive, the rear may go in the opposite way after the first skid. This does not happen with front-wheel drive cars. With both kinds of drive, always steer in the direction the rear wheels are skidding. Don't jam on the brakes, but pump gently and often. When skidding stops steer the car back so that the front wheels point straight ahead. Now gently put your foot on the gas pedal. The message is clear: know how to respond properly when your car goes into a skid.

Stated main idea: It is important to know what to do when your car goes into a skid.

Guided Practice 9–6: Detail: Restatement—B

Directions: For each of the following paragraphs, underline or highlight both the main idea and the detail that restates it.

1. Oil companies blend gasoline to meet the driving needs of the part of the country where you live. Special blends are made for different climates, that is, cold weather, or hot weather. And special blends are made for high altitude or low altitude. Some brands of gasoline may perform better in your car than others. But you can be reasonably sure that any gasoline you buy is blended to meet local needs.

2. The first Europeans to visit Australia could hardly believe the animal life they saw. Who'd ever heard of a furry, duck-billed mammal that laid eggs? Or a hopping creature that carried its young in a pouch? But these animals did exist. The Australian animals simply amazed the first European visitors.

3. I have heard it said that bears, like elephants, have poor eyesight. I don't know how such tales get started. I know that brown bears, at least, can see quite well. For example, I've watched them watching other bears over great distances. And I know they have spotted me as far away as I was able to see them with unaided eyes. I don't question brown bears being able to see well.

4. When you're stuck with strong feelings that won't go away, try burning them off. Go out and weed the garden. It's hard to be angry when there's mulch on your hands, dirt under your fingernails, and wet grass under your knees! Try washing the car, riding your 10-speed, playing tennis, jogging three times around the track. It really doesn't matter what you do to burn off that extra energy. What matters is that you do burn off those strong feelings.

5. Arrows are the most important part of the bowhunter's equipment. They must be matched to each other, to the bow being used, and to the hunter's draw length. One or more of these three things about arrows is often overlooked by the new hunter. This is a mistake. Arrows are more important than anything else the bowhunter uses. So choose them with care.

SKILL PRACTICE: DETAILS—EXAMPLE, REASON, AND RESTATEMENT

A. Directions: Read each main idea and the details below it. Mark the details with the following letters to show how they relate to the main idea: **E** for example, **R** for reason, and **RS** for restatement.

1. **Main idea:** Buying something on an installment plan can prove to be costly.
   a. Another way of buying something may be cheaper than buying on an installment plan. _____
   b. When interest is added to the cost of what you bought, the payments may be high. _____
   c. What you bought might be cheaper if bought in a discount store for cash. _____
   d. Installment buying can cost the buyer a lot of money. _____
   e. If you don't keep up with the payments, you may have to return what you bought and lose all you have paid. _____

2. **Main idea:** Sewing of menswear has now joined the making of women's and children's clothing at home.
   a. The same fabrics used in menswear factories are now on sale to everyone. _____
   b. The same notions and trimmings used in factory-made menswear are now on sale to everyone. _____
   c. It is now possible to make garments for men, women, and children at home. _____
   d. Companies are now providing a selection of patterns to meet the clothing needs of men and boys. _____
   e. Courses in making menswear are being given for those who want to learn the skill. _____

3. **Main idea:** Prince William Forest Park once provided the Indians who lived there with almost everything they needed.
   a. They used the trunks of tall yellow poplars that grew in the forest to make dugout canoes. _____
   b. Deer, bear, elk, cougar, and many smaller creatures of the forest were the Indians' food supply. _____
   c. The Indians did not have to leave their homes in Prince William Forest Park to get things they needed in order to live. _____
   d. Fish traps were made from poles cut in the forest. _____
   e. Clothing was made from skins of animals that lived in the forest. _____

4. **Main idea:** Time your hiking and camping trips according to the expected weather in the places you will visit.
   a. You will know what kind of weather to expect and be prepared for it. _____
   b. In the Colorado mountains, the best time for hiking and camping is from June 15 to October 1, when the weather is just right for these activities. _____
   c. Hiking and camping trips should be planned according to the weather where you are going. _____
   d. The best time for hiking and camping in the Northern Rockies is between July 15 and September 15, when the weather is most pleasant. _____
   e. If you go hiking or camping at the wrong time of year, you may run into snow, high streams, soft trails, or other problems caused by weather. _____

5. **Main idea:** Time plays an important role in our lives.
   a. Every day, hundreds of thousands of people buy time when they drop coins into parking meters, coin-operated washers, dryers, and dry-cleaning machines. _____
   b. Homemakers trust their cakes and roasts, their clothing, and their fine china to timers on ovens, washers, and dishwashers. _____
   c. In other words, we are creatures involved with time. _____
   d. Businesses pay thousands of dollars for the use of a computer's time. _____

e. We all pay telephone bills based on the number of minutes we spend talking to family or friends across the country. _____

B. Directions: Read the following paragraphs. Find the main idea in each. If the main idea is **stated,** write **MI** next to the sentence number. If the main idea is **implied** write it in your own words under the paragraph. Then look at the numbered details. Tell if each is an example (**E**), reason (**R**), or restatement (**RE**). Write your answers on the lines under the paragraphs. For a sample of what to do, look back to the bottom of page 268.

1.   (1) The alligator has been called the keeper of life in the Everglades swamp. (2) With feet and snouts, alligators clear out holes that save animal life in the swamp. (3) In the dry season, alligator holes become watering places when large numbers of fish, turtles, snails, and other freshwater animals move right in with the alligators. (4) Living with alligators, enough of these water creatures are able to live through the dry season to populate the swamp when the rains return. (5) Birds and mammals feed upon some of the creatures in the alligator holes to stay alive until the rains come. (6) Thus, it can be said that alligators help to keep the Everglades swamp alive.

Main idea (if implied): _____

_____

Sentence 1: _____   Sentence 4: _____
Sentence 2: _____   Sentence 5: _____
Sentence 3: _____   Sentence 6: _____

2.   (1) Plan an extra day at the staging camp so that the mountain climbers will start fresh and well organized. (2) Climbers often make the mistake of "rushing" onto the mountain and arrive at a fairly high altitude tired from travel and last-minute preparations. (3) The extra day will prevent tiredness and lack of organization. (4) The time can be well spent in careful planning and the prepackaging of menus for high-camp use. (5) The climb can be started with climbers fresh and their gear in order.

Main idea (if implied): _____

_____

Sentence 1: _____   Sentence 4: _____
Sentence 2: _____   Sentence 5: _____
Sentence 3: _____

3.   (1) The busy honeybee visits more different plant types than does any other insect. (2) In a single day, one bee may visit several thousand flowers during a dozen or more trips from the hive. (3) But on each trip, it usually visits only one kind of plant; it collects one kind of nectar and leaves one kind of pollen. (4) At the same time, thousands of bees from the same hive are doing the same. (5) On the many visits to plants, the honeybee's large and hairy body helps it collect and leave a great deal of pollen.

Main idea (if implied): _____

_____

Sentence 1: _____   Sentence 4: _____
Sentence 2: _____   Sentence 5: _____
Sentence 3: _____

DETAIL: FILLER

Sometimes writers include details in a paragraph that are not related to the main idea at all. They may be there because the writer thinks they add interest to the paragraph. At times, it seems that they are there just to make the paragraph longer. Whatever the reason, these details do not support the main idea. Nor do they help you understand it. Since these details usually add nothing of real value to the paragraph, think of them as **filler**—words that just fill in space. Such filler can be found anywhere in a paragraph.

You know how to pick out details that are examples, reasons, or restatements. It is just as important to learn how to pick out filler. The best way to do this is to ask yourself if each detail in a paragraph supports its main idea by giving specific information about that main idea. If a detail does not support the main idea, don't be afraid to say that it is filler. Learn to pay no attention to that detail. By getting rid of unrelated details, you will form a solid block of information that goes together. You will thus find it easier to understand and remember the important parts of what you read.

In some of the paragraphs used so far in this chapter, there are sentences that do not relate to the main ideas. In this part of the chapter, you will become even more aware of these unrelated sentences, or filler. You will find out how different filler is from related details.

Read the following two sample paragraphs to see how writers may include filler in paragraphs.

Sample A

(1) Frank Hale has been a beekeeper for over 40 years. (2) According to Frank Hale, there are ways to protect yourself from bee stings. (3) Stinging is the only weapon the bee has when it feels itself in danger. (4) But there are some things you can do to make sure you are not stung. (5) First, dress so that most of your body is covered. (6) Second, make sure that there aren't any wide openings around your wrists or ankles for bees to get in. (7) Third, use some kind of netting to protect your face and head. (8) Finally, use a light does of smoke to stun the bees before you try to take honey from the hive.

Stated main idea: According to Frank Hale, there are ways to protect yourself from bee stings. (sentence 2)

Filler: Sentence 1

Filler: Sentence 3

In Sample A, sentence 4 is a restatement of the main idea. Sentences 5 through 8 are examples of how to protect yourself from bee stings. Sentences 1 and 3 do not support the main idea. They do not tell you how to protect yourself. Thus, they are filler. Reread these two sentences if you did not pick them out as filler. You should see that they do not fit in with the rest of the sentences.

Sample B

(1) I paid $600 for a new color TV set from John Doe's Bargain Barn. (2) For the first time, I watched all of my favorite programs in color. (3) My very favorite star, Rock Henry, looked even more handsome than in black and white. (4) After two days, the set went on the blink. (5) It's been three months now, and I've taken it back three times. (6) Doe won't fix the set, and the factory doesn't pay any attention to my letters. (7) Doe says he doesn't like the way I act and not to come back. (8) I've complained to everybody I can think of—and still no results! (9) I want my money back!

Implied main idea: This person is very unhappy with what has happened since buying a color TV set.

Filler: Sentence 1

Filler: Sentence 2

Filler: Sentence 3

In Sample B, sentences 4 through 9 relate to the implied main idea by telling reasons why this person is very unhappy with what has happened since buying a color TV set. Sentences 1, 2, and 3 do not support the main idea at all. They discuss other subjects.

Reread these sentence if you did not pick them out as filler. You should see that they don't fit in with the rest of the sentences.

Guided Practice 9–7: Detail: Filler

Directions: The main idea of each of the following paragraphs has been found for you. Look at the details in each paragraph. Decide which details relate to the main idea. Write the numbers of the sentences that are filler.

1. (1) There is a law that says caps on drug bottles must be childproof. (2) Every year, thousands of children are poisoned by taking drugs from bottles they can open. (3) Children pry open drug bottles to eat what they think is candy. (4) Sometimes adults are angry because these caps are so hard to take off. (5) But they shouldn't be. (6) Childproof caps protect America's children.

> **Stated main idea:** There is a law that says that drug bottles must be childproof. (sentence 1)
>
> **Filler:** Sentence _____
>
> **Filler:** Sentence _____

2. (1) To protect your credit rating, learn how to correct mistakes or misunderstandings in bills you need to pay. (2) Mistakes can happen to anyone. (3) Misunderstandings are not that unusual between people and the companies they deal with. (4) It will save you time and money if you know what to do. (5) When there's a problem try to deal directly with the person or company to whom you owe the money. (6) Remember to use credit laws if you need them to settle without trouble.

> **Stated main idea:** To protect your credit rating, learn how to correct mistakes or misunderstandings in bills you need to pay. (sentence 1)
>
> **Filler:** Sentence _____
>
> **Filler:** Sentence _____

3. (1) There are dry, semimoist, and moist pet foods. (2) All three types can give your pet what it needs to stay healthy. (3) Most pets find canned and semimoist foods the most tasty and

enjoy them the most. (4) Some owners think this makes it worth spending the extra money for them. (5) There are many TV ads for pet food. (6) They use cute dogs or cats in these ads to make you think that the animal is very fussy about its food. (7) They make you think that the animal chooses one brand above another. (8) A dry food is just as healthy as moist or semimoist food. (9) If not mixed with water, it also keeps tartar from building up on the pet's teeth. (10) Dry foods that cost the least are bought most often.

Implied main idea: This paragraph tells about three types of pet foods and what they do for your pet.

Filler: Sentence _____
Filler: Sentence _____
Filler: Sentence _____
Filler: Sentence _____

4. (1) Medicare Part A payments for your bills are based on benefit periods. (2) A benefit period begins the first day of Medicare covered service in a hospital. (3) It ends when you have been out of a hospital or nursing home for 60 days in a row. (4) Some nursing homes offer better services than others. (5) So be careful when you choose a nursing home. (6) If you go to a hospital again after 60 days, a new benefit period begins and your Part A benefits are renewed. (7) There is no limit to the number of benefit periods you can have.

Stated main idea: Medicare Part A payments for your bills are based on benefit periods. (sentence 1)

Filler: Sentence _____
Filler: Sentence _____

5. (1) Grains such as rice, wheat, and corn are the main part of the diet for millions of people. (2) Depending on the country, these grains are grown in different ways. (3) They are also prepared for the table in different ways. (4) The price of grain goes up and down; when there's a lot of grain around, the price is low. (5) But when the weather has been bad or insects have eaten some of the crop, the supply of grain drops and the price goes up. (6) Millions of people around the world already spend

as much as 80 percent of their money on food. (7) They don't have any money left to pay higher prices for grain. (8) So many times they do without. (9) Some people may even go hungry because they cannot afford to buy grain at high prices.

Implied main idea: This paragraph is about the price of grain and how it affects people around the world.

Filler: Sentence _____

Filler: Sentence _____

The Summary Sheet on page 289 shows the four details covered in this chapter and how they do or do not relate to a main idea. Use it to help you master what you have learned about main ideas and details.

SKILL PRACTICE: DETAILS—EXAMPLE, REASON, RESTATEMENT, AND FILLER

A. Directions: Read each main idea and the details below it. Mark the details with the following letters to show how they relate to the main idea: **E** = example, **R** = reason, **RS** = restatement, and **O** = filler, since filler adds nothing to the main idea.

1. **Main idea:** Drugs are chemicals that are taken into the body for some purpose.
   a. Most drugs are used as medicine. _____
   b. Drugs can cost a lot of money. _____
   c. Some people take drugs to help them relax. _____
   d. There is usually a reason for taking any kind of drug. _____
   e. Drugs can be harmful. _____

2. **Main idea:** Graphs in books can help the reader see how things relate to each other.
   a. Line graphs use a line to show how related things have changed over a period of time. _____
   b. It is easier to see how things relate in a graph than in many words. _____
   c. Bar graphs use bars of different sizes to show how things relate to each other. _____
   d. Some readers do not know how to use graphs. _____
   e. Pie graphs show how parts of a whole relate to each other. _____

3. **Main idea:** People have eaten and enjoyed mushrooms for thousands of years.
   a. Mushrooms taste very good raw or cooked with other foods. _____
   b. The Romans were very fond of mushrooms. _____
   c. Mushrooms grow best in dark, damp places. _____
   d. For many, many years, mushrooms have been a part of our dict. _____
   e. Some mushrooms can cause death if eaten. _____

4. **Main idea:** A soldier who is brave in the face of danger may earn a medal.
   a. Many other soldiers do not earn medals. _____
   b. The Purple Heart medal is awarded to soldiers who are wounded in action. _____
   c. Awarding a medal to a soldier is payment for bravery. _____
   d. The highest honor for a brave soldier is to be awarded the Medal of Honor. _____
   e. A soldier may be awarded a medal for saving the lives of other soldiers in battle. _____

5. **Main idea:** Only a little grooming is usually needed to keep a dog in good health.
   a. Short-haired cats need no grooming at all. _____
   b. Dogs do need to be bathed but not often. _____
   c. Some dogs can stand hot weather better if their hair is clipped short. _____
   d. Unless a dog runs on rough ground or concrete, its nails should be clipped from time to time. _____
   e. It does not take much grooming to have a healthy dog. _____

B. Directions: Read each of the following paragraphs and find the main idea in each. If the main idea is **stated,** write **MI** next to the sentence number. If the main idea is **implied,** write in your own words under the paragraph. Then look at the numbered details. Tell if each detail is an example **(E),** reason **(R),** restatement **(RS),** or filler **(O).** Write your answers on the lines under the paragraph.

1. (1) There are hidden costs that customers pay. (2) Shoplifted cameras, coats, and razor blades are paid for by higher prices for other customers. (3) Shoplifters can go to jail if caught. (4) Bruised, pinched bananas and other fruits and vegetables raise the cost of food. (5) Customers' use of credit cards and other services also means higher prices for goods. (6) Yes, customers pay for more than they know.

Main idea (if implied): _____

_____

Sentence 1: _____   Sentence 4: _____
Sentence 2: _____   Sentence 5: _____
Sentence 3: _____   Sentence 6: _____

2.   (1) Fastened safety belts lower the number of injuries and deaths when accidents happen. (2) They also keep little accidents from becoming big ones. (3) All accidents are serious to the people they happen to. (4) Fastened safety belts may even prevent some accidents from happening in the first place. (5) Without your safety belt fastened, a minor crash could throw you away from the steering wheel while driving, making the car go out of control. (6) Yet there are always some people who have excuses for not fastening their safety belts.

Main idea (if implied): _____

_____

Sentence 1: _____   Sentence 4: _____
Sentence 2: _____   Sentence 5: _____
Sentence 3: _____   Sentence 6: _____

C. Directions: Write your own details for each stated main idea. Use complete sentences. Read the main idea and details you have written. They should result in short paragraphs that do not have any filler in them.

Main idea: Be careful when you buy a house.

a. Example: _____

_____

b. Reason: _____

_____

c. **Restatement:** _____

_____

Main idea: Always try to eat a well-balanced diet.

a. **Example:** _____

_____

b. **Reason:** _____

_____

c. **Restatement:** _____

_____

D. Directions: Choose three paragraphs from any reading material. Copy the paragraphs on a copy machine and attach them to this Skill Practice. Number the sentences in the paragraphs. Show main ideas and details as you did in part B above.

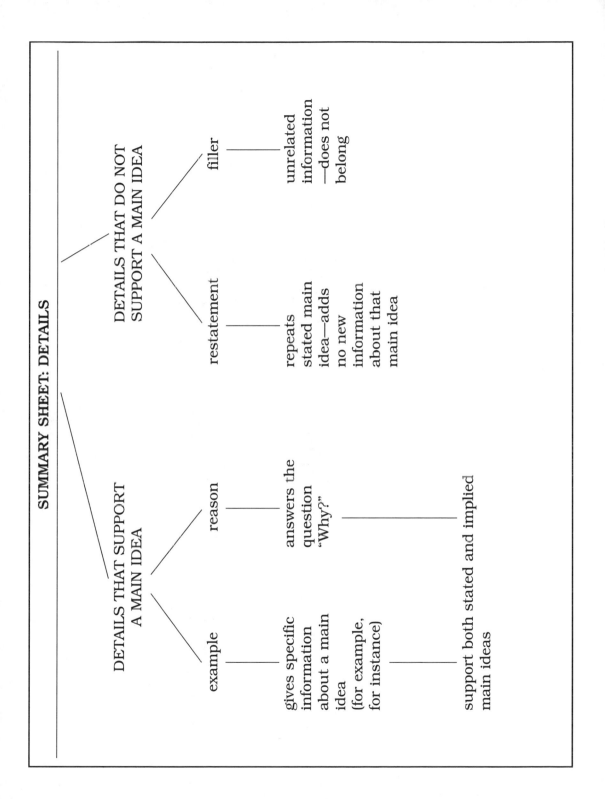

SUMMARY SHEET: DETAILS

DETAILS THAT SUPPORT A MAIN IDEA

example
gives specific information about a main idea (for example, for instance)

reason
answers the question "Why?"

support both stated and implied main ideas

DETAILS THAT DO NOT SUPPORT A MAIN IDEA

restatement
repeats stated main idea—adds no new information about that main idea

filler
unrelated information —does not belong

CHAPTER 10

Main Ideas and Details in Selections

IIn Chapters Eight and Nine, you practiced finding main ideas and details in paragraphs. Using paragraphs is a fine way to learn these two important skills. However, most reading is done in selections that are longer than single paragraphs. Thus, what you have learned about main ideas and details must now be carried over to longer selections. For our purposes, a selection is anything longer than a single paragraph.

In this chapter, you will work with selections to

1. Find main ideas.
2. Relate details.
3. Recognize restatements.
4. Pick out filler.

MAIN IDEAS IN SELECTIONS

Locating the main idea of a selection is done the same way as it is in a paragraph. You ask the same two questions. But now, you ask the questions about a selection:

1. *Who or what is the selection about?*
2. *What does the writer really want you to know about that "who" or "what"?*

The answer to the first question gives you the topic of the selection. The answer to the second question is the main idea of the selection.

Main ideas of selections can be **stated** or **implied.** If stated, the main idea may appear in different parts of the selection. For example, it may be found in the first or last paragraphs. Or it may be in a paragraph somewhere in the middle of the selection. It may be just part of a paragraph. Or it may be the whole paragraph. Remember, if a main idea is stated, you can find it and underline or highlight it. If the main idea is implied, you must look for clues in the selection and then come up with an implied main idea in your own words in a sentence.

In working with selections, you sometimes have an extra clue to the main idea. The selection may have a title that restates the main idea. Or the title may give you an idea of the implied main idea. Warning: Be very careful with titles. Sometimes writers use titles that have little to do with the main idea of a selection. They may be written to catch the reader's eye and to make the selection sound interesting. Therefore, you must always ask yourself if the title really relates to the main idea of a selection. If it does, use it when you check the main idea. If the title doesn't relate, treat it like any other filler. Don't pay attention to it.

When you check the main idea of a selection, do not look at each sentence. That takes too long and is not necessary. Instead, look at whole paragraphs. Use the main ideas of these paragraphs as you did the sentences of single paragraphs. It is the main ideas that are checked for fit under the umbrella statement. They can each stand for the whole paragraph. For example, here is a way you can check a selection with four paragraphs. The main idea of this selection is stated in the first paragraph.

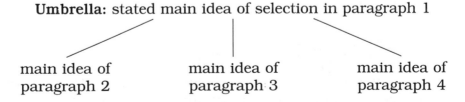

Umbrella: stated main idea of selection in paragraph 1

main idea of paragraph 2   main idea of paragraph 3   main idea of paragraph 4

Implied main ideas of selections are checked in the same way. Again, the main ideas of paragraphs within the selection are checked for fit under an umbrella statement. For instance, checking a selection with three paragraphs might look like this:

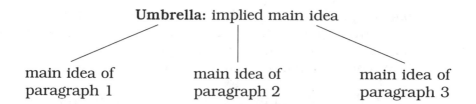

Umbrella: implied main idea

main idea of
paragraph 1

main idea of
paragraph 2

main idea of
paragraph 3

Read the following two sample selections. Then note how their main ideas are found.

Sample A

> (1) Home fire drills may sound silly. And a bad fire is no fun to talk about. But a little time spent planning ways to escape from your home can be very important. Practice what to do if the smoke detector goes off. Planning and practice may save lives in case of fire in your home.
>
> (2) Walk through the main ways to escape from your home several times. Try it in the dark or with your eyes closed. Learn the number of steps between things that might get in your way. Also learn the number of steps between turns. If a piece of furniture keeps getting in the way, move it to clear the path.
>
> (3) Plan different ways to escape from each room. If the main way were blocked by fire or smoke, how would each family member get out? If bedroom windows are too high for safe jumping, perhaps you should buy rope or chain escape ladders to keep at a window in each bedroom.
>
> (4) Your smoke detector is one of the best improvements in home fire safety ever made. But its worth depends on your own efforts to prevent and to escape fires.

Who or what is the selection about?
    escaping from your home in case of fire
What does the writer want you to know about escaping from your home in case of fire?
    Plan and practice for a safe escape from your home in case of fire.

The main idea of the selection is stated in the first paragraph. Most of the sentences in that paragraph tell you to plan and practice for escape from your home in case of fire. If you use the first paragraph as an umbrella statement, you will find that the other two paragraphs fit under it. The last paragraph does not fit. It does not tell anything about planning or practicing for a safe escape from your home in case of fire. Therefore, it is filler.

Umbrella: Plan and practice for a safe escape from your home in case of fire. (implied main idea of paragraph 1)

There are ways to practice escaping from your home. (implied main idea of paragraph 2)

Plan different ways to escape from each room. (stated main idea of paragraph 3)

The title almost restates the main idea, but not quite. Instead, it is too broad to fit under the umbrella statement and gives only the topic of the selection.

Sample B

Floors

(1) Have you noticed what has happened to floors in recent years? There are now many different kinds of floors from which to choose. Buyers are limited only by cost and their own tastes. Gone are the days when most homes had hardwood floors.

(2) Varnished, waxed, or oiled wood floors should never be washed. Varnished floors keep their color and shine best if no water is used on them. Very dirty floors may be wiped with a damp cloth. Then dry and polish with an oiled cloth or mop. A wood floor that doesn't get much wear needs waxing only two or three times a year. It is a mistake to use too much wax.

(3) To clean linoleum floors, use water mixed with mild soap or detergent. Don't overwet the floor. When the floor is dry, put on wax in a thin, even film. Never use anything harsher than fine steel wool to remove spots.

(4) Wash asphalt tile floors only after they have been in place for about two weeks. It is important to allow the tiles to set. In the meantime, wipe the floor with a slightly damp mop. Use soap or detergent and water. Asphalt tile floors should be waxed after washing.

Who or what is the selection about?
   floors
What does the writer really want you to know about floors?
   Take care of different kinds of floors

    The main idea of this selection is implied. Thus, it must be written in a sentence in your own words. Remember, your words may not match those of this writer, but the idea should be the same.

    When you use the answer to the second question as an umbrella statement, you find that the main ideas of three out of the four paragraphs fit under it. Paragraph 1 serves as an introduction but actually does not fit with the other information. Thus, it is filler.

Umbrella: Take care of different kinds of floors.

Take care of wood floors. (implied main idea of paragraph 2)	Take care of linoleum floors. (implied main idea of paragraph 3)	Take care of asphalt floors. (implied main idea of paragraph 4)

    The title "Floors" is too broad. It answers the first question and is the topic of the selection. However, it does not give you any idea as to what the writer really wants you to know about floors.

Guided Practice 10–1: Main Ideas in Selections

    Directions: Read each of the following selections. Use the two questions you have learned to help you find the main idea of the selection. Then check that main idea. Make an umbrella statement. See if all, or most, of the main ideas of the paragraphs fit under it. Also, see if the title fits under the umbrella statement.

1.
Trees

    (1) Of all America's riches, trees are among our most treasured. We would be a poor nation indeed without them. As liv-

ing, growing things, they give us beauty. As wood, logged and milled, they serve us in many, many ways.

(2) The first colonists to arrive in America found a billion acres of trees. Forests stretched almost unbroken from the Atlantic to the Great Plains. Then they went beyond the Plains to the Pacific.

(3) We can count more that 700 different kinds of native tress. In addition, trees have been brought to this country from other lands. However, our forestlands have decreased over the last 300 years.

(4) Our nation has grown from one of farms and small villages to one of factories and large cities. The useful products and services from trees have also grown. They have multiplied many times over.

(5) The major use of trees is for wood. The need for wood to build homes is greater than our ability to supply lumber. The list of different kinds of wood products is almost endless.

(6) We find that trees serve many necessary and enjoyable purposes. They improve the quality of our environment. They shade our homes and streets. They beautify our parks and highways. They build and protect the soil, help prevent floods, and provide homes for wildlife.

Who or what is the selection about?

_____

What does the writer really want you to know about that "who" or "what"?

(in your own words)

_____

Underline or highlight the main idea of the selection if it is stated.

Check main idea of selection:

Umbrella: _____

_____   _____   _____   _____

_____   _____   _____   _____

2.

(No Title)

(1) The lights are out. The clock has stopped. And the heater is not working. There's a power failure! It may be that the electric power in only one house has gone off. Or the whole city may be having a "blackout." The threat of any kind of power failure puts fear into the hearts of many people all across the country.

(2) In recent years, more and more Americans have added food freezers to the list of appliances they own. These freezers may be bought as part of a refrigerator, or they may be just freezers alone. Either way, they are used to store frozen foods for future use.

(3) Power failures mean that the freezer stops working. This causes food in the freezer to thaw and, perhaps, spoil. With the high price of food, the loss can be quite costly. Therefore, it is very important for the freezer-owner to know what to do if the freezer stops working in a power failure.

(4) The first thing is not to open the freezer door! Don't check to see what's happening to the food inside. If the door is kept tightly shut, a fully loaded freezer will stay cold enough to keep foods frozen for two days. However, if the freezer is less than half full, the food may not stay frozen for more than one day.

(5) If you don't think the electric power will be back on in time to keep the food from thawing, use dry ice. If you put dry ice in the freezer soon after the power goes off, 25 pounds should do the job. It will keep the temperature below freezing for 2–4 days, depending upon how much food is in the freezer. Put the dry ice on cardboard or small boards on top of the packages of food. Again, don't open the freezer except to put in more dry ice!

(6) If the power failure is in your home, you can decide if you want to move the frozen food from your own freezer. If you do, use thick boxes and layers of paper around the food to prevent thawing. The food can then be moved to someone else's freezer or to a rented locker.

(7) Knowing what to do when there is a power failure can make a difference for the freezer-owner. It can mean saving many dollars' worth of food from spoiling. It can also reduce panic and, thereby, result in actions that solve the problem.

Who or what is the selection about?

_____

*What does the writer really want you to know about that "who"
or "what"?*

(in your own words)

_____

Underline or highlight the main idea of the selection if it is stated.

Check main idea of selection:

Umbrella: _____

_____   _____   _____   _____

_____   _____   _____   _____

In chapter Eight, you learned how to check the main idea of a
paragraph in your mind. You can do the same kind of check
for the main idea of a selection. As you did in the first two
selections in this chapter, find the main idea of the selection.
Underline or highlight the selection main idea if it is stated.
Use your own words in a sentence if the main idea is implied.
Then check that main idea in your mind by making it into an
umbrella statement. See if all, or most, of the main ideas of the
paragraphs fit under it.

3.   **See You in Court!**

(1) A new American pastime seems to be that of going to
court. Matters that once were settled between parties now
become court cases. As a result, the courts are overcrowded. It
often takes a long time for cases to be settled.

(2) Are you having trouble with a company that says that
you owe money? If so, chances are that you may end up in
court. In many states, businesses use small claims courts
when they want to collect money they believe is owed to them.

(3) It can be very frightening to find out that you are being taken to court. You imagine all kinds of terrible things that can happen to you. Understanding what is to happen can prevent some of your worry. Know what to do if you are being sued by a company that says you owe money.

(4) If you agree that you owe the money, contact the company that began the suit. Try to arrange to pay the debt without going to court. The company may even let you pay on an installment plan. If you make an arrangement with the company, have it put in writing.

(5) If you don't think you owe the money in question, prepare to go to court. There you can tell the judge your reasons. Don't feel that you probably will lose the case. Give the court a chance to help you.

(6) When you are sued, you will get papers telling you that a claim has been filed against you. The papers will include a summons telling you the date, time, and place of the hearing or trial. Be sure to appear in court on the date set. Otherwise, the case may be settled in favor of the company.

(7) Being sued is not a pleasant thing to have happen to you. It can happen to anyone; it happens all the time. However, the wise person knows what to do when sued by a company for money it says is owed to them.

Who or what is the selection about?

_____

What does the writer really want you to know about that "who" or "what"?
(in your own words)

_____

Underline the main idea of the selection if it is stated.

Check the main idea of the selection in your mind.

4. **What's in a Name?**

(1) It has been said that we remember places better than people. If this is true, it may be because we connect events and

feelings with places. The names we give and use for places are very important to us. They are part of our everyday language. They allow us to exchange ideas about the world around us.

(2) The largest collection of American place names can be found on the 30,000 or more maps put out by the U.S. Department of the Interior. There are about 3 million place names on these maps. This is about two-thirds of the place names used today.

(3) In a way, place names are the language in which our country's story is written. Over 500 years of American history are shown in place names like Sandy Point, Bald Knob, Yorktown, The Maiden, Rough and Ready, Bean Blossom Creek, and Independence.

(4) Place names echo every part of American life, past and present. Over 100 languages have been used in American place names. We have named a place for a Swedish singer (Jenny Lind), a French crusader (Saint Louis), a Roman soldier (Cincinnatus), a French pirate (Lafitte), and a Russian ruler (Alexander).

(5) Yes, place names are important to us. They give us a feeling for the history of our country. And they let us describe places so others may know them.

Who or what is the selection about?

_____

What does the writer really want you to know about that "who" or "what"?

(in your own words)

_____

Underline the main idea of the selection if it is stated.

Check the main idea of the selection in your mind.

5. ### AIDS and You

(1) AIDS stands for *acquired immune deficiency syndrome* (a-kwird´ ĭ-myoon´ dĕ-fĭsh´ənse sĭn´drom´). It is a disease caused by a virus that can destroy the body's ability to fight

off illness. The AIDS virus makes you unable to fight other diseases that invade your body. These diseases can kill you. There is presently no cure for AIDS.

(2) Regardless of what you may have heard, you cannot become infected with AIDS through casual contact with persons who have the virus. There isn't any danger of infection through casual contact at parties, bars, or other social meeting places. You won't catch AIDS in a crowded elevator with someone who has the virus. Nor do you have to worry about shaking hands, hugging, or even kissing.

(3) AIDS cannot be caught by using things that a person with AIDS has used. You can't get it by swimming in a pool where a person with the AIDS virus has been swimming. You won't get the AIDS virus from towels in a locker room, or the shower, or the whirlpool, or by using exercise equipment. It won't be passed through a glass or eating utensil.

(4) No one has ever gotten the AIDS virus from a mosquito or any other insect bite. Even if these insects have bitten someone with AIDS, they cannot infect the next person they land on and bite.

(5) Actually, there are very few ways you can be infected by the AIDS virus. It is transmitted through body fluids. You can become infected by having sex with an infected person or by sharing a needle and syringe with a drug user. Babies of women who have been infected with the AIDS virus may be born with the infection because it can be transmitted to the baby before or during birth.

(6) It is now rare that one can become infected with the AIDS virus through blood transfusions. Before 1985, people with a disease called hemophilia and others who needed blood were in danger of being infected with the AIDS virus through transfusions. This was before the virus was identified. Today, all donated blood in the United States is tested to make it as safe as possible for those who need it.

Who or what is the selection about?

_____

What does the writer really want you to know about that "who"
or "what"?

(in your own words)

_____

Underline the main idea of the selection if it is stated.

Check the main idea of the selection in your mind.

SKILL PRACTICE: MAIN IDEAS IN SELECTIONS

Directions: Use the two questions you have learned to find the main idea of each selection. If the main idea is **stated,** underline or highlight it. If the main idea is **implied,** write it in your own words in a full sentence under the selection.

1.   **A Prickly Problem**

Cactus plants, with their sharp spines, look as if they can take care of themselves. Indeed, there were once so many that they caused problems for western-bound wagon trains. But in recent years, their numbers have gone down. In fact, nearly one-third of the different kinds of cacti in this country are now about to disappear.

One reason is that places where cacti grow are being used for mining, grazing, and land development. Another reason is that people uproot truckloads of plants to sell or take home.

In Arizona, there have been laws to protect cacti since 1929. "Cactus cops" patrol the desert. Pickers without permits face fines. They may even face prison sentences. In the last few years, the same kinds of laws have been passed in California, Nevada, and New Mexico.

Perhaps more people will become aware of the threat to cactus plants. Then the market will shift from wild to greenhouse-grown cacti. Homeowners will no longer take cacti from where it grows wild or buy it from those who do.

Main idea (if implied): _____

_____

2.   **Our Planets at a Glance**

From Earth we have gazed up to the sky for untold thousands of years. The ancient astronomers saw points of light that appeared to wander among the stars. They called these objects planets, which means wanderers. They then named the planets after Roman gods: Jupiter, Mars, Mercury, Venus, and Saturn.

During the seventeenth century, astronomers pointed a new device called a telescope at the heavens. Now they were able to get a better look at the planets, and they made startling new discoveries.

The past 25 years have been a golden age for exploring planets. Advances in rocketry during the 1950s made it possible to break the grip of Earth's gravity and travel to the Moon and to the planets.

American robot craft have landed on and reported from the surfaces of Venus and Mars. Our spacecraft have orbited Mars and Venus and gained much information about them. Other spacecraft have made close-range observations while flying past Mercury, Jupiter, and Saturn.

Main idea (if implied): _____

_____

3. ### What's Happened to the Old Time Madstone?

The madstone was used by pioneers to draw poison from a rabid dog bite, snake bite, or poisonous spider bite. It was in popular use until Pasteur's work in 1885 led to other treatment against rabies.

Many folks pinned their hopes for recovery on madstone magic. Madstones are stones found in the bodies of cud-chewing, multistomached, horned animals such as the deer and cow. The madstone found in a white deer was most highly prized for its power. So strong was the belief in madstones that persons would ride hundreds of miles to use one.

Madstones were first used in America by the Indians. But how the Indians discovered their magic power can only be guessed. Pioneer settlers first called them "Indian stones." If a child was bitten by a rabid animal, he was taken to an Indian camp for treatment. The Indians were hunters. They found the stones in the bodies of deer that they killed for food. White settlers began calling them "madstones" since they cured bites from rabid, or mad, animals.

Main idea (if implied): _____

_____

4. **Land**

What are the chances for getting government land? Is there a lot of free land around? How hard is it to buy public land? How much land is for sale each year?

These are only a few of the questions asked of the government every day. Many people read ads that give them the idea Uncle Sam is giving away land. They think the government is still giving "free" or "surplus" public land for homesteading. Or they think the government is selling land for next to nothing as in the days of the Old West, in the eighteenth, nineteenth, and early twentieth centuries.

There is no truth to claims about free public land. There is no free public land. The little land the government sometimes does sell costs as much, or perhaps more, than nearby nonpublic land. Homesteading on public lands in the western lower 48 states is a thing of the past.

Main idea (if implied): _____

_____

5. **A Matter of Time**

Some of the earliest clocks ever made have lasted to the present time. They were built in Egypt. The Egyptians built both sundials and water clocks.

The Greeks and Romans depended on water and sand clocks. Sometime between the eighth and eleventh centuries, the Chinese built a "mechanical" clock. But this was still a kind of water clock.

Many different types of Chinese water clocks were built. By the early thirteenth century, there was a whole group of water-clock makers in Germany. However, there were problems. The water clock did not keep good time. And it froze during the winter.

Sand clocks were invented in the fourteenth century. They solved the freezing problem. But there was another problem. The sand was too heavy. Thus, the clock could only measure short periods of time such as an hour. That's how it came to be called an "hourglass."

Main idea (if implied): _____

_____

DETAILS IN SELECTIONS

In Chapter Nine, you learned that the main idea of a paragraph can be supported by sentences that are related details. These details can be **examples** of the main idea or **reasons** for it. The same two kinds of related details are used to support the main idea of a selection. Related details in selections, however, are not single sentences. It would take too long to relate each sentence to the main idea of a selection. And it is not necessary. Instead, use the main ideas of paragraphs within the selection to stand for the whole paragraph. These paragraph main ideas, stated or implied, serve as details of the selection's main idea. Then relate these as details to the main idea of the selection. For example, if a selection has four paragraphs, details might relate to the main idea of the selection as follows.

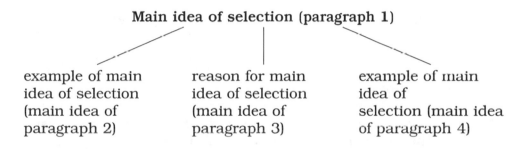

Main idea of selection (paragraph 1)

example of main idea of selection (main idea of paragraph 2)

reason for main idea of selection (main idea of paragraph 3)

example of main idea of selection (main idea of paragraph 4)

As with paragraphs, details in a selection may all be of one kind. There may be all four kinds of details in the same selection. Or a detail may support a main idea in more than one way. For instance, it may be an example and reason at the same time.

As you fit the main ideas of paragraphs under the main idea of the selection, they may simply repeat the same information given in that main idea. These details are restatements. Or you may find some details that do not relate at all. They are filler. They are filler for the same reason that some sentences were filler when you worked with related details in single paragraphs. They tell nothing at all about a main idea. If you can pick out filler, you remove details that are not important. You don't have to bother with them. The rest of the selection consists of ideas that are all related and, thus, is easier to understand and remember. Look again at the Summary Sheet on page 289. The information about a main idea and details applies to selections as well as to paragraphs.

In this part of the chapter, you will use selections for which you have already found the main idea. In some cases, you have also seen which main ideas of paragraphs fit under the main idea of the selection. Now you will look at these main ideas carefully to see *how* they support the main idea of the selection. Are they **examples** of that main idea, or **reasons** for it? If the details sound like the stated main idea, they are restatements. Of course, if they don't fit at all, they are filler.

The following two sample selections will show you how the main ideas of paragraphs can act as details that relate to the main idea of the selection

Sample A

Plan and Practice for a Safe Escape

(1) Home fire drills may sound silly. And a bad fire is no fun to talk about. But a little time spent planning ways to escape from your home can be very important. Practice what to do if the smoke detector goes off. Planning and practice may save lives in case of fire in your home.

(2) Walk through the main ways to escape from your home several times. Try it in the dark or with your eyes closed. Learn the number of steps between things that might get in your way. Also learn the number of steps between turns. If a piece of furniture keeps getting in the way, move it to clear the path.

(3) Plan different ways to escape from each room. If the main way were blocked by fire or smoke, how would each family member get out? If bedroom windows are too high for safe jumping, perhaps you should buy rope or chain escape ladders to keep at a window in each bedroom.

(4) Your smoke detector is one of the best improvements in home fire safety ever made. But its worth depends on your own efforts to prevent and to escape fires.

Implied main idea:	Plan and practice for a safe escape from your home in case of fire.
Paragraph 1:	*Main idea*
Paragraph 2:	*Example* (The main idea of this paragraph is implied: There are ways to practice escaping

from your home. This paragraph's main idea is an example of the practice mentioned in the main idea of the selection.)

Paragraph 3: *Example* (The main idea of this paragraph is stated and has been underlined for you. It tells you to plan ways to escape from your home. Thus, it is an example of the planning mentioned in the main idea of the selection.)

Paragraph 4: *Filler* (This paragraph says nothing at all about planning or practicing for escape from your home. It tells about smoke detectors and is, therefore, unrelated to the main idea.)

The title "Plan and Practice for a Safe Escape" is a little too broad. The plan and practice in the title could be a safe escape from anything, not just a fire.

Sample B

Floors

(1) Have you noticed what has happened to floors in recent years? There are now many different kinds of floors from which to choose. Buyers are limited only by cost and their own tastes. Gone are the days when most homes had hardwood floors.

(2) Varnished, waxed, or oiled wood floors should never be washed. Varnished floors keep their color and shine best if no water is used on them. Very dirty floors may be wiped with a damp cloth. Then dry and polish with an oiled cloth or mop. A wood floor that doesn't get much wear needs waxing only two or three times a year. It is a mistake to use too much wax.

(3) To clean linoleum floors, use water mixed with mild soap or detergent. Don't overwet the floor. When the floor is dry, put on wax in a thin, even film. Never use anything harsher than fine steel wool to remove spots.

(4) Wash asphalt tile floors only after they have been in place for about two weeks. It is important to allow the tiles to set. In the meantime, wipe the floor with a slightly damp mop. Use soap or detergent and water. Asphalt tile floors should be waxed after washing.

Implied main idea: Take care of different kinds of floors.

Paragraph 1: *Filler* (This is an interesting paragraph but not related to the main idea of the selection. It does not tell anything about the care of floors.)

Paragraph 2: *Example* (The main idea of this paragraph is implied: how to take care of one kind of floor—wood. Thus, the main idea of this paragraph is an example of the main idea of the selection: take care of different kinds of floors.)

Paragraph 3: *Example* (The main idea of this paragraph also is implied: take care of one kind of floor—linoleum. Thus, this main idea is an example of the main idea of the selection: take care of different kinds of floors.)

Paragraph 4: *Example* (The main idea of this paragraph is implied: how to take care of yet another kind of floor—asphalt tile. This paragraph is also an example of the main idea of the selection: take care of different kinds of floors.)

Guided Practice 10–2: Details in Selections

Directions: Read the selections on pages 295 to 302 again. Now copy the main idea of each selection. Then show how each paragraph main idea serves as a detail. Paragraph main ideas may be example (**E**), reason (**R**), restatement (**RS**), or filler (**O**). Also, note how the title is related to the main idea of the selection.

1. **Trees (page 295)**

Main idea (if implied): _____

_____

Paragraph 1: _____   Paragraph 4: _____
Paragraph 2: _____   Paragraph 5: _____
Paragraph 3: _____   Paragraph 6: _____

2.　　　　　　　(No Title) (page 297)

Main idea (if implied): _____

_____

Paragraph 1: _____　　　　Paragraph 5: _____
Paragraph 2: _____　　　　Paragraph 6: _____
Paragraph 3: _____　　　　Paragraph 7: _____
Paragraph 4: _____

3.　　　　　　　See You in Court! (page 298)

Main idea (if implied): _____

_____

Paragraph 1: _____　　　　Paragraph 5: _____
Paragraph 2: _____　　　　Paragraph 6: _____
Paragraph 3: _____　　　　Paragraph 7: _____
Paragraph 4: _____

4.　　　　　　　What's in a Name? (page 299)

Main idea (if implied): _____

_____

Paragraph 1: _____　　　　Paragraph 4: _____
Paragraph 2: _____　　　　Paragraph 5: _____
Paragraph 3: _____

5.　　　　　　　AIDS and You (page 300)

Main idea (if implied): _____

_____

Paragraph 1: _____　　　　Paragraph 4: _____
Paragraph 2: _____　　　　Paragraph 5: _____
Paragraph 3: _____　　　　Paragraph 6: _____

Name _____

SKILL PRACTICE: DETAILS IN SELECTIONS

Directions: Read each of the following selections. The main idea of each has been identified for you. Show how each paragraph relates to that main idea [example (**E**), reason (**R**), restatement (**RE**), or filler (**O**)].

1.   **Health Claims: Fact vs. Fantasy**

(1) Health care may well be the number one interest in America today. Americans are more conscious than ever of the importance of staying healthy. However, on the negative side, this interest in health care has also resulted in the growth of health fraud. In fact, health fraud has become a major cause for concern.

(2) Billions of consumer dollars are wasted on useless remedies and devices. They are spent to purchase products that promise a "quick and easy cure." Ads for these products use key words such as "miraculous," "exclusive," "secret," or "ancient" and are full of interesting case histories that are too good to be true.

(3) Health fraud is a business that sells false hope. It preys on persons who are victims of diseases such as arthritis, multiple sclerosis, and certain forms of cancer. Medical science is continually seeking cures for these diseases, but this takes time. Meanwhile, dishonest promoters are quick to market useless concoctions and call them medical "break-throughs."

(4) Other harmful health frauds are those that turn people away from proper medical diagnosis and treatment. Instead, they encourage sick people to try fake products that in themselves may be dangerous. They waste valuable time before getting proper medical attention. That delay may do serious harm and endanger lives.

Stated main idea: Health fraud has become a major cause for concern.

Paragraph 1: _____   Paragraph 3: _____
Paragraph 2: _____   Paragraph 4: _____

2.   (No Title)

(1) The first step is a check of cabinets under the kitchen sink, or any cabinets through which water pipes, drain pipes, or heating pipes pass. Is any food stored there? Sacks of onions or potatoes, or perhaps some liquids or canned goods? Food should never be stored in these cabinets. They will attract insects and possibly rats through openings that are almost impossible to seal. Also, leakage from the pipes can damage food products. Or it can cause cans to become over-heated or rusty.

(2) Next, take a look around your kitchen. Is any food sitting out? Meat thawing at room temperature? A carton of milk you'll put away "in a minute"? Foods that should be refrigerated or frozen must always be handled with special care. Bacteria in such foods can multiply quickly outside the refrigerator or freezer. Always remember to keep cold foods cold.

(3) Take a look at where you put your bread. Bread usually keeps fresher longer at room temperature than in the refrigerator. But in hot sticky weather, bread is better protected against mold in the refrigerator.

(4) Next, look at storage areas near warm spots such as the stove. Foods should not be kept in cabinets above the stove. Even dry mixes will not keep well.

(5) Now take a look at the food you bought. Have you bought all the foods needed for a healthy diet? Have you stayed away from junk foods? If not, make a list of healthy foods to take with you when you shop. Stick to that list!

Implied main idea: Check your kitchen to see if you are storing food the right way.

Paragraph 1: _____   Paragraph 4: _____
Paragraph 2: _____   Paragraph 5: _____
Paragraph 3: _____

3. (No Title)

(1) When you walk into a car showroom—are you thinking only of price, gas mileage, color, style, power, and "extras"? Are you ready to believe whatever the salesperson tells you about the car?

(2) You inspect the car by walking around it a few times, kicking the tires, slamming a door. Maybe you even open the hood and peek at the engine. You often do not really know what you are looking for. You may sit in the front seat. But you never give any thought to the fact that you have tall children who may have to sit in the back seat. They may not have enough head and leg room. You think there is a spare tire and a jack in the trunk. But you don't check. You may drive the car around the block and say you have test-driven it. You note a flaw in the paint. Or you see that one of the rear doors won't close all the way. The salesperson promises these will be taken care of later.

(3) Once you make up your mind to buy, you are in a hurry. You want your car right away. You don't know that all new cars need dealer servicing before they will perform and look their best. You usually pay for this, anyway. As a careless buyer, you're willing to take the car on the promise that an ill-fitting hood, noisy heater/air conditioner, motor, or missing knobs on the dash will be taken care of later.

(4) If you are a careless buyer, you usually wind up thinking that you've been had. Yet you have fallen into a pit you've dug for yourself. If you are a careless buyer, you do not go about buying your car the right way.

Paragraph 1: _____   Paragraph 3: _____
Paragraph 2: _____   Paragraph 4: _MI_

4. Full Moon Madness

(1) There are some who believe that the way people behave changes when the moon is full. These changes don't just happen in werewolf movies. Recent studies show that a full moon brings out all kinds of "lunacy."

(2) Scientists can't give reasons. But some crimes including assault and arson, do go up during the full moon. There

are also more stress-related illnesses such as heart attacks and ulcers at this time of month. Many blood banks report a sharp rise in requests for blood.

(3) Belief in the magical effects of the moon is very old. In some early groups, women were married by the light of full moon. It was believed that the moon would help them to have many babies. In other early groups, moon goddesses were thought to have the power to drive men mad.

(4) Many have tried to shed light on the subject of the full moon's effects. Some say that criminals use the extra light for carrying out crimes. Others say that there is a slight change in the earth when the earth, sun, and moon are lined up. They are lined up this way during a full moon. It is said the change in the earth somehow changes the way we feel.

(5) At least one thing we know to be true. During the full moon, there is more of a gravity pull. This pull produces bigger tides, which pull small fish closer to shore. The small fish are followed by larger ones that feed on them.

(6) On the sixteenth of this month, the moon will be full. Your best bet may be to just go fishing.

Implied main idea: The full moon affects people.

Paragraph 1: _____	**Paragraph 4:** _____
Paragraph 2: _____	**Paragraph 5:** _____
Paragraph 3: _____	Paragraph 6: _____

5.   **Drug-Free Schools: Who Can Help?**

(1) Today's schools at all levels are often faced with drug and other social problems that affect students. Even though many of the causes of these problems are beyond any school's ability to change, schools are called on to help solve them. Schools can help. However, schools alone cannot prevent drug use by students. Studies show that drug prevention works best when it goes beyond the school day and involves a variety of people from the community. Making schools and communities drug-free is a shared effort that needs help from every part of society.

(2) **Students.** Students have two responsibilities. The first is to remain drug-free and to obey family rules, school policies, and community laws. Their second responsibility is to help those who have drug problems. Students listen to other students and, thus, may be encouraged not to use drugs or alcohol.

(3) **Families.** Families are the first line of defense against drugs. The standards set at home are the strongest means for children to stay off drugs. Parents should make it clear to their children that they will not put up with the illegal use of any drugs, including alcohol. They should work with other parents, the schools, and the community to make sure that drug prevention policies are carried out.

(4) **Schools.** It is important for schools at all levels, from preschool through college, to know that drug prevention education is not enough. This drug prevention effort must be supported by school policies, programs, and services that include the needs of students both in and out of school. Along with the family, schools and colleges are critical in the war on drugs.

(5) **Community.** In every community, many people and organizations play important roles in the lives of young people. These people and organizations can help the school's drug education and prevention efforts. For example, religious institutions and civic groups can give moral leadership and guidance. Law enforcement can keep schools and neighborhoods safe. Health and social services can treat students with drug problems. Community groups may need to reach out and become involved in individual students' lives and problems.

(6) **Government.** The government's first responsibility in making schools drug-free is to give leadership and direction. Enough funds for drug prevention programs should be given, and they should be spent wisely. Schools should get help from the government in developing and operating their programs when they need it. Government leaders should be role models for the entire community.

(7) **Media.** The media—television, videos, radio, movies, music recordings, newspapers, and other publications—has great power to influence people. Many students spend more time watching television or videos than they do in school or on family, religious, or community activities. Use of the media is a great way to inform students of all ages about the dangers of drugs and alcohol.

(8) The war on drugs cannot be won by any single person or group. Each of the above named parts of society can and must help to overcome the drug problem in America's schools. Drug-free schools and communities can result from all parts of society working together in this case.

Stated main idea: Making schools and communities drug-free is a shared effort that needs help from every part of society.

Paragraph 1: _MI_ **Paragraph 5:** _____

Paragraph 2: _____ **Paragraph 6:** _____

Paragraph 3: _____ **Paragraph 7:** _____

Paragraph 4: _____ **Paragraph 8:** _____

SKILL PRACTICE: MAIN IDEAS AND DETAILS IN SELECTIONS

A. Directions: Read each selection. Use the two questions you have learned to find the main idea. If the main idea is **stated,** write **MI** on the line next to the paragraph where it is located. If the main idea is **impied,** write it in a sentence under the selection. Then show how each paragraph relates to that main idea [example (**E**), reason (**R**), restatement (**RE**), or filler (**O**)].

1.   **Daydream Your Problems Away**

(1) "Stop that daydreaming! You should be doing your schoolwork!" It's a scolding that has been heard by countless children. Many people think of daydreams as time-wasters. But psychologists are now finding that daydreams may be good for us.

(2) According to a study by psychologist Leonard Giambra, many daydreams help us solve problems. Sometimes, answers seem to come from "out of the blue." They are often the result of this kind of daydreaming.

(3) In a study of 1,200 men and women, Dr. Giambra found that people of all ages daydream. They daydream more about solving personal or job-related problems. They daydream less about such matters such as sex, success, or failure.

(4) Dr. Giambra also found that women of all ages daydream more than men. Both sexes daydream less and less as they get older. However, there is a spurt of daydreaming between the ages of 45 and 49.

(5) The elderly don't dream only about the good old days as many people believe they do. Instead, like everyone else, old people daydream equally about the past, present, and future. And although their overall daydreaming goes down, it still involves problem solving.

(6) Dr. Kathleen Staley adds, "People should take more time to daydream, since daydreams not only solve problems but can provide entertainment or relief from stress."

Main idea (if implied): _____

_____

Paragraph 1: _____   Paragraph 4: _____
Paragraph 2: _____   Paragraph 5: _____
Paragraph 3: _____   Paragraph 6: _____

2.   (No Title)

(1) Southern hardwood forests are the home of the white-tailed deer and the wild turkey. America's wetlands are host to millions of ducks, geese, and shorebirds each year. Mountains and meadows are the stomping grounds for elk and grizzly bears, while streams and lakes teem with salmon, trout, and bass. These are just a few of the species and habitats (places where animals and plants live) on the 191 million acres that make up the national forests and grasslands of America. The national forests and grasslands area is roughly the size of Texas and Louisiana rolled into one.

(2) America's national forests and grasslands are managed by the Forest Service. Nearly 1,100 Forest Service biologists and botanists manage wildlife, fish, and rare plant habitats. They work closely with state and other federal agencies to plan how the national forests and grasslands will be managed and used. Nationwide partnerships have been set up with groups and persons who are interested in working with the Forest Service. As a result, special programs have been developed and in recent years partners have donated labor, material, and money to benefit wildlife, fish, and rare plants.

(3) The national forests and grasslands are home to thousands of species of fish, amphibians, reptiles, birds, mammals, insects, and plants. Most live out their lives under the watchful eye of the Forest Service in these protected habitats. Some threatened or endangered species depend on special programs in national forests and grasslands for their very survival. This means the careful management of their food, water, space, and shelter. Through such management, for example, the endangered grizzly bear is making a dramatic comeback.

(4) Twenty-two million people visit America's national forests and grasslands each year. Many come to enjoy wildlife, fish, and rare plants through photography, viewing, and nature study. Others come to enjoy fishing, a popular outdoor activity. Whether it's trolling for salmon in Alaska or casting for bass in Florida, fishing is great in the national forests and grasslands. Still others use these areas to hunt for game and waterfowl such as ducks. The rich and different national forests and grasslands with their wild inhabitants belong to all Americans.

Main idea (if implied): _____

Paragraph 1: _____   **Paragraph 3:** _____
Paragraph 2: _____   **Paragraph 4:** _____

3.   How to Be a Water Miser

(1) Water is something we can't afford to waste. Trying to save water does make a difference. You may be surprised at how much you can save in your own home. You must simply find and limit water wasters.

(2) The average showers uses 3 gallons of water a minute. A filled tub has 25 gallons per bath. A dishwasher uses about 21 gallons per load. And a toilet uses between 5 and 7 gallons with each flush.

(3) To save water, put something in your faucets and shower to make water pressure go up as it cuts the flow of water in half. Some shower units allow you to turn the water off while you soap up. Then, when you turn the water back on, it is the right temperature.

(4) Keep showers short—about 5 minutes. To get children to hurry, have them take showers during breaks in their favorite TV shows. When taking baths, fill the tub only halfway.

(5) Cut down on the amount of water used with each toilet flush. Fill a plastic bleach bottle with water and stone to weigh it down. Place it in the tank. The bottle should be out of

the way of moving parts.

(6) If you wash dishes by hand, do so in a basin instead of under running water. Otherwise, run a full load in the dishwasher to save water. Don't let the tap run while you brush your teeth, shave, or clean counters. This is also very wasteful.

Main idea (if implied): _____

_____

Paragraph 1: ____	Paragraph 4: ____
Paragraph 2: ____	Paragraph 5: ____
Paragraph 3: ____	Paragraph 6: ____

4.

Early American Flags

(1) Hear someone mention the American flag and you instantly picture white stars on a field of blue and stripes of red and white. And rightly so, since the pattern and colors have been a symbol of the United States for a very long time. The stars and stripes has been in use since the time of the American Revolution. With the admission of new states, stars were added, but the basic flag, with its colors and stripes, is the same today as it was then.

(2) This history of flags in America really begins with the early settlers. As soon as the first colonists settled in America, they created flags of their own. Wide differences in colonies led to a wide variety of flags. Flags at this time were symbols of the colonists' struggles with the wilderness of the new land. Beavers, pine trees, rattlesnakes, anchors, and various other insignia were affixed to different banners with mottoes such as "Hope," "Liberty," "Appeal to Heaven," or "Don't Tread on Me."

(3) In the early days of the Revolution, there were colonial and army regimental flags by the score. The Boston Liberty flag, made up of nine red and white horizontal stripes, flew over the Liberty Tree, a fine old elm in Hanover Square in Boston, where the Sons of Liberty met. Still another was a white flag with a green pine tree and the saying "An Appeal to Heaven." This particular flag became familiar on the seas as the sign on the cruisers commissioned by General George Washington.

(4) Flags with a rattlesnake theme also were popular with colonists. The slogan, "Don't Tread on Me" almost always appeared on rattlesnake flags. A flag of this type was used by the South Carolina Navy. Another, the Gadsden flag, had a yellow field with a rattlesnake in a spiral coil, ready to strike, in the center. Below the snake was the motto, "Don't Tread on Me." Similar was the Culpepper flag, banner of the Minutemen of Culpepper (now spelled Culpeper) County, Virginia. It had a white field with a rattlesnake in a spiral coil in the center. Above the rattlesnake it said "The Culpepper Minute Men" and below, the motto "Liberty or Death" as well as "Don't Tread on Me."

(5) The Moultrie flag was the first really American flag displayed in the South. It flew over the fort on Sullivan's Island, which lies in the channel leading to Charleston, South Carolina. The flag was blue, as were the uniforms of the men of the garrison, and it bore a white crescent (shape of a quarter moon) in the upper corner next to the staff, like the silver crescents the men wore on their caps, inscribed with the words "Liberty or Death."

(6) The Maritime Colony of Rhode Island had its own flag. It bore an anchor, 13 stars, and the word "Hope." Its white stars in a blue field are believed by many to have led to the design of our national flag.

(7) During the Revolution, the Army preferred to use its regimental flags on the battlefield instead of the Stars and Stripes. However, the Army also used the Stars and Stripes with 13 stars in a circle. The Stars and Stripes was officially used in Army artillery units in 1834, and in infantry units in 1842.

Main idea (if implied): _____

_____

Paragraph 1: _____   **Paragraph 5:** _____
Paragraph 2: _____   **Paragraph 6:** _____
Paragraph 3: _____   **Paragraph 7:** _____
Paragraph 4: _____

5. ## How Can You Mend a Broken Heart?

(1) Hey, wait! Don't reach for a whiskey and soda to drown your sorrows. Don't puff a cigarette to soften your hurt. You should know that there are other cures for your broken heart!

(2) The cure for lost love may not be as simple as "Take two aspirins and get plenty of rest," but there are things you can do to get over the depressing breakup period. Zev Wanderer, for example, has some good points in his book, *Letting Go.*

(3) Wanderer claims that people don't grieve enough for their lost love. He suggests that you take out all those photographs and presents that were given to you by your ex-lover. Cry as long as you want over them. You'll get bored. They'll become nothing more than objects.

(4) Many people get excited every time a car that looks like the one driven by their ex-sweetheart passes them on the street. Wanderer suggests taking photographs of every car in the neighborhood that is the same. Then spread all the pictures out. Tell yourself that all of those cars don't belong to him or her. Then just watch when any white T-bird goes by.

(5) While you're at it, write down all your ex's bad habits on a piece of paper. Think about those instead of mooning over that cute smile or those blue eyes.

(6) Sometimes it hurts to return to a favorite restaurant. All the memories keep flooding back. Here you have to use "override." By all means return to the same restaurant. But this time take along a new group of friends. Join in the laughter and joking. Have fun. This will override your memories with new good times.

(7) Do avoid seeing that special person "accidentally on purpose." If you know when he works or she goes to the library on Tuesdays, stay away. Don't be mean to yourself. Work out your day so you run across the person as little as possible.

(8) Finally, the best cure is time. Have faith that someday this chapter of your life will be seen warmly and without pain.

Main idea (if implied): _____

_____

Paragraph 1: _____   Paragraph 5: _____
Paragraph 2: _____   Paragraph 6: _____
Paragraph 3: _____   Paragraph 7: _____
Paragraph 4: _____   Paragraph 8: _____

B. Directions: Find a short selection (at least three paragraphs) and copy it on a copying machine. Attach the selection to this Skill Practice. Number the paragraphs. Show the main idea and details in the selection as you did in Part A above.

CHAPTER 11

Paragraph and Selection Mapping

Some paragraphs and selections may be hard to understand even if you read them several times. You may then ask yourself, "What was that about?" The reason for your problem with this reading material is that the writer may have included so many facts that you may have trouble sorting out the information so that you can understand what the writer is telling you. One way to work with such paragraphs or selections is to use a skill called **mapping**. Mapping is a way of taking paragraphs or selections apart and putting the information in another form—a written picture. Mapping also puts information together to form packages of related information. You can actually see what you need to know. You will be surprised at how clear the information will become. Also, writing the information in the map will help you remember the facts included in paragraphs or selections of any length.

The form of mapped information should look familiar to you. Some of the Summary Sheets in this book are in the form of maps. For example, look at the Summary Sheet on page 289. This is what a map can look like.

You have already done some mapping in Chapter Eight when you worked with umbrella statements. There you checked main ideas by looking at the sentences in the paragraph to see if these details related to that main idea. Then, in Chapter Nine you learned *how* these details relate to a main idea. In Chapter Ten you went beyond single paragraphs to longer selections. Again you worked with main ideas and related details. These three chapters have prepared you for mapping as presented in this chapter. You are ready to go a step further and use mapping when you need a clear picture of all related information that is included in a paragraph or selection. Think of a map as a package of related information.

In this chapter, you will learn how to

1. Identify major and minor details.
2. Map paragraphs.
3. Map selections.

MAJOR AND MINOR DETAILS

A map always begins with the main idea. That main idea may be stated or implied. Information about that main idea is found in related details called **major details.** These major details may be related to the main idea as examples or reasons. Restatements and filler are never included in a map. They do not belong in a package of related information. Restatements have already been said and do not need to be repeated. Filler, as you remember, just takes up space and adds nothing to what you need to know.

When a writer wants you to know specific information about the major details, this information is found in details called **minor details.** Minor details can relate to major details as examples or reasons. Once again, restatements or filler are not included as minor details.

Picture a map as an upside-down triangle. The main idea is at the top, the widest part of the triangle, because it gives the most general information. The major details are in the middle section because they are less general in the information they give about the main idea. The minor details are at the narrowest part of the triangle because they give very specific information about the major details. At times, in selections you might even have very, very specific information about the minor details. Think of these additional minor details as the very point of the triangle.

You worked with the following sample paragraph in Chapter Nine. It is used in the following to show you how to identify major and minor details.

Sample A

> (1) Proper lighting above the bathroom sink is needed for grooming and shaving. (2) It is hard to do a good job of these if your face is only dimly seen in the mirror. (3) In a large bathroom, good overhead lighting is most important. (4) Otherwise, parts of the room will be dark. (5) If the bathroom includes a shower, a second overhead light in or near the stall can be most helpful. (6) A night light should always be set up just inside the bathroom door. (7) If the night light is turned on each evening, your bathroom becomes a safer place.

Implied main idea: There are ways to light a bathroom.

Major Details	Minor Details
(1) Proper lighting above the bathroom sink is needed for grooming and shaving. (example of way to light a bathroom) ⟷	(2) It is hard to do a good job if your face is only dimly seen in the mirror. (reason to support sentence 1)
(3) In a large bathroom, good overhead lighting is most important. (example of way to light a bathroom) ⟷	(4) Otherwise, parts of the room will be dark. (reason to support sentence 3)
(5) If bathroom includes a shower, a second overhead light in or near the stall can be most helpful. (example of way to light a bathroom) ⟷	None
(6) A night light should always be set up just inside the bathroom door. (example of way to light a bathroom) ⟷	(7) If the night light is turned on each evening, your bathroom becomes a safer place. (reason to support sentence 6)

In this sample paragraph, the major details were all examples of the main idea and the minor details were reasons for the major details. This is not always the case. As you found when working with details in Chapter Nine, there is no set pattern of examples or reasons. Also, be aware that some major details may not have minor details to support them. This was true for sentence 5 in this paragraph. The use of different kinds of details depends on the writer's style.

MAPPING A PARAGRAPH

The first step in mapping a paragraph is to use the two important questions you learned in Chapter Eight to find the main idea. Remember that the main idea can be stated or implied. Write this main idea at the top of what will be your map.

Second, identify the major details and write them below the main idea. All of these major details will be example and/or reason details that relate to the main idea of the paragraph. This means that they will supply less general information about that main idea.

Next, identify the minor details that relate to the major details and write them below those major details. These minor details can relate by being examples and/or reasons. This means that they will supply specific information about the major details.

Check your map to be sure that you have not included restatements or filler in your map. They do not belong there because they add nothing to information presented by major and minor details.

Finally, connect the main idea, major details, and minor details with lines that show they are related. You should now be able to see a package of related information that is easier to understand and remember.

Sample B, which follows, will show you the placement of information for a map of the same paragraph in Sample A.

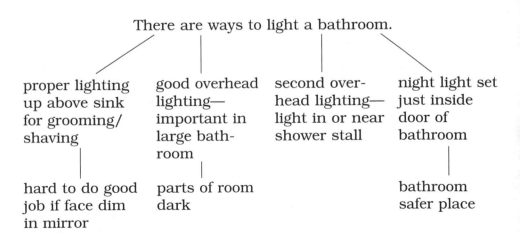

There are ways to light a bathroom.

| proper lighting up above sink for grooming/ shaving | good overhead lighting— important in large bath- room | second over- head lighting— light in or near shower stall | night light set just inside door of bathroom |

| hard to do good job if face dim in mirror | parts of room dark | | bathroom safer place |

Notice that the main idea is written in a complete sentence. The details are written in phrases, so they are very brief. Do not copy the sentences to show details. In some cases you might just use single words to stand for the details. You choose how much information you want to include in a major or minor detail and can use your own words. But be sure that you have not lost the meaning of that detail. Remember that the purpose of mapping is to be able to pick out related information and to be able to see that information at a glance.

Guided Practice 11–1: Mapping a Paragraph

Directions: Use these steps to map the two paragraphs that follow. You worked with both paragraphs in Chapter Eight.

1. *Use the two questions you learned in Chapter Eight to find the stated or implied main idea. Write this main idea at the top of what will be your map.*
2. *Identify the major details. They will give information about the main idea. Write these major details below the main idea.*
3. *Identify the minor details that give information about the major details, and write them below major details to which they relate.*
4. *Connect the main idea, major details, and minor details with lines that show they are related.*
5. *Check to be sure that you do not have restatements or filler any place on your map.*

Paragraph 1

You may be better off working for someone else rather than being boss in your own business. First, your working hours are probably shorter. Think of all the times you have left work while your boss stays behind to finish extra things. Second, you don't have to worry about meeting a payroll. If business is good or bad, you still get your paycheck. Third, you are not the one to take care of major problems. They are turned over to the boss. Finally, you may be happier when someone else is in charge. Not everyone is a leader. Some people are happier as followers.

MAP

Paragraph 2

Cross-country skiers enjoy being alone in forests and fields as they glide on their way. They enjoy the silence and the beauty of the countryside. Downhill skiers enjoy these things, too. But they get more kick from the plunge down a steep trail, showing their skills by mastering whatever springs up on the path. They really enjoy the thrill of going at great speeds.

MAP

MAPPING A SELECTION

Although a selection has much more information than a single paragraph, it is mapped in much the same way.

The first step in mapping a selection is to use the two questions you learned in Chapter Ten to find the main idea. Remember that the main idea can be stated or implied. Write this main idea at the top of what will be your map.

Second, the main idea of each paragraph in the selection will become a major detail. These major details will give related information about the main idea of the selection. Identify these major details and write them below the main idea. They may be example and/or reason details.

Next, the details in each paragraph will be the minor details that relate to the major details. They will give specific information about the major details. They may be example and/or reason details. Identify these minor details and write them below the correct major details.

Check to be sure you do not have restatements or filler in your map. They do not belong there because they add nothing to the package of related information presented by major and minor details. In fact, if included in the map, they may prove to be confusing when you look at the map.

Finally, connect the main idea, major details, and minor details with lines which show that they are related. You should now be able to see a package of related information that is easier to understand and remember than the original selection.

Sample C below should make it easier for you to understand how to map a selection. This is a selection you worked with in Chapter Ten and you may use the information on pages 313 and 314.

Health Claims: Fact vs. Fantasy

(1) Health care may well be the number one interest in America today. Americans are more conscious than ever of the importance of staying healthy. However, on the negative side, this interest in health care has also resulted in the growth of health fraud. In fact, health fraud has become a major cause for concern.

(2) Billions of consumer dollars are wasted on useless remedies and devices. They are spent to purchase products that

promise a "quick and easy cure." Ads for these products use key words such as "miraculous," "exclusive," "secret," or "ancient" and are full of interesting case histories that are too good to be true.

(3) Health fraud is a business that sells false hope. It preys on persons who are victims of diseases such as arthritis, multiple sclerosis, and certain forms of cancer. Medical science in continually seeking cures for these diseases, but this takes time. Meanwhile, dishonest promoters are quick to market useless concoctions and call them medical "breakthroughs."

(4) Other harmful health frauds are those that turn people away from proper medical diagnosis and treatment. Instead, they encourage sick people to try fake products that in themselves may be dangerous. They waste valuable time before getting proper medical attention. That delay may do serious harm and endanger lives.

Sample C

Main idea of selection: Health fraud has become a major cause for concern. (Paragraph 1)

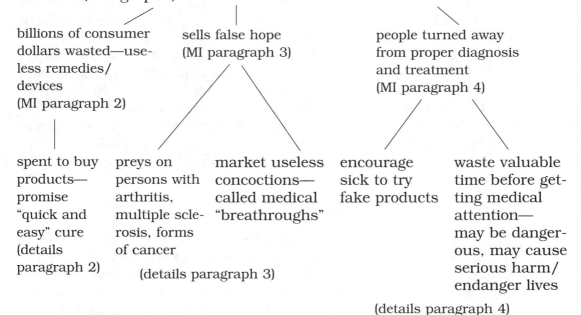

billions of consumer dollars wasted—useless remedies/devices
(MI paragraph 2)

sells false hope
(MI paragraph 3)

people turned away from proper diagnosis and treatment
(MI paragraph 4)

spent to buy products— promise "quick and easy" cure (details paragraph 2)

preys on persons with arthritis, multiple sclerosis, forms of cancer

market useless concoctions— called medical "breathroughs"

(details paragraph 3)

encourage sick to try fake products

waste valuable time before getting medical attention— may be dangerous, may cause serious harm/endanger lives

(details paragraph 4)

Notice that this writer has used her own words to reduce the information in both the major and minor details. If you had mapped this selection, the wording might have been slightly different. In paragraphs 3 and 4 there are two important details that needed to be included. They are placed side by side under the major details to which they relate. You can now see all of the important information in the selection. It should be easier to understand and remember what you have read in that selection.

Guided Practice 11–2: Mapping a Selection

Directions: Use these steps to map the two selections below. You worked with both selections in Chapter Ten and you may use the information on pages 310 and 322.

1. *Identify the main idea of the selection. It may be stated or implied. Write this main idea at the top of what will be your map.*
2. *Identify the major details. They will be the stated or implied main idea of each paragraph in the selection. Write these major details below the main idea.*
3. *Identify the minor details that relate to the major details. They will be the important information found in each paragraph in the selection. Write these minor details below the major details to which they relate.*
4. *Connect the main idea, major details, and minor details with lines that show they are related.*
5. *Check to be sure that you do not have restatements or filler any place on your map.*

Selection 1

How to Be a Water Miser

(1) Water is something we can't afford to waste. Trying to save water does make a difference. You may be surprised at how much you can save in your own home. You must simply find and limit water wasters.

(2) The average shower uses 3 gallons of water a minute. A filled tub has 25 gallons per bath. A dishwasher uses about 21 gallons per load. And a toilet uses between 5 and 7 gallons with each flush.

(3) To save water, put something in your faucets and shower to make water pressure go up as it cuts the flow of water in half. Some shower units allow you to turn the water off while you soap up. Then, when you turn the water back on, it is the right temperature.

(4) Keep showers short—about 5 minutes. To get children to hurry, have them take showers during breaks in their favorite TV shows. When taking baths, fill the tub only halfway.

(5) Cut down on the amount of water used with each toilet flush. Fill a plastic bleach bottle with water and stone to weigh it down. Place it in the tank. The bottle should be out of the way of moving parts.

(6) If you wash dishes by hand, do so in a basin instead of under running water. Otherwise, run a full load in the dishwasher to save water. Don't let the tap run while you brush your teeth, shave, or clean counters. This is also very wasteful.

MAP

Selection 2

Floors

(1) Have you noticed what has happened to floors in recent years? There are now many different kinds of floors from which to choose. Buyers are limited only by cost and their own tastes. Gone are the days when most homes had hardwood floors.

(2) Varnished, waxed, or oiled wood floors should never be washed. Varnished floors keep their color and shine best if no water is used on them. Very dirty floors may be wiped with a damp cloth. Then dry and polish with an oiled cloth or mop. A wood floor that doesn't get much wear needs waxing only two or three times a year. It is a mistake to use too much wax.

(3) To clean linoleum floors, use water mixed with mild soap or detergent. Don't overwet the floor. When the floor is dry, put on wax in a thin, even film. Never use anything harsher than fine steel wool to remove spots.

(4) Wash asphalt tile floors only after they have been in place for about two weeks. It is important to allow the tiles to set. In the meantime, wipe the floor with a slightly damp mop. Use soap or detergent and water. Asphalt tile floors should be waxed after washing.

MAP (or use page 338)

SKILL PRACTICE: MAPPING PARAGRAPHS AND SELECTIONS

A. Directions: Use the five steps presented on pages 331 and 333 in this chapter to map the following paragraph and selection.

Evidence given by a witness in a court case is often called "eye-witness" evidence. This is putting it too simply. Direct evidence is really the product of all five of a person's senses. Thus, sight, touch, taste, smell, and hearing should all be included as direct evidence. The person who saw the accused pulling a revolver from his belt is giving direct eyewitness testimony. Had he also testified "I heard three shots," he would be giving an example of direct "ear-witness" testimony. The person who testifies "It smelled like smoke" is a nose-witness. And the person who testifies "I felt his wrist and got no pulse" is a touch-witness. "It tasted like bitter almonds" is, of course, an example of direct evidence based on the witness's sense of taste.

MAP

Stress in the Workplace

Employers pay attention when problems in the workplace begin to affect the company's profits. A serious problem that results in both human and money losses is stress in the workplace. Stress is probably present in any job. However, the stress can be reduced if the company tries to lessen it. Today, more and more companies are making major efforts to reduce stress in the workplace.

Company fitness programs are the most popular method used to deal with stress in the workplace. These programs may be company-sponsored walking and jogging groups, aerobics, or exercise classes. Workers are also encouraged to use community or company fitness centers where special equipment is available.

Another company approach to stress in the workplace is to try to reduce mental stress by offering special benefits to its workers. These benefits include counseling (both personal and family), programs for weight reduction, cigarette smoking, alcohol, and drug abuse. The increased use of flextime, in which employees can choose their working hours, is another kind of stress reduction benefit.

MAP

B. Directions: Choose a paragraph and a selection from any reading material. The selection should have at least three paragraphs. Copy the paragraph and selection on a copy machine and attach them to this Skill Practice. Use your skills to map both the paragraph and selection below.

PARAGRAPH MAP

SELECTION MAP

Fighting Oil Well Fires

In August 1990, Iraqi armed forces invaded the country of
Kuwait and would not leave. The United States and twenty other
countries, under the guidance of the United Nations, began the Gulf
War on January 16, 1991. After a short war, the defeated Iraqis left
Kuwait. But before they left, they set Kuwait's oil fields on fire.
Special firefighters rushed to Kuwait to put out these fires.

Some of the special firefighters worked for the Red Adair
Company, Inc. This company was founded by a man who has fought
oil well fires all over the world. This selection tells about Red Adair
and how oil well fires can be brought under control.

Far down in an oil well, great pressure begins to build. Oil is
pushed through the pipe and up against the derrick at the top of
the well. Suddenly, part of the derrick gives way. The oil flows out
of control and shoots into the air. Chunks of rock and windblown
sand strike the metal derrick, causing sparks that set off an explosion. The well turns into a giant torch.

Oil company crews may try to put out the fire. But the flames
are often too hot. Nothing works. What do they do? They often call
Red Adair.

Paul "Red" Adair is a special kind of firefighter. He is president
of Red Adair Company, Inc., in Houston, Texas. Red and his seven-

man team fight dangerous blowouts and well fires all over the world.

An oil or gas well fire starts with a blowout. A blowout happens when oil spurts out of control in a well. One small spark can turn a blowout into a raging fire.

Red's job is to put out the fire and then get the well back into operation. Most firefighters use hoses to spray water on a fire. But water won't put out an oil fire. So Red's team must use special methods. They clear the well of broken machinery. Then they wrap explosives in fireproof material and attach them to the end of a long metal pole. They lower the explosives over the well and set them off. The blast usually blows out the fire.

Once the fire is out, the Adair team tries to stop the flow of oil. First, they replace the broken machinery on the well. Using brass tools, which don't cause sparks, they install shut-off fixtures, called valves. The men work carefully and quickly. One mistake could start another fire.

If the new machinery doesn't stop the blowout, the team may pump drilling mud into the well. Drilling mud is a mixture of heavy clay, water, and chemicals that can force the oil back down into the well. The weight of the mud is greater than the pressure of the oil.

Once the blowout is brought under control, the oil crew makes other repairs. Then the well can operate normally again.

Red has been working with fires since he was a child. His father was a blacksmith. Red's job was to keep the fire going in the forge.

During World War II, Red worked as a member of an Army bomb squad. The experience was helpful when he went to work fighting oil and gas well fires. He found that explosives often put out a fire when no other methods worked.

Throughout his career, Adair has never had a failure. No blowout or fire has been too much for him. He has had some close calls. Once a bulldozer hit him and broke his hips. Doctors said he probably would never walk normally again. But four months later, he was back on the job. Another time, a protective suit he was trying out began to shrink in the heat and almost smothered him before he could get it off.

Is Red ever afraid? He says he isn't. "As long as you know your job, your equipment, and the people you're working with, you feel safe. Then you can get the job done."

Directions: Use a separate sheet of paper to answer the following questions and to write your reaction to the selection.

1. What happens to an oil well when the oil flows out of control?

2. If oil company crews can't put out a fire in an oil well, what might they do?

3. Who is "Red" Adair?

4. An oil or gas well fire starts with a blowout. What is a *blowout*?

5. What are the two parts to Red's job?

6. The selection tells you that Red's team must use special methods. In a general way, what are *methods*?

7. What must be brought under control before a well can be used again?

8. How did Red get experience working with fire as a child?

9. What experience did Red have in World War II that helped him to fight oil and gas well fires?

10. From what you have read in this selection, how do you know that Red is good at what he does?

YOUR REACTION: After reading this selection, would you describe Red as a very brave man? Defend your answer in one or two paragraphs.

Water Over the Dam

Frank E. Heard

We all make mistakes. And sometimes those mistakes come back to haunt us years after they have happened. This selection is about a man who made a very big mistake, paid for that mistake, and went on to change his life, only to find that new life in danger.

I had no idea what would greet me that day. My work for a large printing company keeps me on the road a lot. I was driving behind a school bus on a dusty country road, thinking about nothing more than the good dinner I hoped to enjoy after one more call.

The yellow bus ahead slowed, its flashing red lights indicated a stop at the next side road. I put on the brakes and ground to a halt a few yards behind.

I watched the driver climb down. He unfolded a wheelchair, set it down at the bus door, and climbed back into the bus. He then reappeared, a thickset man, carrying a frail-looking girl in his arms. Lowering her gently into the wheelchair, he smiled and patted the child awkwardly on the head. The little girl looked up and smiled her thanks.

I frowned as I watched the episode. Where have I seen that fellow before? I wondered. Then I dismissed the thought from my mind as the bus pulled away from the intersection.

I moved into the passing lane, and as I passed the slower-moving bus, I glanced toward it. I saw the driver looking back at me with a funny look. I thought I detected a flash of recognition in his face.

Where *have* I seen that chap before? The question gnawed at me all the way into Dorchester.

As I drove down the main street of the small town, I noticed several school buses in front of a garage. Pulling over to the curb, I got out and strolled over to a group of drivers chatting together after completing their runs.

I approached the nearest man.

"Say, Mac," I said. "I just passed a school bus down the road, and I think I may know the guy driving it. White hair, ruddy face, rather stocky. Would you know his name?"

The man rubbed his chin slowly. "Sounds like you might mean Sam Jackson," he said.

"Sam Jackson? Doesn't ring a bell. Has he lived around here long?"

"Must be close on to 15 years now. Don't rightly know where he came from before that—say, here comes Sam now! You can ask him yourself."

I turned as a bus swung off the dusty street and pulled up beside us. The door opened, and the white-haired driver climbed down.

"Hi, Jeff!" He greeted the other man with a grin.

"Hello Sam. Say, feller here wants to talk to you. Thinks he knows you from somewhere."

Jackson turned and looked at me sharply, his friendly expression turning to a scowl.

I stuck out my hand. "I'm sure I know you, don't I, Sam?"

"You don't know me, and I don't know you, mister!" Jackson's face was grim as he turned away. Ignoring my outstretched hand, he walked quickly across the street to a small coffee shop. Without a backward glance, he pushed open the door and vanished inside.

I stared at him, shrugging my shoulders.

"That sure ain't like Sam Jackson to behave thataway," said Jeff. "Can't be feeling too good today. Best-natured feller in the world—good driver too. Never misses a run. Got the best safety record in the gang."

I walked over to the coffee shop and went inside. Jackson sat at the counter, his eyes downcast. Taking a stool next to him, I ordered a cup of coffee.

"Sam," I said, turning to him, "please forgive my curiosity. I thought I knew you, but I guess I was wrong."

"Guess so," said Jackson curtly, staring straight ahead.

As Jackson lifted his cup, I glanced at his hand. I stared. That ring! It was the same as my own, presented years ago for winning the high school conference football title back in Ridgeville!

Now it all fell into place. "Sorry, Rocky," I murmured softly, sliding from the stool. "See you around."

"Wait a minute! What did you call me?" Jackson turned quickly and grabbed my arm. He glared as I gently broke his grip.

"Let's sit over there." I motioned to an empty booth against the wall. Jackson followed me and sat down heavily.

I leaned forward. "I called you Rocky because you are—or used to be—Rocky Bellingham. Right?"

"OK, Duke, you've nailed me—figured you probably knew me when you passed the bus. I sure recognized you."

"But, why—?" I gestured helplessly.

"Look, will you do me a big favor?" He suddenly looked old. "If I tell you why I'm living here under a new name, will you forget you ever saw me?"

I was shocked by the look on his face.

"Sure, sure—if that's the way you want it." I looked at the bus driver questioningly.

"OK. You remember me back in the old days in Ridgeville, eh? A pretty wild kid—hot rodder, fighter, hard to control even on the team. Ran with a tough gang after high school."

"Yeah, I remember."

"Well, I left town to see more of the bright lights—Detroit. Tied in with a wild bunch. Started boozing real heavy, dope—the whole bit."

"One night after a session in some bar I figured I could still drive. I couldn't. I—I hit a kid." Jackson's face grayed and he swallowed convulsively. "I panicked and ran. The kid died. They picked me up—hit-and-run and drunken driving. I did five years." He swallowed again.

"I had a lot of time to think in the pen. Well, that's the story. I moved out here when I got out. Been living here over 15 years and stayed out of trouble. Nobody here knows about my record."

He looked at me anxiously. "I like it here, Duke."

I smiled, "All right Rocky," I said quietly. "As far as I'm concerned, it's all water over the dam."

I stood up.

"Sorry, Mr. Jackson," I said loudly. "I was sure I knew you but I guess I had you mixed up with someone else. So long!"

I never saw him again.

Directions: Use a separate sheet of paper to answer the following questions and to write your reaction to the selection.

1. Why is the writer of this selection on the road a lot?

2. When did the writer first think he knew the bus driver?

3. The writer says that a question gnawed at him. What does *gnawed* mean in this context?

4. Why did Sam Jackson act the way he did toward the writer at the garage?

5. What did Jeff, the man in the garage, tell the writer about Sam Jackson?

6. How did the writer finally know who Jackson was?

7. Who was Sam Jackson?

8. When Jackson told his story, his face grayed and he swallowed convulsively. What does *convulsively* mean in this context?

9. Jackson said he had "a lot of time to think in the pen." ("Pen" is slang.) What does *pen* mean in this context?

10. How do you know that Jackson's secret will be kept?

YOUR REACTION: Do you agree with the way Duke treated Sam Jackson at the end of this selection? Defend your answer in one or two paragraphs.

READING SELECTION 3

Do You Have the Time?

Students often complain that they are short of two important things: money and time. While you can get more money in any number of ways, time cannot be increased. There are twenty-four hours each day and that is it. Although you cannot add to the number of hours, you can increase what you do in those hours. This selection will let you in on some ways to make the most of your time.

An old saying tells us that if you want something done, ask a busy person to do it. Surely, you have met busy people who are able to do more in one day than the rest of us and, all the while, they remain calm. The key to their success is organization. Such organization does not mean becoming like a robot, marching in lock step through your day. It does mean organizing your time through use of an action plan, organizing your study times, and organizing your materials. Like so many students who have tried the following suggestions and found that they work, you will be able to do more with the time you have.

DEVELOP AN ACTION PLAN

The first step in organizing your time is to develop an action plan that will help you to use time in the best way. You will need a form like the following printed one. Since you need to write on it, draw one that is larger or have this one enlarged on a copy machine.

Time	Mon.	Tues.	Wed.	Thurs.	Fri.	Sat.	Sun.

Begin your action plan by filling in the times of day in the left-hand column. Start at the top with the time you get up in the morning, and fill in the hours until you usually go to bed at night.

You are now ready to develop your action plan. Write three important kinds of activities on your action plan.

1. Definites

Definites include everything you definitely *must* do. They include class times, work times, personal duties, and any other tasks you must do at a set time.

2. Study Times

Study times are set aside for all the work you must do for your classes. This may include studying textbook chapters, working on research papers, completing projects, reading assigned books, and so forth.

When you plan your study times, consider the following suggestions:

- Try to plan study times just before or after a class. If you study before class, you will be better prepared for what will happen there and you will learn more. If you study right after class, you will strengthen what you have just learned, making it easier for you to remember.

- Schedule study times for when you work best. Some people are day people who rise early and go to bed early. They have the most energy early in the morning, so that is when they do their best work. Night people, on the other hand, rise late and go to bed late. They work best late in the day. Decide on your best time to work, and plan to study then. If you are a day person you will get as little from late study times as a night person will get from early morning study.

- At the beginning of a course, you will not know how much time to plan for study. For the time being, set aside at least one hour for each course that will require outside work. With experience, you will find that one hour is either too little or too much time. You can then adjust study times to suit your own needs.

- Shade in your study times on the action plan. In this way, they stand out from the rest of your schedule. They let you know that it is now time to get down to the hard work of being a student.

3. Leisure-Time Activities

If you plan to fill every possible hour of the week with some school-related activity, you will soon be tired, bored, or both. Plan for some hours, or even a day if possible, during the weekend when you can relax and enjoy yourself. This is time well spent. You will start the new week refreshed and ready to go.

After you have written your "definites," study times, and leisure-time activities on the action plan, go back and check what you have scheduled. Analyze the way you will spend each week. Ask yourself if you can follow this plan. Any plan that cannot be easily followed is useless—get rid of it and develop a new plan that works for you. Keep an important fact in mind: An action plan is not etched in stone. It can, and should, be changed as your life or your needs change.

ORGANIZE YOUR STUDY TIMES

Add up the number of hours you will spend studying. If you are like most students, you will find that you must spend many such hours if you are to do well. To get the most benefit from study times, it helps to organize them. Carefully select what you must do in each study period. This involves the use of a priority system. How do you know which assignments should be given top priority during a study time? Use a calendar that can be inserted in your looseleaf notebook.

Buy a monthly calendar that has boxes large enough to write in. First, enter all of the important school and personal dates in the proper months. Carry the calendar with you to classes. Write in all assignments and exam dates as soon as they are mentioned by the instructor. Write them in the boxes that show when they are due. Now you can see at a glance what you must prepare for on any given day in an entire month. It is now possible to decide which assignments should be given priority over others. You will be using your study time according to your own needs.

Now that you know what you are going to study, be realistic in your idea of how much you can do in any given study time. If you set your goals too high, you will never reach them. You will probably feel defeated before you begin to work. In time, you will learn with experience how much you can really expect of yourself. Adjust your study time goals accordingly.

Try to find a quiet place to study. You will find that it is easier to get down to studying when you use the same place all of the time. It is as though your mind is ready to get down to work. Keep all your study supplies in this place. You don't want to interrupt what you are doing to sharpen a pencil or go out to the store to buy supplies in the middle of studying—it takes too long to get back into what you were doing before the interruption.

ORGANIZE YOUR COURSE MATERIALS

Part of managing your time involves organizing your materials. If you have ever spent time looking for that lost sheet of paper an instructor said you'd better study for an exam, you know how upsetting it can be. And what a waste of time, too.

Instructors usually give handouts to students during a course. These may include the course syllabus, or outline, study guide, and other information the instructor wants students to have in addition to the assigned textbook. Keep these handouts with your class notes. You should also keep exams as they are returned to you. You can then review and analyze these exams. They can be very useful when studying for future exams. All of these course materials need to be kept together and handy for use. In other words, they need to be kept in an organized way.

It is easy to organize your course materials if you use a loose-leaf notebook system. First, buy a good-sized looseleaf notebook and paper to fit. Use separators to mark off a section for each course you are taking. Label the section so you can find it quickly and easily. Second, invest in a hole puncher and use it on all materials given out in class and anything else related to that course. File everything in its proper section. Now you have only a single notebook to take to class or to use during your study times—one that has everything you might need.

This simple notebook system gives you more than just organization. It is a flexible system. You can add handouts or take out an entire section to study. If you miss a class, you can still keep your notes in order by date. Just insert a copy of what you have missed in its proper place.

Finally, be sure that you have enough pens, pencils, and other supplies or materials you will need for class. Don't waste your time and the time of another person from whom you are trying to borrow materials in class.

The title of this reading selection asks the question "Do You Have the Time?" Try the suggestions that have been offered here. Then you should be able to answer this question with a loud and definite **YES**.

READING SELECTION 3: QUESTIONS

Directions: Use a separate sheet of paper to answer the following questions and to write your reaction to the selection.

1. According to this selection, what is the first step in organizing your time?

2. What are the "definites" that need to be written into an action plan?

3. Why is it important to shade in your study times?

4. Why should you schedule leisure time in your action plan?

5. The selection tells you to analyze your action plan. In this context, what does *analyze* mean?

6. How can you keep your action plan up to date?

7. You are told to use a priority system to select what must be done in a study time. As used here, what is a *priority system*?

8. When should you mark assignments on your monthly calendar?

9. What are two advantages of the notebook system?

10. Why is it important to have all the supplies and materials you need with you in class?

YOUR REACTION: Think about the suggestions offered for organizing time, study, and materials. In one or two paragraphs, describe how you see yourself best applying these suggestions.

How Close Is Too Close?

Michael S. Quinton

Recently, there have been a number of cases of bears attacking people. Victims of such attacks have appeared on television or had their stories published in newspapers and magazines. Even though they were badly mauled, all felt they had been very lucky to be spared from a horrible death.

This selection tells about one man's meeting with a grizzly bear and his experience with a strange kind of animal behavior.

The dark grizzly was munching crowberries when I blundered over a rise and surprised him and myself. Mistake! His hair stood up, and he walked toward me on stiff legs in a fierce way.

I sidled away slowly, trying to keep some distance between us. We went across a river bar about 100 feet apart. I muttered, "Keep cool!"

But then the bear lay down, rested his head on his paws, and closed his eyes. Puzzled, I stopped and stood there looking at him. My curiosity overcame my carefulness. I even took a few steps toward him. That could easily have been my last mistake.

I'm a wildlife photographer and I live in Idaho. When what I just described took place, I was in Alaska's Denali National Park trying to photograph grizzlies at very close range. After I took the photographs, I decided that no one should ever do what I did. I risked my life. And if I had been attacked, park rangers might have been forced to risk their lives to save me.

However, I learned something while taking those photographs that could be of great use to anyone who comes into close contact with a grizzly. In my two weeks at Denali, I met many bears. They supported an important idea about animal behavior. In recent years, biologists have come up with the idea of "displacement behavior." It holds that many animals have two completely opposite drives. One drive is fierce and the other is peaceful. An animal may be torn between making an attack and backing off from possible danger. Because it can't decide, it may go from outright fierce behavior to meek actions such as lying down, seemingly to sleep. This kind of behavior was shown by the bear I described before. Unsure whether to attack or not, he lay down and even closed his eyes.

Shortly afterward, however, he came out of his seeming sleep and angled toward me. His inborn drive to defend his land was overcoming his wish for peace and quiet. I stood up and backed away, but his step quickened into springy lunges. I couldn't outrun him, so I stood still facing him. At 40 feet, he charged. I threw one arm into the air in a traffic policeman's stop signal and yelled "Yo!" at the top of my lungs. It sounded loud, and startled me just as much as it did the bear. He skidded to a stop just 10 feet away. The bear was growling and grinding his teeth. Then the grizzly walked away, back toward the berry bushes. But he looked back at me a few times.

Understanding displacement behavior is important to anyone who deals with wild animals. If a seemingly fierce animal suddenly changes his behavior (such as stopping to graze or eat berries), don't think that the danger is over. Peacefulness may be suddenly displaced by an all-out drive to kill.

I saw many examples of what I think was displacement behavior. I remember that one bear came toward me at a fast trot with his nose high and his ears up to find out more about me. The closer he came, the madder he became until his ears were laid back and his hair was standing on end. At 20 yards, he stopped, sniffed, and then rolled on his back and began to scratch himself. He wanted to be elsewhere just as much as I did. Jumping up, he ran away until he came to a small bush. As though to remind me that he was boss, he tore the bush from the ground.

I came upon that same bear a few days later and sat down near him. He knew that I was there. But he seemed to ignore me.

He listened and sniffed. He pounced and swept up a mouse. He gulped it down, and then he charged straight at me. Fortunately, I wasn't the only living thing in his path. Before I could yell, a bird exploded from the grass under the bear's nose. I'm still not sure if he was after me or the bird. The bear hit the brakes when it flew.

Looking back at the danger I was in while making those photographs, the fate of Alan Lee Precup is often on my mind. In 1976, he went to Glacier Bay National Monument to photograph bears. Rangers found a few remains and grizzly bear tracks. They recovered his camera and one of the last exposures showed a big grizzly. My advice to anyone who wants to photograph grizzlies is to take up another hobby.

READING SELECTION 4: QUESTIONS

Directions: Use a separate sheet of paper to answer the following questions and to write your reaction to the selection.

1. The writer starts out by telling how he met a bear. How did this bear act when he was first surprised by the writer?

2. The writer says that he sidled away slowly trying to keep distance between himself and the bear. What does *sidled* mean in this context?

3. What did the writer do that he felt no one should ever do?

4. What is *displacement behavior?*

5. An animal can go from fierce behavior to meek actions. What are *meek* actions? Give one example of a meek action.

6. How did the bear described in the first part of the article show displacement behavior?

7. Why is it important for anyone who deals with wild animals to understand displacement behavior?

8. There is an example of displacement behavior in which an angry bear stopped 20 yards from the writer. How did this bear then show that he was boss?

9. Why did Alan Lee Precup's fate bother the writer?

10. Why does the writer advise anyone who wants to photograph grizzlies to take up another hobby?

YOUR REACTION: Imagine yourself as the author of this selection. Write one or two paragraphs that describe how you would have felt as the bear showed different kinds of displacement behavior.

"It's the Books that Changed Me"

Peter Swet

Sean Connery, as James Bond and in some other film roles, seems to be a man who has always been wealthy and well-polished. Also, you most likely see him as a well-educated man. While Sean Connery is now wealthy, elegant, and well-read, it was not always so. You will probably be surprised as you read this selection to learn about his background and how Sean Connery says he changed his life.

As a young boy in Scotland, Thomas Sean Connery was put to bed each night in the bottom drawer of the family wardrobe. "When my brother Neil came along," he remembered, "he got the wardrobe, and I graduated to the settee (small sofa)."

Connery was recalling Edinburgh during the Depression. "There was a lot of industry there, and every house had coal, so there was also a lot of smoke. We lived in a tenement—no electricity or hot water, six floors up with four flats per floor, and one hallway toilet for each two flats. My dad was a laborer who brought in £2 [$10] a week and was glad to have it."

We were seated in the garden of a hotel in Marbella, Spain, a resort on the Costa del Sol that is known for its gleaming white buildings, warm sun, and soft Mediterranean breezes. At 61, Sean Connery was still fit, trim, and handsome—even without the toupee he often wears in films. A major international star since he first created a sensation as James Bond in 1962, the actor has a home in Marbella, another in Monaco, and yet a third in the Caribbean. I wanted to know how he had escaped the mean streets of a poor, smoke-filled neighborhood to become what is, for many, an example of wealth, fame, and elegance. Had he known, as a child, that he was poor?

"No, I don't think so," Connery said. "As a kid, you're not concerned about life's unfairness or how disadvantaged you are. You just do what you have to. Me, I went to work when I was 9 and delivered milk by horse cart seven days a week. I was at the job 6 A.M., then straight to school, which I left at age 12. It was 1943. The war was on, and schools were dispersed into people's homes because of the bombs. And there was a shortage of men, which meant work to be had."

His earnings went to the family, with Connery's "mum" setting aside just enough for his expenses. Meanwhile, "Big Tam," as he was called by pals, grew tall and strong, devoting what little free time he had to soccer and swimming at the public baths—"which you did often," he explained, "just to keep clean."

"I grew up with no notion of a career, much less acting," Connery continued with a smile. "When I was 16, I signed into the Navy for 12 years but was out in three because of ulcers. Obviously, I wasn't suited for the service. I mean, someone who gets ulcers has got certain feelings of anxiety. I wanted something to do in life but didn't know what, so I came back to various laborer jobs, then learned that as a disabled vet I was entitled to schooling to learn a trade: barber, upholsterer, tailor, or French polisher. I chose the latter, which meant putting the finishes on things like pianos and coffins."

One day in 1953, a friend talked him into going down to London to enter the Mr. Universe contest. The trip proved to be fateful. Not only did Connery place third in the tall men's category, but he also was told about auditions at the Drury Lane Theatre for the male chorus in *South Pacific*. "I thought, 'What the hell, it's an easy way to make a living for a few hours' work,'" he recalled. "Well, I got on stage and sang good and loud, and did some handstands. I must've looked right as a sailor, because I got the job, and that's what started me as an actor."

"This American in the cast, Robert Henderson, helped me," Connery continued. "Gave me a list of books to read." He started ticking off the works: "All of George Bernard Shaw, *An Actor*

Prepares and *My Life in Art,* by Stanislavsky, all of Thomas Wolfe, all of Oscar Wilde, all of Ibsen, *Remembrance of Things Past,* by Proust, Joyce's *Finnegan's Wake* and *Ulysses.*:

What was it like to face these masterworks as a 22-year-old who hadn't been to school since he was 12? "Well, it was tough going!" he said. "But the power of those works does seep through. Plus, I had a dictionary at my side." Connery laughed, his face turning bright red. "I spent my *South Pacific* tour in every library in Britain, Ireland, Scotland, and Wales," he said, "and on the nights we were dark, I'd see every play I could, meet the actors and learn. But it's the books, the reading, that can change one's life. I'm the living evidence."

READING SELECTION 5: QUESTIONS

Directions: Use a separate sheet of paper to answer the following questions and to write your reaction to the selection.

1. What did you read about Sean Connery's early life that tells you he was very, very poor?

2. Connery's youth is compared with his present life. How would you describe Connery today?

3. Connery is described as handsome even without the toupee he often wears in films. As used in this context, what is a *toupee*?

4. Why did Connery leave school at age 12?

5. Why did Connery use the public baths in the way that he did?

6. Why did Connery leave the navy after 3 years instead of the 12 years he had planned on?

7. How did Connery get to learn a trade?

8. What was Connery's first acting job?

9. What happened on that job that changed Connery's life?

10. Connery says it was tough to face the masterworks he read. In this context, what are *masterworks*?

YOUR REACTION: Sean Connery says that reading can change one's life and that he is the "living evidence." Write one or two paragraphs describing what you think he means by that statement.

Practice Makes Perfect

Patricia Barnes Svarney

Sometimes we get so used to events in our lives that we stop thinking of them as being very special. In this way, we have come to accept air travel and missions into space. We tend to forget all that goes into these events that make them happen. This selection tells about the preparation of pilots and astronauts for their journeys far above the earth.

Astronauts cannot fly or try out for the Space Shuttle before they go into space; they have to train while the spacecraft is on the ground. But how do they practice liftoffs, maneuvers in space, and landings? By using an invention called the flight simulator.

We all know what practice means. We practice to play a musical instrument, or even when we want to learn how to ride a bike. Pilots and astronauts have to practice long and hard to fly their craft. And to do this, they use a simulator.

What is a simulator? It is a mock-up or model of the inside of a plane or spacecraft. All the buttons, dials, and switches are exactly like the ones on the real plane or spacecraft—but the machine never leaves the ground! To make the mock-up as accurate as possible, a computer is used to create the sights a pilot would see during an actual flight.

Simulators are mounted on special stands that can make the mock-ups move, twist, and turn much like real spacecraft and planes. This allows astronauts and pilots to practice "flying" many long hours and to get used to how the craft feels.

A BETTER IDEA

The simulator was developed many years ago by inventor and scientist Edwin Albert Link, Jr. Link was born in Huntington, Indiana, in 1904. He was always interested in flying. As a young man, Link took flying lessons. He realized that there was something wrong with learning how to fly: The only way to "practice" was in the air, watching the more experienced pilots at the controls.

The inventor soon found a better way to train pilots. Using parts of an organ from his father's piano manufacturing company, Link built the first simulator in Binghamton, New York, in 1927.

Simulators became important for pilots during World War II. The mock-ups of airplanes were called "blue boxes" because they were painted blue. Simulators helped train over half a million fliers. And today, most pilots who fly airplanes, helicopters, and jets have trained in simulators.

Simulators have been used in the space program almost from the beginning. Gemini, Apollo, Skylab, Spacelab, and Space Shuttle crews have all trained in simulators.

Astronauts who rode to the Moon and back in the Apollo command modules first trained in the Apollo simulator. The three Apollo mock-ups used for practice were the largest and most complex training simulators ever built—each was 9 meters (30 feet) high and weighed over 40 tons!

Along with the Apollo command modules went the LEMs—the lunar excursion modules—that landed on the Moon. In order to land the LEMs on the moon, astronauts had to practice. And of course, they trained in the LEM simulator.

SIMULATORS TO THE RESCUE

Perhaps the most famous simulator story involved the *Apollo 13* mission to the Moon. Launched on April 11, 1970, *Apollo 13* was to have been the third lunar landing mission. Two days into the mission, astronaut John Swigert radioed Mission Control:

"O.K., Houston, we've had a problem here." An explosion in an oxygen tank had left the spacecraft with little power, heat, or water.

For the next four days, astronauts back on Earth used the Apollo simulators to work out a plan to bring *Apollo 13* safely home. Hour after hour, the Earth-bound astronauts practiced the maneuvers. After the tests were completed in the simulators, they relayed the information to the *Apollo 13* crew. On April 17, the *Apollo 13* command module splashed down safely in the Atlantic Ocean.

The first Space Shuttle simulator was "flown" by many of the astronauts. Before the first Shuttle flight in 1981, crew members John Young and Robert Crippen each spent more than 1,300 hours practicing in the Shuttle simulator! "We had a thousand landings in the simulator and the vehicle flies just like the simulator," said astronaut Young after flying the real Space Shuttle *Columbia*.

The Space Shuttle has more than 2,000 separate displays and controls. In order to learn which switch to turn or button to push, the astronauts need to practice. The Shuttle simulator looks just like the real Shuttle cockpit, and even its motions, scenes, and sounds are realistic. The only thing missing is zero gravity.

The main reason for training in a simulator is simple: safety. Practice does make perfect. Practice in a simulator sharpens skills and reflexes. It helps astronauts and pilots fly better and prepares them to handle almost any situation—without ever leaving the ground!

Directions: Use a separate sheet of paper to answer the following questions and to write your reaction to the selection.

1. What is a flight *simulator*?

2. Why is the flight simulator an important part of astronaut training?

3. What has been done to make simulator training as realistic as possible?

4. How do pilots and astronauts practice "flying" and getting used to how their crafts feel?

5. Why did Link invent the simulator?

6. What does pilot training for airplanes, jets, and helicopter's have in common?

7. Why has the space program used simulators from its very beginning?

8. The selection states that astronauts and pilots practice maneuvers on the simulator. As used in this context, what are *maneuvers*?

9. What two kinds of simulators were used to train astronauts who went to the Moon?

10. How did the Apollo simulators help to bring *Apollo 13* safely back to Earth?

YOUR REACTION: Imagine yourself as an astronaut in training. Based on what you learned in this selection, write one or two paragraphs describing your reactions to your training on simulators.

Walnut Canyon: Then and Now

The canyon and the buildings look as they did about 800 years ago. You feel as though you have gone back in time to when this canyon was alive with people and their activities. You are visiting Walnut Canyon National Monument, the former home of the Sinagua (See-NAH-wah) Indians, seven miles from Flagstaff, Arizona. In this selection you will find out about the Sinagua and how they lived.

The wind howls through the empty canyon. Other than the sound of the wind, there is silence. This was not always so. Sounds of people once echoed from the walls of Walnut Canyon. It was here, in north central Arizona, that the Sinagua Indians made their homes.

The Sinagua arrived at Walnut Canyon about 800 years ago. They brought with them new ideas and skills. These came from the exchange of ideas and customs with other friendly tribes. The Sinagua came with a special new skill: masonry. They put it to use in building more than 300 small cliff rooms in caves within the canyon's limestone walls. They simply extended their houses into these caves. Thus, the Sinagua gained protection from the weather and possibly from other tribes.

But Walnut Canyon offered the Sinagua more than cozy home-sites. A dependable supply of water flowed along the streambed on the floor of the canyon. Fertile soil lay within two miles of both rims of the canyon. A great variety of trees, for fuel and implements, grew within the canyon and on the mesa. Other wild plants, a source of food and medicines, lined the banks of the stream and blanketed the slopes. Game, furred and feathered, haunted canyon and mesa top.

The Sinagua made the canyon a place of activity. On a spring morning 800 years ago, the scene might have looked something like this: Six girls, carrying clay pots filled with water, pause at the rim of the canyon to gasp for breath. They have just climbed up the steep trail from the stream. After a few minutes of rest, they continue on the trail to the fields.

Men and women stop their work with digging sticks as they notice the approach of the water-bearers. They are slight but muscular, and have dark hair and eyes and brown skin. Some of the men wear woven cotton blankets around their waists, kilt-like; others wear breechcloths of woven cotton. The women wear "skirts," or "aprons," of yucca cord. Small fur blankets, which they will drape around their shoulders when they leave the fields, hang from bushes near the trail. Sandals of plaited yucca fiber rest beside the bushes.

The field workers quench their thirst and enjoy a needed rest, but soon return to planting the seed of corn, beans, and squash. If these seeds fail to fulfill their promise, the coming winter will be one of hunger.

A grandmother, twisted and bent by arthritis, sits on a stone on the ledge in front of her house and watches tiny children playing about her. When a child toddles too near the edge or strays too far up the trail, her call brings it back. She smiles a toothless smile as she guards the small ones. Bits of stone, unavoidably mixed with cornmeal, have worn away her teeth.

In another shallow cave in the opposite wall of the canyon, two men and two women are adding another 12- by 14-foot room to an existing house. Walls, made of slabs of limestone, are double thick, the space between being filled with mud. Mud is also used as mortar and plaster, and—firmly packed and dried—it will be used as a floor. A hole above the small doorway is intended as an outlet for smoke from the fire that will be built inside the room. During cold weather, an animal skin will be hung over the doorway.

A group of women, chatting and laughing, kneel beside the stream as they weave baskets of yucca fiber. Nearby, other women gather clay from which they will fashion their pottery.

Several men and older boys appear at the lower end of the canyon walking along the trail that parallels the stream. They are equipped with bows and arrows, throwing sticks, and stone-bladed knives. Proudly they display the results of their successful hunt: two deer, a fox, six rabbits, a porcupine, pack rats, a brace of jays, and a great horned owl.

In front of his house in one of the topmost caves, a young man bends over his fire-making equipment and twirls a hardwood spindle rapidly between his palms; with one foot, he holds the cottonwood hearth firmly. Smoke rises from the hearth, and he will soon be able to blow a spark to flame.

The excited barking of dogs near the rim announces the arrival of strangers in the community. All eyes peer at the three figures coming down one of the trails, figures that are instantly recognized. They are traders from the south. In proper time, they will exhibit the finished shellwork that they obtained by trade from other Indians. And when the traders return to the south, they will take some of the local products: pinyon nuts, black walnuts, baskets, and pottery. From other traders, the Sinagua will obtain salt, turquoise, decorated pottery, and raw cotton.

Thus, the Sinagua lived in Walnut Canyon for almost 150 years. Then they left their homes. Why? No one knows. Perhaps it was lack of rain, worn-out soil, pressure from enemy groups, disease—any, all, or none of these. Whatever the reason, they are gone. Today, the only people in the canyon are those who come to see what is left of the Sinagua way of life. They look at the cliff dwellings and try to imagine what life was once like in Walnut Canyon.

READING SELECTION 7: QUESTIONS

Directions: Use a separate sheet of paper to answer the following questions and to write your reaction to the selection.

1. How did the Sinagua get new ideas and skills that they brought with them to Walnut Canyon?

2. When did the Sinagua Indians arrive at Walnut Canyon?

3. What is a *canyon*?

4. How did the Sinagua use their masonry skills?

5. Why was it a good idea to extend the houses into caves in the canyon's walls?

6. The selection says that game, furred and feathered, haunted canyon and *mesa* top. What is a *mesa*?

7. The selection also says that there was a great variety of trees for fuel and implements. What are *implements*?

8. Why was Walnut Canyon such a good place for the Sinagua to live? Give at least three reasons.

9. How did the Sinagua get products that were not local?

10. Why is the disappearance of the Sinagua from Walnut Canyon a mystery?

YOUR REACTION: Put yourself into the Walnut Canyon described in the selection. In one or two paragraphs, tell how your life in the canyon 800 years ago would have been different than the way it is now.

Are You Really Listening?

Margaret Lane

Have you ever played a game called "whispering down the lane"? In this game, one person whispers a message to another person, who whispers to a third person, and so on down a line of people. It is always interesting, and sometimes funny, to hear what happened to the message as it traveled down the line. It is not funny, however, when we don't listen to messages that are important to us. Sometimes, the results of not listening carefully can even be very serious. This selection offers suggestions on how to improve your listening skills.

A hostess once decided to test how well people listen. Serving appetizers, she remarked, "Do try one. I've filled them with poison." Not a single guest hesitated. "Lovely," they said. "I must have your recipe."

We all like to think of ourselves as good listeners. But the fact is, most of us speak at about 120 to 180 words a minute and think at four or five times that rate. So our attention wanders, and we often pick up only about half of the other person's message. Yet the ability to listen and respond can make all the difference in any relationship—on the job, in the home, with friends.

Years ago, fresh out of college and being interviewed for a job on a small-town newspaper, I learned the hard way. My interview had been going well. The editor began telling me about his winter ski trip. Wanting to make a big impression with a tale of my own backpacking in the same mountains, I tuned him out and started planning my story. "Well," he asked suddenly, "what do you think of that?" Not having heard a word, I babbled foolishly, "Sounds like a marvelous holiday—great fun!" For a long moment he stared at me. "Fun?" he asked in an icy tone. "How could it be fun? I've just told you I spent most of it hospitalized with a broken leg."

How can we improve our ability to listen? To find out, I talked with many professional listeners—psychiatrists, family counselors, social workers. Here is what they recommend:

Listen with your whole self. Tapping your fingers or jiggling a foot is fine if you're listening to music—but not to people. Nothing is more damaging to another person's ego. And if that person is your mate, boss, or customer, nothing is more damaging to you.

So try to block out everything—that fly buzzing in the corner or the dental appointment you have later in the day. Show you are listening through eye contact, a nod of the head, a hand movement that urges the speaker to go on. Even the way you sit, if it's relaxed and attentive, shows interest as clearly as words.

When the conversational ball bounces into your corner, don't feel you've got to hang on to it. Bounce it back. Early in life most of us are led to believe that making the grade socially depends on the ability to hold our own in conversation. The wife of a Foreign Service officer once described for me the agonizing hours she'd spent at parties early in her husband's career: "Here I was, a small-town girl form Nebraska, in a roomful of marvelously articulate people who'd lived all over the world. I'd find myself desperately searching for something to talk about—instead of simply listening to what other people were saying."

Finally, one evening, she confided her problem to a quiet, well-liked senior diplomat. "Long ago," he told her, "I discovered that every talker needs a listener. Believe me, a good listener is as welcome at a party—and as rare—as spring water in the midst of the Sahara."

One of the most engaging women I've ever known is neither beautiful nor especially witty. But when she's listening to you, her attention is so complete that she can make you feel you're the most interesting person on earth. A good listener has a power: the ability, the magic, to make other people feel important.

Help draw the other person out by using brief questions or comments that show you're listening—even if you are reduced to "Really?" or "Tell me more." Talking to someone who doesn't respond is like shouting over a dead telephone: you soon feel foolish and quit.

Suppose, for instance, you're having lunch with a longtime friend who tells you he's had a terrible fight with his wife and hasn't slept much all week. If you're like many of us—afraid of prying—you might say, "Well, every marriage has its ups and downs. You having the chef's salad or pastrami on rye?" Indirectly you've told him he'd better keep his problem to himself.

But what if you responded positively? "I don't wonder you can't sleep," you could say. "You must've gone through a lot of agony over this." Given a chance to release those pent-up feelings, your friend will feel much better. Few of us are so self-sufficient that we don't sometimes need to tell our troubles to a friend who knows how to listen.

"We think listening is easy, but it isn't," says Dr. Irwin Rosen of the famed Menninger Foundation. "True listening means exposing oneself to the fright or rage or despair of another person—and perhaps, to those same feelings within ourselves."

Develop a sensitivity for what is left unsaid in most messages: the inner thoughts that words often hide. The most successful real-estate agent in our town credits his success to the fact that he listens not only to what clients tell him but to what they fail to say. "Nothing's too good for my family," a client claims as he is told the price of a house. But the agent notes the slight hesitancy in the voice, the tight smile, and knows his client is caught in a conflict between what he wants and what he can afford.

"Before you decide," the real-estate agent says tactfully, "maybe you'd like to look at a few more houses." The result of this kind of listening? Everybody wins: the client gets a house he can afford and the agent has a satisfied customer and referrals that will lead to further sales.

Even with the people we love most, it's easy to hear only words and miss the real message. An angry attack—"What do you *mean,* you're out of money? All this family does is spend, spend, spend!"—may have nothing to do with the family's spending. The real message? "I've had a terrible day at work. I'm ready to explode."

If you know how to listen, you'll recognize the hidden hurt and frustration behind the criticism. In a calmer moment, a few words that show you care ("You look tired. Rough day?") can help the one who's hurting to vent feelings in a more constructive way. What might have been a bitter quarrel becomes, instead, the quiet sharing that strengthens any marriage.

Listen without being judgmental. We are always eager to set standards or right and wrong, and hand down judgments. But by judging instead of listening, we cut all lines of communication.

University of California psychiatrist Dr. Barbara Shipley says it is essential to show people you care about that while you may not approve of their behavior, you still approve of *them.* Listening does this. When a teen-ager walks in at 3 a.m., it's not easy for concerned parents to keep in mind the importance of listening. The impulse is to shout, "I don't want to *hear* what happened!" This reaction not only destroys communication, but—far more seriously—it further weakens the teen-ager's regard for himself. By all means, let him know how his behavior has made *you* feel: "We've been terribly worried and upset." But then permit him to tell his side of it. Psychiatrist caution that it often takes years of therapy to rebuild the self-esteem of those who've grown up in a home where parents never listened.

All of us hunger to be heard. Psychiatrists offices are filled with people in need of a listener. In most instances, communication gets blocked because there are no listeners—only talkers. One family counselor with an enviable record for healing broken relationships says: "I really don't do much of anything to get families back together. I simply give each member a chance to talk while the others listen—without interrupting. Often, it's the first time they've listened to each other in years." Listening is an act of caring, a selfless act that permits us to escape the isolation of our separate selves and enter into the warm circle of human kinship—and friendship.

READING SELECTION 8: QUESTIONS

Directions: Use a separate sheet of paper to answer the following questions and to write your reaction to the selection.

1. What is the main idea of this selection?

2. How does the writer's story about the hostess show that people do not listen?

3. Why is the difference between the way we speak and the way we listen important?

4. How did the writer ruin a job interview?

5. What are two of the ways you can listen with your whole self?

6. The selection tells about damaging another person's ego. What is one's *ego*?

7. You are advised to show that you are listening through eye contact. How do you make *eye contact*?

8. Why is it important to use questions or comments that show you are listening?

9. Why is true listening hard to do?

10. Why is it important to listen without judging?

YOUR REACTION: Do you think the five suggestions to improve your listening skills will be of help to you? Write one or two paragraphs to defend your answer.

The Last "Witches" of Salem

Jane Scherer

We often hear complaints that the wheels of justice move too slowly. What about waiting more than 250 years to pardon six people who were convicted in Salem, Massachusetts, in 1692?

This selection tells about the results of the Salem witch trials in the late seventeenth century. One man worked against the odds to see justice done and an ancestor's name cleared.

The terrible Salem witch hunts began in February 1692 and ended in November of the same year, but not until August 1957—265 years later—were the last "witches" finally pardoned.

The madness had ended as quickly as it had begun. The good people of Salem were shocked at what had happened and were sorry for the suffering that had been inflicted on innocent people. After the trials, the court and the church set aside days of penance and prayer, which were observed for many years afterward. Four years later, in January 1696, twelve of the jurors, a judge, and one of the principal accusers signed a statement of remorse.

In 1711, the General Court of Massachusetts set aside the convictions of thirteen of the people who were executed when the victims' relatives asked them to do so. Six of the people were not

Source: From COBBLESTONE's October 1986 issue: *Witchcraft,* ©1986, Cobblestone Publishing Company, 30 Grove Street, Suite C, Peterborough, NH 03458. Reprinted by permission of the publisher.

cleared because their family and friends had either died or moved away.

While jailed, the accused "witches" had to pay for their own food and other services, as all imprisoned people had to do at the time. Also, as was the general practice at the time for people in prison, they even had to pay for the chains that bound them, and they had to stay in jail until the fees were paid. As the weeks and months passed, the debts grew, and in many cases, their property was taken from them. At least one woman died in jail because she did not have the money to pay her fees. Tituba, the West Indian slave whose stories of the black arts may have helped set off the hysteria, was sold to pay her fees.

In 1709, twenty-one of the survivors or their families sued the court for compensation for the loss of their civil rights and property. Not until a few years had passed were they awarded any money.

In the following years, the general court received many pleas to set aside the convictions of the remaining victims. These petitions were always rejected. Some people were afraid that if the accused were pardoned, their relatives would sue the state to recover the victims' property or to receive compensation for its loss. Others felt that history should not be changed. Some people even said that since Salem was an English colony in 1692, the pardon should come from the queen of England.

Then in 1948, a strange thing happened halfway across the country. L. Vance Greenslit, who lived in New Orleans, Louisiana, took an interest in genealogy. Because his family name was unusual, he was curious about its origins. Checking into his family history, he found that Ann Greenslade Pudeator, one of the women hanged as a witch, had been his many-times-great-grandmother. He also learned that she was one of the unpardoned "witches."

Studying her life, he felt that a great injustice had been done. Widowed with five children, she had nursed the sick, later remarried, and was left with property and money. Furthermore, she had declared her innocence until her death. (Only those people who had refused to confess were put to death.)

Greenslit (the family name had changed through the years) wanted to clear her name. It became an obsession with him. Since he had friends among the lawmakers in Massachusetts, a bill to pardon the woman eventually was drafted. When it was presented to the court, however, it contained two petitions: one to pardon Ann Greenslade Pudeator and her companions and the other to do the same for a religious agitator who had been banished from Salem in 1637.

At the public hearings preceding passage of the bill, several objections were raised. The most damaging objection came from the secretary of the Massachusetts bar, a person interested in New England history, who said that pardoning the victims would be "fooling with history."

When the bill was defeated, Greenslit was even more determined to right the ancient wrongs, and after a few years, he tried again. And then again. There were always objections, especially from those who were afraid that Greenslit might try to reclaim Ann Pudeator's property, which would be very valuable today. Greenslit argued that he had no interest in the property; he just wanted to clear his relative's name.

Finally, in August 1957, the governor of Massachusetts signed a resolution stating that Ann Pudeator and five others may have been illegally tried according to a "shocking" law of the time and that descendants of the accused at last could be free of their burden of inherited guilt and shame. More than two and a half centuries after the fact, the last of Salem's "witches" finally were pardoned.

Directions: Use a separate sheet of paper to answer the following questions and to write your reaction to the selection.

1. What three actions mentioned at the beginning of this selection tell you there was regret for the Salem witch hunts?

2. What made the difference in whether or not executed victims had their convictions set aside in 1711?

3. The selection says in 1709 that twenty-one survivors of the witch hunts and their families sued the court for compensation. As used in this context, what is *compensation*?

4. After 1711, why did the general court reject pleas to set aside the convictions of the remaining victims of the witch hunts?

5. What did L. Vance Greenslit learn about his ancestor, Ann Greenslade Pudeator?

6. Clearing Ann Greenslade Pudeator's name became Greenslit's obsession. In this context, what is an *obsession*?

7. The selection states that the bill to pardon the woman and her companions also contained a pardon for a religious agitator who was banished from Salem in 1637. As used in this context, what is an *agitator*?

8. Why was that bill defeated?

9. Why were later bills to pardon Ann Pudeator also defeated?

10. What did the resolution the governor of Massachusetts signed in 1957 say about Ann Pudeator and five others?

YOUR REACTION: At the beginning of this selection, there is a description of how the victims of the witch hunts were treated when jailed. In one or two paragraphs, give and defend your opinion of this kind of treatment.

Block Island Lights

Elinore DeWire

Lighthouses are found along sea coasts, usually where the shore is considered to be dangerous. They have tall towers with lights at the top to guide ships at night. While you may never have actually visited one, chances are that you have seen a picture of a lighthouse in a book or in a movie. That should make it easier for you to picture the lighthouses in this selection and how they came to be.

Midway between Newport, Rhode Island, and Montauk, New York, is an island that resembles a giant pork chop adrift on the sea. Block Island is its official name, but New Englanders affectionately call it the *Bermuda of the North*, since its beaches are tawny and inviting, and the weather is milder than anywhere else in the Northeast. Winters here are chipper, with a continual nipping wind, but rarely does snow lay or the island's many ponds freeze over. In other seasons, Block Island lives up to its nickname. Kissed by cool, fresh breezes and plentiful sunshine, and blessed with an old-fashioned environment, it has become a major vacation spot.

In the age of sail, Block Island was a popular stopover for ships running between Boston, New York, and Philadelphia, in spite of the many hazards to navigation surrounding it. Benjamin Franklin was among the famous people who regularly visited the island, but there were no lights in his time to guide vessels into

Block Island's two main ports. Ships relied on bonfires that burned at both the northern and southern points, as well as on Beacon Hill, 211 feet above sea level at the center of 7-mile-long Block Island.

Local Indians called the island Manisses—Isle of the Little God—but in 1614 Dutch navigator Arian Block chanced upon the sport and gave it his own name. Almost 50 years later the first settlers arrived to farm and fish. They would later discover the island's lure as a vacation spot and turn to tourism for their livelihood. Even so, only a few hundred people currently live on the island year-round.

Shipping losses in the area of Block Island were costly in the years immediately following settlement. Some estimates put the number of wrecks as high as 1,000, with most occurring off the island's north point. Not until 1829, however, was any effort made to mark the treacherous spit of sand and shoal believed to be what was left of a land bridge that once connected Block Island with Rhode Island proper.

Two short towers attached to either end of a 25-foot house were the first official lighthouses on the island. They served sailors for about a decade before erosion and complaints about their inefficiency forced the government to replace them. The second set of double towers fared no better and were abandoned in the 1850s in favor of a single tower. It lasted until the Civil War; then sand and water destroyed it.

The fourth and final lighthouse at Sandy Point was built in 1866, a sturdy granite house with a small tower rising from its roof. It was confidently called *Old Granitesides* in hopes the erosion problem was halted, but the elements began a renewed attack and sand was soon stripped from its base. A solution came in 1873 when the immediate area around the lighthouse was paved with blocks to stabilize the lighthouse plot. Erosion continued, but at a snail's pace, and the old North Light still stands today.

Shortly after the lighthouse was established at Sandy Point, a second sentinel was built atop the Mohegan Bluffs on Block Island's southern shores. Southeast Light, perched 204 feet above sea level, is the highest lighthouse in New England.

The lighthouse overlooks the sea where the fabled Palatine Lights are sometimes seen. According to legend, the ship *Palatine* caught fire off Block Island. All aboard were rescued except for a frightened woman who had hidden below. As flames consumed the ship, her screams echoed across the water to the watchers on shore. Islanders say strange, unexplained lights sometimes appear on the sea around Block Island, usually on calm, clear nights; and occasionally the lights are accompanied by the distant wail of a woman in distress. Many people believe these are the ghosts of the lost ship *Palatine* and her ill-fated passenger.

A number of Block Island lightkeepers and their children have shared memories of life on the island in the days before automation of the lighthouses. Barbara Beebe Gaspar, for example, has fond recollections of growing up at both of the Block Island lights where her father served some 20 years beginning in the 1920s. Barbara walked across the long spit at Sandy Point to catch the bus to Old Harbor School. Blowing sand stung her face, and during one windstorm her raincoat was shredded. In winter, the block pavement around the lighthouse iced over, and Barbara's father had to pull her up to the door on a rope, which she considered great fun.

Marie Carr, wife of lightkeeper Earl Carr, lived at Southeast Light during the 1938 hurricane. The storm threw stones up the cliff and hurled them through her living room window. Electricity failed in the afternoon, kicking on the emergency generator that powered the beacon, but the keepers still had to turn the lens by hand, since the rotating mechanism was not emergency powered. While the tower suffered little damage, 25 feet of the cliff behind the lighthouse washed into the sea.

Additional storms have brought the edge of the cliff to within 55 feet of the lighthouse. Another storm like that of 1938 could undermine it completely. The Southeast Lighthouse Foundation has raised $1.8 million to relocate the historic tower 200 feet back from the cliff, but there's little time. Engineers say the structure cannot be moved once the distance separating it from the sea narrows to 40 feet. The relocation project was scheduled for the summer of 1992 and be accomplished with hydraulic jacks that lift the 60-foot tall lighthouse onto a railway and slowly roll it to its new location. Samuel Drake once said, "Nothing moves the imagination like a lighthouse." It this case, nothing moves a lighthouse like imagination!

READING SELECTION 10: QUESTIONS

Directions: Use a separate sheet of paper to answer the following questions and to write your reaction to the selection.

1. Check a map of the United States. Where is Montauk, New York?

2. What is the main idea of this selection?

3. How were sailing vessels guided into Block Island's two main ports?

4. Where did Block Island get its name?

5. How did the people who live on Block Island year-round change in the way they earned their living?

6. Why was an effort made in 1829 to mark what had once been a land bridge between Block Island and Rhode Island?

7. Why were the first official lighthouses on the island replaced?

8. The selection mentions an erosion problem at Sandy Point. In this context, what is *erosion*?

9. What are the Palatine Lights?

10. How was Southeast Light to be relocated?

YOUR REACTION: You have read a little about life on Block Island. Would you like to live on Block Island as one of its year-round residents? Write one or two paragraphs to defend your answer.

Guided Practice Answers

CHAPTER ONE

Guided Practice 1-1: Sounds of **c** (page 14)

You should have marked: 1. once, 2. fence, 4. spruce, 7. decide, and 10. peace with **s**; the **c** in each of these words has a soft sound. You should have marked: 3. college, 5. recount, 6. cool, 8. course, and 9. common with **k**; the **c** in each of these words has a hard sound.

Guided Practice 1-2: Sounds of **d** (page 15)

The usual sound of **d** (dime) is heard in: 1. dark, 2. hide, 3. diet, 5. does, 7. stored, and 8. lady. The **j** sound of **d** is heard in: 4. gradual and 6. education.

Guided Practice 1-3: Sounds of **g** (page 16)

You should have marked: 1. hinge, 3. urge, 5. ranger, 6. stage, 8. lodge, and 10. rage with a **j**; each of these words has the soft **g** sound. The words 2. gold, 4. gift, 7. God, and 9. govern should have been marked with a **g**; they all have a hard **g** sound.

Guided Practice 1–4: Sounds of n (page 17)

You should have marked: 1. many, 3. notice, 5. money, 6. answer, 8. open, and 10. nun with **n;** these words all have the usual sound of **n.** The words 2. ink, 4. lanky, 7. wink, and 9. ankle should have been marked with **ng;** the **n** in each of these words has the **ng** sound.

Guided Practice 1–5: Sounds of s (page 18)

The usual sound of **s** (<u>s</u>on) is heard in: 2. sandy, 3. pipes, and 6. perhaps. The **z** sound of **s** (<u>z</u>ip) is heard in: 1. shores, 4. avoids, 7. trades, 9. chose, and 10. Thursday. The **zh** sound of **s** (trea<u>s</u>ure) is heard in: 5. leisure and 8. pleasure.

Guided Practice 1–6: Sounds of x (page 19)

You should have marked: 2. excite, 3. sixty, 5. next, 6. coax, 8. except, and 9. excuse with **ks;** they all have the **ks** sound of **x** in them. The words 1. exhaust, 4. example, 7. exist, and 10. examine should have been marked with **gz,** since they all have that sound of **x.**

Guided Practice 1–7: L Blends (page 25)

You should have circled: 1. (pl) ace, 2. (cl) ock, 3. (sl) eet, 4. (fl) eet, 5. (gl) ue, 6. (fl) op, 7. (cl) aw, 8. (spl) it, 9. (pl) ot, and 10. (bl) eed.

Guided Practice 1–8: R Blends (page 25)

You should have circled: 1. (tr) ip, 2. un (fr) iendly, 3. (pr) etty, 4. (br) at, 5. (dr) ug, 6. (fr) ank, 7. (cr) y, 8. (pr) each, 9. (tr) ack, and 10. un (br) reakable.

Guided Practice 1–9: S Blends (page 26)

You should have circled: 1. (sc) at, 2. (spr) inkle, 3. (Sc) otch, 4. (scr) een, 5. (sm) ear, 6. (sw) ear, 7. (sn) oop, 8. (str) etch, 9. fir (st), and 10. de (sk).

Guided Practice 1-10: Other Blends (page 27)

You should have circled: 1. bu (nk) , 2. fie(ld) , 3. pai (nt) er, 4. la (nd) ing, 5. fe (nd) er, 6. ho (ld) er, 7. wa (nt) ed, 8. se (nd) , 9. ra (nk) , and 10. we (ld) er.

Guided Practice 1-11: Consonant Digraphs—New Speech Sound (page 34)

You should have circled: 1. (sh) oe, 2. (wh) eeze, 3. (sh) ip, 4. (wh) ip, 5. four (th) , 6. wi (sh) , 7. mo (th) er, 8. (wh) isk, 9. fla (sh) er, and 10. (sh) arp.

Guided Practice 1-12: Consonant Digraph ch (page 35)

The following words should be marked with a **ch**: 1. reach, 4. change, 7. branch, 8. ditch, and 10. choke; they all have the new sound of **ch** (chip). The words marked with **k** should be: 2. backache, 6. Christmas, and 9. chorus, since the **ch** in each of these words has a **k** (kind) sound. The words marked with an **sh** should be: 3. Chicago and 5. moustache, as both have **ch** consonant digraphs with an **sh** (she) sound.

Guided Practice 1-13: Silent Consonants (page 42)

You should have crossed out: 1. silent **t** in listen, 2. silent **b** in thumb—silent after **m**, 3. silent **gh** in sigh, 4. silent **c** in scent, 5. silent **l** in stalk, 6. silent **p** in psychology, 7. silent **l** in pillow—only hear one **l**, 8. silent **w**—silent before **r**— and silent **c**—before **k** in wreck, 9. silent **s**—only hear one **s**—and silent **g**—before **n** in assign, and 10. silent **k**—before **n**—and silent **gh** in knight.

CHAPTER TWO

Guided Practice 2-1: Long Vowels (page 51)

The words should be marked: 1. base, 2. Utah, 3. tote, 4. flute, 5. high, 6. choke, 7. Pete, 8. hope, 9. kite, 10. flake, 11. wipe, 12. she, 13. late, 14. we, and 15. chute.

Guided Practice 2-2: Silent **e** (page 51)

The words in the bottom line should be marked: fate, hope, made, use, and tone.

Guided Practice 2-3: Long and Short Vowels (page 52)

You should have marked the vowels: 1. i, 2. ŭ, 3. u, 4. o, 5. ĭ, 6. ă, 7. ŏ, 8. a, 9. ĕ, and 10. e.

Guided Practice 2-4: Vowel Sounds of **y** (page 54)

You should have marked the vowel sounds of y: 1. i, 2. e, 3. ĭ, 4. e, 5. ĭ, 6. e, 7. i, 8. e, 9. ĭ, and 10. ĭ and e.

Guided Practice 2-5: Sound of **au** and **aw**, Sound of **oi** and **oy** (page 60)

The words marked with **aw** are numbers 3, 4, 6, 7, and 9. The words marked with **oy** are numbers 1, 2, 5, 8, and 10.

Guided Practice 2-6: Sounds of **ow** (page 61)

The words should be marked: 1. b, 2. b, 3. a, 4. a, 5. b, 6. b, 7. b, 8. a, 9. b, and 10. a.

Guided Practice 2-7: Sounds of **ou** (page 62)

The words should be marked: 1. b, 2. c, 3. a, 4. a, 5. b, 6. c, 7. a, 8. b, 9. b, and 10. c.

Guided Practice 2-8: Sounds of **oo** (page 63)

You should have marked these sounds of **oo**: 1. zoo, 2. broŏk, 3. shoŏk, 4. bloom, 5. noose, 6. hoŏd, 7. groom, 8. woŏl, 9. proof, and 10. rooster.

Guided Practice 2-9: Decoding Nonsense Words (page 74)

1. caild:
   c not before **e, i, y,** = **k** sound
   ai = double vowel, usually = **a**
   ld = blend—go together
   k + **a** + **ld**
   Pronounced: kald

2. sproad:
   spr = blend—go together
   oa = double vowel, usually = **o**
   d = usual consonant sound
   spr + **o** + **d**
   Pronounced: sprod

3. wremb:
   wr = usually = silent **w** = **r**
   | consonant | vowel | consonant | pattern = ĕ
   mb = silent **b**
   r + ĕ + **m**
   Pronounced: rĕm

CHAPTER 3

Guided Practice 3-1: Hearing Syllables (page 79)

You should have marked the following number of syllables for each word: 1. window (2), 2. please (1), 3. addresses (3), 4. altogether (4), 5. property (3), 6. accept (2), 7. during (2), 8. count (1), 9. danger (2), and 10. quarter (2).

Guided Practice 3-2: Visible Clue 1—VC/CV (page 85)

Check to see if you marked the words: 1. pĭt/cher, 2. ĕn/joy, 3. hănd/some— note **nd** blend, 4. ĕx/plain—note **pl** blend, 5. wor/ship, 6. fur/ther—vowel + **r**—note **th** digraph, 7. mŏt/to, 8. con/vince—note **o** in first syllable has ə sound, 9. swăl/low, and 10. prĕt/zel.

Guided Practice 3-3: Visible Clue 2—V/CV (page 86)

The words should be divided as follows: 1. e/qual, 2. U/tah, 3. no/tion, 4. re/flex, 5. spo/ken, 6. pre/view, 7. ti/tle, 8. na/ture, 9. o/pen, and 10. trea/son—note that the double vowel **ea**, with a long **e** sound and silent **a**, is treated as a single vowel.

Guided Practice 3-4: Visible Clue 2—VC/V (page 87)

The words should be divided as follows: 1. sĕc/ond, 2. hăb/it, 3. tăx/i, 4. pĭt/y, 5. Lăt/in, 6. dĕv/il, 7. wĕap/on—note the double vowel **ea,** which stands for the single vowel sound of ĕ, 8. lĕv/el, 9. prĭs/on, and 10. ŏl/ive.

Guided Practice 3-5: Visible Clue 3—**consonant + le** (page 88)

The words should be divided as follows: 1. buck/əl, 2. tum/bəl, 3. pick/əl, 4. sta/bəl, 5. ri/fəl, 6. crip/pəl, 7. dou/bəl, 8. spack/əl, 9. dan/gəl, and 10. wrin/kəl.

Guided Practice 3-6: Visible Clue 4—**d** or **t** + **ed** (page 89)

The words that have **ed** as separate syllables are: 2. elected, 3. herded, 6. sighted, 8. branded, 9. greeted, and 10. lasted.

Guided Practice 3-7: Decoding Nonsense Words (page 95)

daiblod

1. **V/CV** pattern—dai—keep **ai** together = double vowel.
   bl = consonant blend—keep together—divide before **bl**
   two-syllable word—dai/blod

2. <u>dai</u>
   d = usual sound
   ai—open syllable with one vowel sound = **a**
   pronounce syllable: da
   <u>blod</u>
   bl- = consonant blend—say together
   closed syllable—o = ŏ
   d = regular sound
   pronounce syllable: blŏd

3. Pronounce word:

   dablŏd

makoded

1. **V/CV** pattern = ma/kod
   ed at end of word = separate syllable after **d**
   three-syllable word = ma/kod/ed

2. <u>ma</u>
   m = usual sound
   a in open syllable = a
   pronounce syllable: ma
   <u>kod</u>
   k = usual sound
   o in closed syllable = ŏ
   d = usual sound
   pronounce syllable: kŏd
   <u>ed</u>
   e in closed syllable = ĕ
   d = usual sound
   pronounce syllable: ĕd

3. Pronounce word:

   | makŏdĕd |

tobflackle

1. **VC/CV** pattern
   split before **fl**—consonant blend—keep together = tob/flack
   ck at end before **le**—le = separate syllable
   three-syllable word—tob/flack/le

2. <u>tob</u>
   t = usual sound
   o in closed syllable = ŏ
   b = usual sound
   pronounce syllable: tŏb
   <u>flack</u>
   fl = consonant blend—say together
   a in closed syllable = ă
   ck = one sound = k
   <u>le</u>
   le = sound of əl

3. Pronounce word:

   | tŏbflăkəl |

CHAPTER FOUR

Guided Practice 4-1: Words with More Than One Meaning (page 103)

1. The context gives a picture of a boy trying to learn about being a knight. Since he is planning on being a Knight of the Round Table one day, he must be trained. Try (a), *boy training to be a knight* in place of *page.*

2. The context tells of wet ground. If an animal walks on that ground, it will leave paw prints. Thus, it may be easier to follow that animal. Try (b), *follow* in place of *track.*

3. The context gives a picture of a man shopping. He must check to see if he can afford something before buying it. What would he check? Try (d), *card that tells cost* in place of *tag.*

4. The context gives a picture of Frank not watching his business as he should. What could happen to sales that would result in Frank closing his shop? Try (a), *go down* in place of *slip.*

5. A careful speaker doesn't state anything in public unless he or she is sure of the facts. What will this careful speaker do? The speaker will make sure of those facts. Try (c), *make sure of* in place of *check.*

Guided Practice 4-2: Word Clues in Context—Definition (page 111)

1. *legitimate:* child born of parents who are legally married to each other. The writer has used parentheses to set off the word meaning from the rest of the sentence.

2. *egotist:* a self-centered person. Here the writer has used commas to set off the word meaning from the rest of the sentence.

3. *illusion:* false idea. The writer has used dashes to set off the word meaning in this sentence.

4. *cascade:* a small, steep waterfall. A dash has been used to set off the word meaning from the rest of the sentence.

5. *sheath:* case. The word meaning is set off from the rest of the sentence by means of parentheses.

Guided Practice 4-3: Word Clues in Context—Example (page 113)

1. *violated:* broke. Each example gives a picture of how Jamie broke the law. She drove a stolen car, did not have a driver's license, and went through red lights. Try *broke* in place of *violated.* It fits in context.

2. *placid:* calm. The examples of how Toby behaves give a picture of the kind of person he is. Very little bothers him and he never gets upset or angry. So he must be a calm person. Try *calm* in place of *placid.* It fits in context.

3. *ample:* plenty of. There are two examples of how there will be *plenty of* material in the garment: enough to let out and enough to let down the hem. Try *plenty of* in place of *ample.* It fits in context.

4. *veteran:* person who served in a military force. Each sentence gives an example of something related to being a soldier or person who served in a military force: the uniform, ribbons, silver bars. Try *person who served in a military force* instead of *veteran.* It fits in context.

5. *liberal:* generous. Each sentence gives an example of Mr. Jackson's *generous* way of spending his money. Try *generous* in place of *liberal.* It fits in context.

Guided Practice 4-4: Word Clues in Context—
Experience (page 118)

1. *ravenous:* very hungry. If the two hikers have not had much food for a week, you know that they are very hungry. Try *very hungry* in place of *ravenous.* It fits in context.

2. *charitable:* kindhearted. Picture the kind of person Molly is. The paragraph tells you that she is very selfish. If Mary is very different from her twin sister, she probably is kindhearted rather than selfish. Try *kindhearted* in place of *charitable.* It fits in context.

3. *competent:* fit. This paragraph gives a picture of a man who is not doing a good job as president of an important company. You know that someone who does the things this president does is not fit to head an important company. Try *fit* in place of *competent.* It makes sense in context.

4. *mutiny:* revolt. A crew can be pushed only so far before it revolts. In this case, a cruel captain is doing the pushing and the revolt happens at sea. Try *revolt* in place of *mutiny.* It fits in context.

5. *exasperate:* annoy. How do you feel when an interesting and exciting TV program is cut off for TV ads? Do you lose track of the story while products are sold on TV? When you have this experience, it can annoy you. Try *annoy* in place of *exasperate.* It fits in context.

CHAPTER FIVE

Guided Practice 5-1: Greek Root Words (page 132)

1. xylophone
2. aristocracy
3. phonics
4. stenographer
5. telescope
6. autohypnosis
7. autopilot
8. graphite

Guided Practice 5-2: Latin Root Words (page 134)

1. spectator
2. dictate
3. mortal
4. audible
5. creed
6. spectacles
7. audience
8. mortician

Guided Practice 5-3: Prefixes non, un, dis (page 138)

You should have written: 1. not obey, 2. not cooked, 3. not agree, 4. not active, 5. not dated.

Guided Practice 5-4: Prefix in (page 139)

You should have put an **x** next to: 2. insert—put in, 3. inward—toward the inside, 6. instill—put in little by little, 7. ingrown—grown into something, 8. inhabit—live in, and 10. inborn—born in a person.

Guided Practice 5-5: Prefix im (page 139)

You should have put an **x** next to: 2. immortal—not mortal, 3. impersonal—not personal, 5. impatient—not patient, 6. imperfect—not perfect, 8. impractical—not practical, and 9. immoral—not moral.

Guided Practice 5-6: Prefix re (page 140)

You should have put an **x** next to: 1. reawaken—awaken again, 2. refasten—fasten again, 3. reform—form again, 4. recapture—capture again, 6. readjust—adjust again, 7. rebuild—build again, 9. reproduce—produce or create anew, and 10. rerun—run again.

Guided Practice 5-7: Noun Suffixes (page 151)

A. 1. employment—state of employing, 2. confession—state of confessing, 3. avoidance—state of avoiding, 4. dependence—state of depending, and 5. adoption—state of adopting.

B. 1. objector—one who objects, 2. governor—one who governs, and 3. talker—one who talks.

C. 1. weakness—condition of being weak, 2. darkness—condition of being dark, and 3. plainness—condition of being plain.

D. 1. sainthood—state of being a saint, 2. citizenship—state of being a citizen.

Guided Practice 5-8: Verb Suffixes (page 153)

1. falsify—cause to be false, 2. tenderize—cause to be tender, 3. shorten—cause to be short, and 4. solidify—cause to be solid.

Guided Practice 5-9: Adjective Suffixes (page 155)

A. 1. powerful—full of power, 2. joyous—full of joy, and 3. windy—full of wind.

B. 1. boyish—somewhat like a boy, 2. sweetish—somewhat sweet.

C. 1. sisterly —like a sister, 2. cowardly—like a coward.

D. 1. faithless—without faith, 2. faultless—without fault.

E. 1. readable—able to be read, 2. predictable—able to be predicted, 3. reducible—able to be reduced. Note that the final e must be dropped in *reduce* before adding the suffix.

Guided Practice 5-10: Adverb Suffix (page 157)

1. dearly—in a dear manner, 2. grandly—in a grand manner.

Guided Practice 5-11: Compound Words (page 164)

Since you used your own words, the meanings may not match exactly to those given here. But they should have the same ideas: 1. crazy man, 2. have too much stock or goods, 3. something used to crack the shells of nuts, 4. someone who stays at home, 5. the falling of rain, 6. shoe of a horse, 7. dog used to catch foxes, 8. nail on your thumb, 9. cloth used for washing, and 10. band worn around one's head.

CHAPTER SIX

Guided Practice 6–1: Alphabetical Order (page 171)

A. 1. w x y z, 2. b c <u>d</u> <u>e</u> f, 3. s t <u>u</u> <u>v</u> w, 4. o q <u>r</u> s, 5. h <u>i</u> j k,
6. f g <u>h</u> <u>i</u> j, 7. m <u>n</u> <u>o</u> p, 8. j k l <u>m</u> <u>n</u> o, 9. a b c <u>d</u> <u>e</u> f, and 10. v w <u>x</u> <u>y</u> z.

B. 1. f, 2. y, 3. q, 4. h, 5. n, 6. j, 7. c, 8. u, 9. v, and 10. y.

Guided Practice 6–2: Alphabetical Order—First Letters (page 172)

List 1a: 1. band, 2. heart, 3. many, 4. offer, and 5. supper. Note the order of first letters: **b h m o s.**

List 1b: 1. absent, 2. comet, 3. friend, 4. really, and 5. water. Note the order of first letters: **a c f r w.**

List 2a: 1. artist, 2. cork, 3. dozen, 4. effect, 5. flame, 6. life, 7. marsh, 8. Sunday, 9. test, and 10. wrapper. Note the order of first letters: **a c d e f l m s t w.**

List 2b: 1. bark, 2. east, 3. junk, 4. model, 5. nation, 6. open, 7. pillow, 8. quick, 9. untidy, 10. X ray. Note the order of first letters: **b e j m n o p q u x.**

Guided Practice 6–3: Alphabetical Order—Second Letters (page 172)

List 3a: 1. able, 2. actor, 3. ankle, 4. apart, and 5. ask. Note the order of second letters: **b c n p s.**

List 3b: 1. wake, 2. well, 3. wind, 4. woman, and 5. write. Note the order of second letters: **a e i o r.**

List 4a: 1. sap, 2. scene, 3, shame, 4. sift, 5. slump, 6. smack, 7. some, 8. spar, 9. step, and 10. Sunday. Note the order of second letters: **a c h i l m o p t u.**

List 4b: 1. case, 2. certain, 3. chop, 4. city, 5. clean, 6. comb, 7. cramp, 8. cut, 9. cycle, and 10. Czech. Note the order of second letters: **a e h i l o r u y z.**

Guided Practice 6–4: Alphabetical Order—Third Letters (page 175)

List 5a: 1. rude, 2. rug, 3. rule, 4. rumble, and 5. rust. Note the order of third letters: **d g l m s.**

List 5b: 1. each, 2. eagle, 3. ear, 4. eat, and 5. eaves. Note the order of third letters: **c g r t v.**

List 6a: 1. habit, 2. hack, 3. hag, 4. hair, 5. hammer, 6. hand, 7. happen, 8. hard, 9. haste, and 10. have. Note the order of third letters: **b c g i m n p r s v.**

List 6b: 1. mice, 2. middle, 3. might, 4. Mike, 5. mild, 6. mince, 7. mirror, 8. mistake, 9. mitten, and 10. mix. Note the order of third letters: **c d g k l n r s t x.**

Guided Practice 6-5: Alphabetical Order—First Letters That Are Different (page 177)

List 7a: 1. tear, 2. tearful, 3. tearing, 4. tearless, and 5. teary. Note the order of letters for 2–5: **f i l y.**

List 7b: 1. passable, 2. passage, 3. passed, 4. passer-by, and 5. passing. Note the order of letters: 1 and 2—first different letters are **b** and **g**; 3 and 4—first different letters are **d** and **r**; 5. **i.**

List 8a: 1. lead, 2. leader, 3. leadership, 4. lead-in, 5. leading, 6. lead-off, 7. leads, 8. leaf, 9. leafless, and 10. leafy.

List 8b: 1. forgave, 2. forget, 3. forgetful, 4. forgets, 5. forgive, 6. forgiven, 7. forgiveness, 8. forgiver, 9. forgiving, and 10. forgivingly.

Guided Practice 6-6: Guide Words (page 181)

You should have circled: 1. father, 4. stain, 5. gone, 7. marble, 8. pipe, and 10. carpet. In line 2, the last guide word begins with pap so pa<u>rt</u> does not fit. In line 3, the last guide word begins with revi, so rev<u>o</u>lt does not fit. In both lines 2 and 3, the words can be found in later pages. In line 6, the first guide word is cra<u>m</u>, so cra<u>d</u>le does not fit. In line 9, the first guide word begins ba<u>c</u>, so ba<u>b</u>y does not fit. In both lines 6 and 9, the words can be found on earlier pages.

Guided Practice 6-7: Syllables (page 183)

Number of syllables in entry words: 1. gallery—3; 2. forerunner—3; 3. irresistible—5; 4. tabernacle—4; 5. tableware—3.

Guided Practice 6-8: Plural Forms of Words (page 184)

Plural forms: 1: tablespoonful –tablespoonfuls; 2. platypus—platypuses; 3. buggy—buggies; 4. cactus—<u>cacti</u> or <u>cactuses</u>; 5. ox—<u>oxen</u>.

Guided Practice 6–9: Pronunciation (page 186)

You should have written: 1. blouse, 2. blunt, 3. team, 4. teen, 5. please, 6. crawl, 7. blur, 8. blotch, 9. herb, 10. crowd.

Guided Practice 6–10: Stress Marks (page 187)

You should have heard the stress and circled the syllables: 1. (pŏp´)yə-lər, 2. (rôr´) ing, 3. te- (boo´) , 4. fôr- (ĕv´) ər, 5. (plĕzh´)ər.

Guided Practice 6–11: Word Origins (page 189)

Word origins: 1. gingerbread—from Old French, Medieval Latin; 2. tablet—Middle English, Old French; 3. crayon—French, Latin.

Guided Practice 6–12: Word Meanings (page 000)

You should have used these word meanings: 1. blues—noun, meaning 1; 2. hog—verb, informal meaning 1; 3. monkey—verb, informal meaning 1; 4. tabby—noun, meaning 3b; 5. gallant—adjective, meaning 2a.

CHAPTER SEVEN

Guided Practice 7–1: PVS (pages 210–214)

Check your cards to see if they look like the ones that follow. What you have written may not match exactly. The pronunciation, definition, and the information about the word should be the same. And, of course, your sentences will not match. When you check your sentences, they are correct if they show that you know what the word means and how to use it correctly in your own context.

1.

Front

kroud

crowd

(prepared food for the <u>crowd</u>)

Back

noun

large number of persons
gathered together

Michael Jackson usually draws a
<u>crowd </u>at each of his concerts.

2.

Front

ted off
teed off
(She was <u>teed</u> <u>off</u> by the many people . . .)

Back

verb
made angy or disgusted
Peggy was <u>teed</u> <u>off</u> at her brother because he wouldn't stop teasing her.

Notice that you must use the past tense in your sentence to match use of the term in context.

3.

Front

kravd
craved
(they all <u>craved</u> her famous onion soup . . .)

Back

verb
had an intense desire for
After not having any ice cream for months, Herbert <u>craved</u> a double scoop of chocolate ice cream.

Again note that you must use the past tense in your sentence to match use of the term in context.

4.

Front

kroo´tonz´ or kroo-tonz´ croutons (onion soup topped off with <u>croutons</u>)

Back

noun Small pieces of toasted or fried bread Use <u>croutons</u> on top of a green salad to make it extra crunchy.

Note that you must use the plural form to match the use of the term in context.

CHAPTER EIGHT

Guided Practice 8-1: Stated Main Ideas—A (page 224)

The stated main idea of each paragraph is shown as an umbrella statement.

1. *Who or what is the paragraph about?* people and jobs

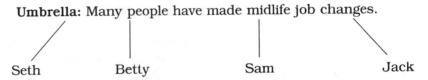

Umbrella: Many people have made midlife job changes.

Seth   Betty   Sam   Jack

2. *Who or what is the paragraph about?* electric power failures

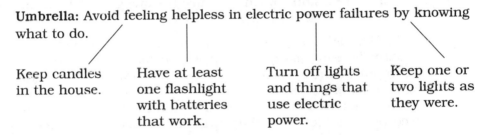

Umbrella: Avoid feeling helpless in electric power failures by knowing what to do.

Keep candles in the house.

Have at least one flashlight with batteries that work.

Turn off lights and things that use electric power.

Keep one or two lights as they were.

3. *Who or what is the paragraph about?* a hot summer

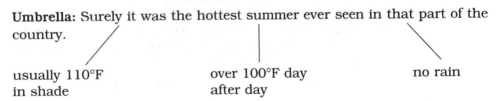

Umbrella: Surely it was the hottest summer ever seen in that part of the country.

usually 110°F in shade

over 100°F day after day

no rain

4. *Who or what is the paragraph about?* tools

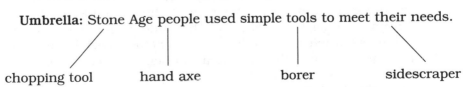

Umbrella: Stone Age people used simple tools to meet their needs.

chopping tool   hand axe   borer   sidescraper

5. Who or what is the paragraph about? farmers

Umbrella: There are fewer farmers today than there were 50 years ago.

New farm machinery needs fewer farmers.	Younger farmers take jobs in cities.	Farmers sell land and go into other work.

Guided Practice 8-2: Stated Main Ideas—B (page 228)

1. *Who or what is the paragraph about?* houses *What does the writer really want you to know about houses?* (main idea as stated in paragraph) The price of new houses is so high that many people are fixing up their homes instead of moving.

Did you check the stated main idea in your mind? Did you picture the answer to question two and the sentences in your mind? If you did not have the correct stated main idea, use the one given here as an umbrella statement and fit the sentences under it.

2. *Who or what is the paragraph about?* shopping *What does the writer really want you to know about shopping?* (main idea as stated in paragraph) Taking a small calculator with you when you go grocery shopping can be very helpful.

Did you check the stated main idea in your mind? If you did not have the correct main idea, use the one given here as an umbrella. Then fit the sentences under it.

3. *Who or what is the paragraph about?* Arizona *What does the writer really want you to know about Arizona?* (main idea as stated in paragraph) Arizona has much to offer those who enjoy the outdoors.

Did you check the stated main idea in your mind? If you did not have the correct stated main idea, use the one given here as an umbrella statement. Then fit the sentences under it.

4. *Who or what is the paragraph about?* lightning in storms *What does the writer really want you to know about lightning in storms?* (main idea as stated in paragraph) There are a number of ways to avoid being struck by lightning if you are caught in a storm.

Did you check the stated main idea in your mind? When you made the umbrella statement in your mind, did you notice that not all the sentences fit under that umbrella? The sentence that says: "Every year, people all over the United States die from being struck by lightning" does not fit. It is not one of the ways to avoid being struck by lightning if you are caught in a storm. However, the stated main idea is still correct. Most, if not all, of the sentences fit under that umbrella.

If you did not have the correct stated main idea, use the one given here and see how the rest of the sentences fit under it.

5. *Who or what is the paragraph about?* people *What does the writer really want you to know about people?* (main idea as stated in the paragraph) People have certain advantages over animals.

Did you check the stated main idea in your mind? Did you notice that the last two sentences do not fit under the umbrella statement? They say nothing about people's advantages over animals. But, the stated main idea is still correct. Most of the sentences fit under the umbrella statement.

If you did not have the correct stated main idea, use the one given here and see how the rest of the sentences fit under it.

Guided Practice 8-3: Implied Main Ideas—A (page 235)

Remember that your words do not have to match the implied main ideas given below. The ideas, however, must be the same.

1. *Who or what is the paragraph about?* smelling gas *What does the writer really want you to know about smelling gas?* There are things to do if you smell gas in the house.
Check implied main idea:

Umbrella: There are things to do if you smell gas in the house.

| Check pilot lights. | Call gas company. | Open all windows. | Turn off main gas shutoff valve. |

2. *Who or what is the paragraph about?* rough-water swimming *What does the writer really want you to know about rough-water swimming?* Take safety measures when rough-water swimming.
Check implied main idea:

Umbrella: Take safety measures when rough-water swimming.

| Swim with friend who has done rough-water swimming. | Stay in area marked for swimming. | Wear a bright colored cap. | Stay close to shore unless a boat goes along. | Don't underrate dangers of open waters. | Don't overrate your fitness and ability to stand the cold. |

3. *Who or what is the paragraph about?* angry people *What does the writer really want you to know about angry people?* People show anger in different ways.

Check implied main idea:

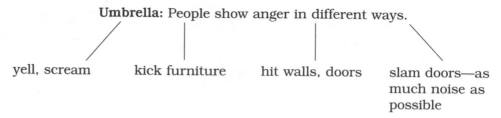

Umbrella: People show anger in different ways.

yell, scream   kick furniture   hit walls, doors   slam doors—as much noise as possible

4. *Who or what is the paragraph about?* a town *What does the writer really want you to know about that town?* The town has become a ghost town.

Check implied main idea:

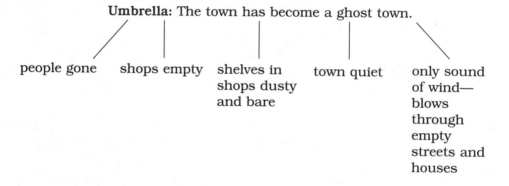

Umbrella: The town has become a ghost town.

people gone   shops empty   shelves in shops dusty and bare   town quiet   only sound of wind— blows through empty streets and houses

5. *Who or what is the paragraph about?* a trip *What does the writer really want you to know about a trip?* There are things to do on a trip that will help you enjoy it.

Check implied main idea:

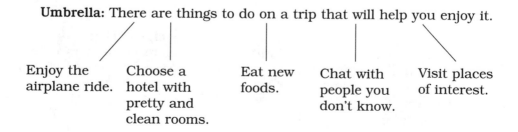

Umbrella: There are things to do on a trip that will help you enjoy it.

Enjoy the airplane ride.   Choose a hotel with pretty and clean rooms.   Eat new foods.   Chat with people you don't know.   Visit places of interest.

Guided Practice 8-4: Implied Main Ideas—B (page 239)

1. *Who or what is the paragraph about?* Jim *What does the writer really want you to know about Jim?* Jim is usually late for work.

Did you check the implied main idea in your mind? If you did not have a correct implied main idea, use the one given here as an umbrella statement. Then fit the sentences under it.

2. *Who or what is the paragraph about?* a woman *What does the writer really want you to know about that woman?* The paragraph tells you what the woman looked like.

Did you check the implied main idea in your mind? If you did not have a correct implied main idea, use the one given here as an umbrella statement. Then fit the sentences under it.

3. *Who or what is the paragraph about?* Mike *What does the writer really want you to know about Mike?* Mike has a very busy life.

Did you check the implied main idea in your mind? Did you notice that one sentence did not fit under the umbrella statement? The sentence that tells about Mike liking to ski in winter and play golf in summer does not tell anything about Mike being busy. Still, the implied main idea is correct. Most, if not all, of the sentences fit under it.

If you did not have a correct implied main idea, use the one given here as the umbrella statement. Then fit the other sentences under it.

4. *Who or what is the paragraph about?* a heart attack *What does the writer really want you to know about a heart attack?* There are things you can do to help a person who may be having a heart attack.

Did you check the implied main idea in your mind? If you did not have a correct implied main idea, use the one given here as an umbrella statement. Then fit the sentences under it.

5. *Who or what is the paragraph about?* a woman *What does the writer really want you to know about that woman?* The woman is bored with her job.

Did you check the implied main idea in your mind? Did you notice that the first two sentences did not fit under the umbrella statement? They tell about the office and not about the woman. The implied main idea is still correct. Most, if not all, of the sentences fit under it. If you did not have a correct implied main idea, use the one given here as an umbrella statement. Then fit the rest of the sentences under it.

CHAPTER NINE

Guided Practice 9–1: Detail: Example—A (page 256)

1. Sentences 2, 3, 4, and 5 are examples of the stated main idea. They each give an example of Robert's golf game getting better. Sentence 6 is a result of it getting better, not an example of it.

2. Sentences 1, 2, 3, 4, and 5 are examples of signs of spring. When you check out sentence 7, you find that it is not a sign of spring.

3. Sentences 1, 3, 5, and 7 are examples of ways to save gasoline. When you check out sentences 2, 4, 6, and 8, you find that they do not tell of ways to save gasoline.

4. Sentences 1, 2, 3, 4, and 5 are all examples of bad things that happened to the Blake family on a fishing trip.

5. Sentences 1, 2, 3, 4, 5, and 6 tell you ways to be a good salesperson. Sentence 7 tells what will happen if you are a good salesperson but not a way to be one.

Guided Practice 9–2: Detail: Example—B (page 258)

1. The main idea, which is sentence 4, is supported by sentences 5, 6, and 7. They give examples of how horses are used in sports. Sentences 1,2, and 3 are interesting but do not support the main idea.

2. The main idea, which is sentence 3, is supported by sentences 4, 5, and 6. They each give an example of using bricks in or around the home. Sentences 1 and 2 do not support the main idea.

3. This paragraph has an implied main idea. As identified by this writer: **There are five steps to follow before opening a business.** Sentences 1, 2, 3, 4, and 5 all support the main idea because each gives a step to follow.

4. This paragraph has an implied main idea. As identified by this writer: **There are ways to light a bathroom.** Sentences 1, 3, 5, and 6 are examples of ways to use lighting in a bathroom. Sentences 2, 4, and 7 do not support the main idea.

5. The main idea is sentence 6. Sentences 1, 2, 3, and 4 support the main idea with examples of advantages of cooking in a microwave oven. Sentence 5 does not support the main idea.

Guided Practice 9-3: Detail: Reason—A (page 261)

1.
1.	R	4.	R
2.	R	5.	R
3.	R		

2.
1.	—	4.	R
2.	R	5.	R
3.	R	6.	R

3.
1.	—	5.	R
2.	R	6.	—
3.	R	7.	R
4.	R	8.	—

4.
1.	R	4.	R
2.	R	5.	—
3.	R		

5.
1.	—	4.	R
2.	R	5.	—
3.	R		

Guided Practice 9-4: Detail: Reason—B (page 263)

1.
1.	MI	4.	R
2.	—	5.	R
3.	R	6.	R

2. Implied MI: Camping out is good for you.
1.	R	4.	R
2.	R	5.	R
3.	R	6.	R

3. Implied MI: People are moving to the sunbelt from other parts of the country.
1.	R	5.	R
2.	—	6.	—
3.	R	7.	R
4.	—	8.	—

4.
1.	MI	6.	R
2.	R	7.	—
3.	—	8.	R
4.	R	9.	—
5.	—	10.	—

5.
1.	MI	4.	R
2.	R	5.	—
3.	R	6.	R

Guided Practice 9-5: Detail: Restatement—A (page 272)

1. The main idea is restated: What joy climbing a mountain is for Tim!

2. The main idea is restated: Some people are hooked on TV.

3. The restatement of the main idea is: Make sure you go to an interview looking your best.

4. The restatement of the main idea is: It is unlikely that you will stay where you are now living.

5. The main idea is restated: The message is clear: respond properly when your car goes into a skid.

Guided Practice 9-6: Detail: Restatement—B (page 274)

1. Stated main idea: **Oil companies blend gasoline to meet the driving needs of the part of the country where you live.** Restatement: But you can be reasonably sure that any gasoline you buy is blended to meet local needs.

2. State main idea: **The first Europeans to visit Australia could hardly believe the animal life they saw.** Restatement: The Australian animals simply amazed the first European visitors. The wording is different, but the ideas are about the same: both express European amazement at Australia's animal life.

3. State main idea: **I know that brown bears, at least, can see quite well.** Restatement: I don't question brown bears being able to see well.

4. Stated main idea: **When you're stuck with strong feelings that won't go away, try burning them off.** Restatement: What matters is that you burn off those strong feelings.

5. Stated main idea: **Arrows are the most important part of the bowhunter's equipment.** Restatement: The arrows are more important than anything else the bowhunter uses. In this case, the words are quite different. But the basic idea is the same: the importance of the right kind of arrows in bowhunting.

Guided Practice 9-7: Detail: Filler (page 281)

1. Sentences 2, 3, and 6 are all related to the stated main idea. They are reasons for it. Sentences 4 and 5 do not relate to that main idea at all. They have nothing to do with the law. Therefore, they are filler.

2. Sentences 4, 5, and 6 relate to the stated main idea: 4. reason, 5. example, and 6. example. Sentences 2 and 3 do not relate to the main idea at all. They do not support the idea of learning how to protect your credit rating. Therefore, they are filler.

3. Sentences 1, 2, 8, 9, and 10 relate to the implied main idea. They are all examples of the main idea. Sentences 4, 5, 6, and 7 do not relate to the main idea. Since they do not tell anything about the three types of pet food or what they can do for your pet, they are filler.

4. Sentences 2, 3, 6, and 7 are related to the stated main idea. They are all examples of how Medicare Plan A payments are paid. Sentences 4 and 5 go off on another subject—nursing homes. They are filler.

5. Sentences 1, 4, 5, 6, 7, 8, and 9 are related to the implied main idea: 1 is a reason why people are affected by the price of grain; 4 and 5

are examples of what happens to the price of grain; and 6, 7, 8, and 9 are all examples of the effect of grain price on people. Sentences 2 and 3 are not related to the main idea. They discuss different subjects. Therefore, they are filler.

CHAPTER TEN

Guided Practice 10-1: Main Ideas in Selections (page 295)

1. *Who or what is the selection about?* trees *What does the writer really want you to know about trees?* Of all America's riches, trees are among our most treasured.
The main idea of the selection is stated in the first sentence.

Umbrella: Of all America's riches, trees are among our most treasured. (paragraph 1)

The useful products and services from trees have grown. (main idea of paragraph 4)	The major use of trees is for wood. (main idea of paragraph 5)	Trees serve many necessary and enjoyable purposes. (main idea of paragraph 6)

The title, *Trees,* is too broad. It answers only the first question; it does not tell you what the writer really wants you to know about trees.

2. *Who or what is the selection about?* freezers *What does the writer really want you to know about freezers?* It is very important for the freezer-owner to know what to do if the freezer stops working in a power failure.

Umbrella: It is very important for the freezer-owner to know what to do if the freezer stops working in a power failure. (stated main idea of paragraph 3)

Don't open the freezer door. (main idea of paragraph 4)	Use dry ice to keep food from thawing. (main idea of paragraph 5)	Move frozen food from your freezer. (main idea of paragraph 6)	Knowing what to do can make a difference for the freezer-owner. (main idea of paragraph 7)

3. *Who or what is the selection about?* being sued *What does the writer really want you to know about being sued?* Know what to do if you are being sued by a company that says you owe money. (stated main idea of paragraph 3)

Did you check the main idea in your mind? If you did not have the correct main idea, use the one given above as an umbrella statement. Then try to fit the main ideas of the paragraphs under it. You will find that most, but not all, of the main ideas fit under the umbrella statement. Notice that the title is too broad to be a restatement of the main idea of the selection.

4. *Who or what is the selection about?* place names *What does the writer really want you to know about place names?* The names we give and use for places are very important to us. (stated main idea of paragraph 1)

Did you check the main idea in your mind? If you did not get the correct main idea, use the one given above as an umbrella statement. Then try to fit the main ideas of the paragraphs under it. You will find that most, if not all, of the main ideas fit under the umbrella statement. The title is very broad. Thus, it serves only as a general clue to the main idea of the selection.

5. *Who or what is the selection about?* the AIDS virus *What does the writer really want you to know about the AIDS virus?* There are ways you can and cannot become infected by the AIDS virus. (implied main idea of the selection)

Did you check the main idea in your mind? You should have a main idea similar to the one given. Your words may differ, but the idea must be the same. If you have a different main idea, try the implied main idea given as an umbrella statement. You will find that most of the paragraph main ideas fit under that selection main idea. Notice that the title is very broad. Thus, it serves only as a clue to the topic of the selection.

Guided Practice 10-2: Details in Selections (page 310)

1. The main idea of paragraphs 4, 5, and 6 are all stated. Paragraphs 1, 4, 5, and 6 are reasons. Each of their main ideas also answers the questions "Why?" trees are among our most treasured riches. Paragraphs 2 and 3 are filler. They have nothing to do with the trees being treasured. Don't pay any attention to these two paragraphs. Note again that the title, *Trees,* is too broad.

2. Paragraphs 1 and 2 are filler. They do not tell anything about the main idea of the selection. The main ideas of paragraphs 4, 5, and 6 are stated in the first sentence of each. They are all examples of the main idea of the selection. Each tells something the freezer-owner can do. The main idea of paragraph 7 is a reason.

3. Paragraphs 1 and 2 are filler. They do not tell anything about the main idea of the selection. The main ideas of paragraphs 4, 5, and 6 are

stated. Each is an example of knowing what to do if you are sued. The main idea of paragraph 7 is a restatement of the main idea of the selection. The words are different but the idea is the same. Note again that the title does not restate the main idea of the selection. It is too broad.

4. Paragraph 2 is filler. It does not tell anything about the importance of place names. The main ideas of paragraphs 3 and 4 are stated and are examples of the importance of place names. They are also reasons for this importance. Thus, the main ideas of paragraphs 3 and 4 relate to the main idea of the selection as both examples and reasons. The main idea of paragraph 5 is a restatement of the main idea of the selection. The title is too broad. It does not answer even the first question used to find the main idea of the selection.

5. Paragraph 1 is filler. It is an introduction to the selection but does not support its main idea. The main ideas of paragraphs 2, 3, and 4 are implied. The main idea of paragraph 6 is stated in the first sentence. Paragraphs 2, 3, 4, and 6 support the main idea of the selection, since they give examples of how you cannot become infected with the AIDS virus. The main idea of paragraph 5 is stated in the first sentence and supports the main idea of the selection by telling how you can become infected with the AIDS virus. The title is too broad, giving only a clue to the selection's topic.

CHAPTER ELEVEN

Guided Practice 11-1: Mapping a Paragraph (page 331)

Your maps may not look exactly like those that follow. Remember that maps are written in the mapper's own words. Be sure that your maps do include the same ideas, make sense, and are in the correct form.

1. **Main idea:** You may be better off working for someone else rather than being boss in your own business. (main idea stated in first sen-

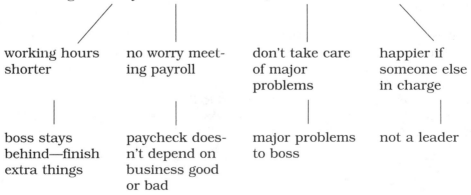

working hours shorter	no worry meeting payroll	don't take care of major problems	happier if someone else in charge
boss stays behind—finish extra things	paycheck doesn't depend on business good or bad	major problems to boss	not a leader

The major details are all reasons why you may be better off working for someone else.... The minor details are also all reasons. They give specific information related to the major details above them.

2. Main idea: Cross-country and downhill skiers enjoy different things about their sport. (implied)

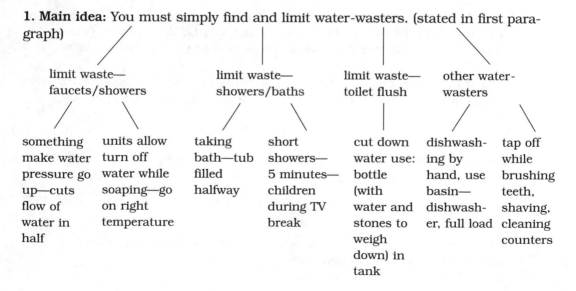

cross-country skiers enjoy — downhill skiers get a kick out of

being alone in forests and fields | silence and beauty of countryside | plunge down steep trail | showing skills—master whatever on path | thrill of going at great speeds

Guided Practice 11–2: Mapping Selections (page 335)

Your maps may not look exactly like those that follow. Remember that maps are written in the mapper's own words. Make sure that your maps do include the same ideas, make sense because they are a package of related information, and are in the correct form.

1. Main idea: You must simply find and limit water-wasters. (stated in first paragraph)

limit waste—faucets/showers | limit waste—showers/baths | limit waste—toilet flush | other water-wasters

something make water pressure go up—cuts flow of water in half | units allow turn off water while soaping—go on right temperature | taking bath—tub filled halfway | short showers—5 minutes—children during TV break | cut down water use: bottle (with water and stones to weigh down) in tank | dishwashing by hand, use basin—dishwasher, full load | tap off while brushing teeth, shaving, cleaning counters

Notice that paragraph 2 is filler and not included in the map. The writer's style in this selection made it hard to map. Thus, the person who maps must organize the minor details so that they include the important information and make sense.

2. Main idea: Take care of different kinds of floors. (implied main idea)

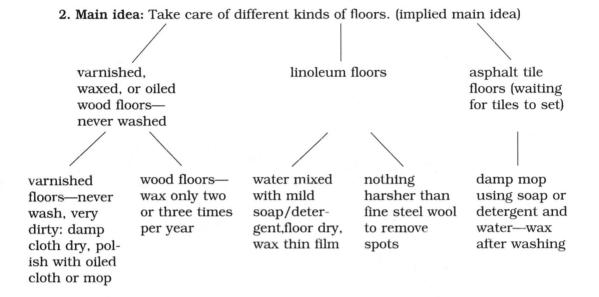

varnished, waxed, or oiled wood floors— never washed

linoleum floors

asphalt tile floors (waiting for tiles to set)

varnished floors—never wash, very dirty: damp cloth dry, polish with oiled cloth or mop

wood floors— wax only two or three times per year

water mixed with mild soap/detergent,floor dry, wax thin film

nothing harsher than fine steel wool to remove spots

damp mop using soap or detergent and water—wax after washing

The title, *Floors*, is too general to be the main idea of the selection. It is the topic of the selection. The first paragraph is filler and not included in the map.

Index

th, 33
wh, 33
Consonants, 11–48
  c, 13–14, 21–22
  d, 14–15
  g, 15–16
  n, 16–17
  q, 17
  s, 17–18
  silent, 40–42
    b, 40
    c, 40
    g, 40
    gh, 41
    h, 41
    k, 41
    l, 41
    n, 41
    p, 41
    s, 41
    t, 41
  that stand for only one sound,
      12–13
  that stand for more than one
      sound, 13–20
  w, 41–42
  summary sheet of, 47–48
  x, 19
  y, 13
  z, 19–20
Context, 101–102
  clues in for words with more than
      one meaning, 102–104
  clues to unknow words in, 109–127
  clues–definition, 109–111
  clues–example, 111–114
  clues–experience, 117–119
  summary sheet of clues in, 127

D

D, sounds of, 14–15
Dec, as prefix, 142
Decoding, 2–3, 11, 70–76, 93–96

using phonics for, 73–74
using phonics and syllables, 93–96
Definition, 109–111, 115–116,
    125–127
Details:
  in paragraphs, 254–258
  in selections, 307–310
  major and minor, 328–329
  summary sheet of, 289
Dictionaries:
  alphabetical order in, 170–177
  how to choose, 169–170
  how to use, 181–198
Digraphs and syllables, 84
Dis, as prefix, 137–138
Double vowels, in one–syllable words,
    78

E

E, silent at end of word, 51
Ea, as double vowel, 58–59
Ed, at end of word, 88–89
Ee, as double vowel, 59
Effective reader, you as, 1
En, as suffix, 153
Ence, as suffix, 150, 152
Entry word, 182
Er, as suffix, 150, 152
Example:
  as context clue, 111–114
  in paragraphs, 254–260
  in mapping, 327–337
  in selections, 291–292
Experience, as context clue, 117–119

F

Filler:
  in selections, 292
Ful, as suffix, 154–155
Fy, as suffix, 153–155

G

G:
  silent, 40
  sounds of, 15–16
Gh:
  consonant digraph, 34
  silent, 41
Greek root words, 132–133
Guide words, 181

H

H, silent, 41
Hemi, as prefix, 142
Hexa, as prefix, 142
Hood, as suffix, 151, 152

I

Ible, as suffix, 155, 156
Im, as prefix, 138–139
In, as prefix, 138–139
Ion, as suffix, 150
Ish, as suffix, 154, 156
Ize, as suffix, 153

K

K, silent, 41
Kilo, as prefix, 142

L

L, silent, 41
Latin root words, 133, 134
L consonant blends, 24–25
Le, at end of word, 87–88
Less, as suffix, 155, 156
Listening vocabulary, 206
Ly, as suffix, 156

M

Main idea, 219–251
  implied in paragraphs, 233–246
  locating, 219–220, 233–235
  mapping, 327–337
  restatement of, 271–274
  in selections, 291–302
  stated in paragraphs, 220–230
  summary sheet, 251
Mapping:
  paragraphs, 330–332
  selections, 333–337
Meaning:
  clues to in context, 101–108
  word, 182–186
Ment, as suffix, 150, 152
Milli, as prefix, 142
Mis, as prefix, 140
Mono, as prefix, 142
Multi, as prefix, 142

N

N:
  silent, 41
  sounds of, 16 17
Ness, as suffix, 151, 152
Non, as prefix, 137, 138
Not, prefixes that mean, 137–138
Noun suffixes, 150–152
Nov, as prefix, 142

O

Oa, as double vowel, 59
Oct, as prefix, 142
Oi, as double vowel, 60
One–syllable words, 78
Oo, as double vowel, 62–63
Open syllables, 86
Or, as suffix, 150, 152
Ou, as double vowel, 61–62

Ous, as suffix, 154
Ow, as double vowel, 60–61
Oy, as double vowel, 60

P

P, silent, 41
Paragraphs:
   details in, 253–289
   implied main ideas in, 235–246
   stated and implied main ideas in,
      220–230
   stated main ideas in, 220–230
   topic of, 220
Parts of speech, 151, 188, 208–209
Penta, as prefix, 142
Ph consonant digraph, 34
Phonics, 7–8, 11
   using to decode words, 70–76
Plural forms, 184
Prefix, 130, 137–143
   anti as, 141
   bi as, 142
   cent as, 142
   dec as, 142
   dis as, 137–138
   hemi as, 142
   hexa as, 142
   im as, 138–139
   in as, 138–139
   kilo as, 142
   milli as, 142
   mis as, 140
   mono as, 142
   multi as, 142
   non as, 137, 138
   nov as, 142
   number, 142, 143
   oct as, 142
   penta as, 142
   pro as, 141
   quadr as, 142
   quin as, 142

re as, 140
semi as, 142
sept as, 142, 143
sex as, 142
sub as, 141
summary sheet of, 148
super as, 141
tetra as, 142
that mean not, 137–138
tri as, 142
un as, 137–138
uni as, 142
Primary stress mark, 187–188
Pro, as prefix, 141
Pronunciation, 185–187

Q

Q, sounds of, 17
Quadr, as prefix, 142
Quin, as prefix, 142

R

R consonant blends, 25
Re, as prefix, 140
Reading, how to learn, 2–8
Reading vocabulary, 206
Reasons:
   in paragraphs, 260–265
   in mapping, 330
   in selections, 307–308
Restatement:
   in paragraphs, 271–274
   in selections, 291–302
Root words, 131–134
   Greek, 133–134
   Latin, 134–135

S

S:
   silent, 41

sounds of, 17–18
Schwa, 54
S consonant blends, 25–26
Secondary stress mark, 187–188
Selection:
    details in, 307–310
    main ideas in, 291–302
    mapping, 333–337
Semi, as prefix, 140
Sept, as prefix, 142
Sex, as prefix, 142
Sh consonant digraph, 32
Ship, as suffix, 151, 152
Sight vocabulary, developing, 3, 7–8
Silent consonants, 39–44
Skills:
    mastering, 1–2
    taught in this book, 8–10
Sounds:
    of c, 13–14
    consonant digraphs that stand for
        new, 32–34
    consonants that stand for only one
        sound, 12–13
    consonants that stand for more
        than one, 13–20
    of d, 14–15
    of g, 15–16
    of n, 16–17
    of q, 17
    of s, 17–18
    of single vowels, 50–53
    of x, 19
    of z, 19–20
Speaking vocabulary, 206
Spelling, 183
Stress marks, 187–188
Sub, as prefix, 141
Suffix:
    able as, 155, 156
    adjectives and, 154–156
    adverbs and, 156, 157
    ance, 152
    en as, 153
    ence as 150, 152

er as, 150, 152
    ful as, 154, 155
    fy as, 154, 155
    hood as, 151, 152
    ible as, 155, 156
    ion as, 150
    ish as, 154, 156
    ize as, 153
    less as, 155, 156
    ly as, 156
    ment as, 150, 152
    ness as, 148
    nouns, 150–152
    or as, 150, 152
    ous as, 154
    ship as, 151, 152
    summary sheet of, 162
    tion as, 150, 152
    verbs, 153
    y as, 154, 155
Super, as prefix, 141
Syllable, 54, 77–99
    closed, 85, 86
    clues for dividing words into,
        84–90, 130–131
    digraphs and, 84
    ed at end of word, 88–89
    hearing, 77–79
    le at end of word, 87–88
    open, 86
    summary sheets, 90, 163

T

T, silent, 41
Tetra, as prefix, 142
Th consonant digraph, 33
Tion, as suffix, 150, 152
Topic:
    of paragraph, 220
    of selection, 291, 292
Tri, as prefix, 142

U

Umbrella statement, 222, 233, 292
Un, as prefix, 137–138
Understanding, of what you are reading, 8
Uni, as prefix, 142

V

Verbs, suffix, 149, 153
Vocabulary:
    developing sight, 3, 7–8
    listening, 206
    reading, 206
    speaking, 206
    system for building, 207–216
    writing, 206
Vowels, 11, 49–63
    at end of short word, 51
    double, 51–63, 78
        ai, 58
        au, 59
        aw, 59
        ay, 58
        ea, 58–59
        ee, 59
        oa, 59
        oi, 60
        one vowel is silent, 58–59
        in one–syllable words, 78
        oo, 62–63
        ou, 61–62
        ow, 60–61
        oy, 60
    e silent at end of word, 51–52
    more than one single sound, 60–63
    new single sounds of double, 59–60
    schwa, 54
    silent, 58–59
    single long, 50–52
    single + r, 52–53
    single short, 52
    sounds of single, 50–53
    summary sheet of, 72
    y as, 53–54

W

W, silent, 41
Wh consonant digraph, 33
Word meaning, 190–195
Word origin, 189–190
Words, clues to unknown in context, 101–127
Word structure, clues in, 129
Writing vocabulary, 206

X

X, sounds of, 19

Y

Y as consonant, 13
    as suffix, 154, 155
    as vowel, 53–54